IFIP Advances in Information and Communication Technology 557

IFIP – The International Federation for Information Processing

IFIP was founded in 1960 under the auspices of UNESCO, following the first World Computer Congress held in Paris the previous year. A federation for societies working in information processing, IFIP's aim is two-fold: to support information processing in the countries of its members and to encourage technology transfer to developing nations. As its mission statement clearly states:

IFIP is the global non-profit federation of societies of ICT professionals that aims at achieving a worldwide professional and socially responsible development and application of information and communication technologies.

IFIP is a non-profit-making organization, run almost solely by 2500 volunteers. It operates through a number of technical committees and working groups, which organize events and publications. IFIP's events range from large international open conferences to working conferences and local seminars.

The flagship event is the IFIP World Computer Congress, at which both invited and contributed papers are presented. Contributed papers are rigorously refereed and the rejection rate is high.

As with the Congress, participation in the open conferences is open to all and papers may be invited or submitted. Again, submitted papers are stringently refereed.

The working conferences are structured differently. They are usually run by a working group and attendance is generally smaller and occasionally by invitation only. Their purpose is to create an atmosphere conducive to innovation and development. Refereeing is also rigorous and papers are subjected to extensive group discussion.

Publications arising from IFIP events vary. The papers presented at the IFIP World Computer Congress and at open conferences are published as conference proceedings, while the results of the working conferences are often published as collections of selected and edited papers.

IFIP distinguishes three types of institutional membership: Country Representative Members, Members at Large, and Associate Members. The type of organization that can apply for membership is a wide variety and includes national or international societies of individual computer scientists/ICT professionals, associations or federations of such societies, government institutions/government related organizations, national or international research institutes or consortia, universities, academies of sciences, companies, national or international associations or federations of companies.

More information about this series at http://www.springer.com/series/6102

Lynette Drevin · Marianthi Theocharidou (Eds.)

Information Security Education

Education in Proactive Information Security

12th IFIP WG 11.8 World Conference, WISE 12
Lisbon, Portugal, June 25–27, 2019
Proceedings

Springer

Editors
Lynette Drevin
North-West University
Potchefstroom, South Africa

Marianthi Theocharidou
European Commission
Joint Research Center
Ispra, Italy

ISSN 1868-4238 ISSN 1868-422X (electronic)
IFIP Advances in Information and Communication Technology
ISBN 978-3-030-23450-8 ISBN 978-3-030-23451-5 (eBook)
https://doi.org/10.1007/978-3-030-23451-5

This Springer imprint is published by the registered company Springer Nature Switzerland AG
The registered company address is: Gewerbestrasse 11, 6330 Cham, Switzerland

Preface

This volume contains the papers presented at the 12th World Conference on Information Security Education (WISE 12) held during June 25–27, 2019, in Lisbon. It was held in conjunction with the 34th IFIP International Conference on Information Security and Privacy Protection (IFIP SEC 2019). WISE 12 was organized by the IFIP Working Group 11.8, which is an international group of people from academia, government, and private organizations who volunteer their time and effort to increase knowledge in the very broad field of information security through education. WG 11.8 has worked to increase information security education and awareness for almost two decades. This year, WG11.8 organized the 12th conference of a successful series under the theme "Education in Proactive Information Security." We received 26 submissions from around the world. Each submission was blind reviewed by at least three international Program Committee members. The committee decided to accept 12 full papers, and thus the acceptance rate for the papers is 46%.

During the conference, a working group discussion addressed the "Graduate Student Pipeline Problem in Cybersecurity." It was chaired by Susanne Wetzel of Stevens Institute of Technology (USA). The topic is driven by surveys and observations in the USA, which indicate a mismatch between open faculty positions in cybersecurity and the number of accepted academic positions from the newly awarded PhDs in cybersecurity. In fact, the majority of them joined industry. The workgroup discussed the effect on education of the next generation of students in cybersecurity and explored options to address the problem. With high-paying jobs in industry that are already available to graduates from bachelor or master programs, what is the incentive for someone to pursue a PhD? What can and needs to be done in order to attract graduates to academic instead of industry jobs?

This conference took place thanks to the support and commitment of many individuals. First, we would like to thank all TC-11 members for continually giving us the opportunity to serve the working group and organize the WISE conferences. Our sincere appreciation also goes to the members of the Program Committee, to the external reviewers, and to the authors who trusted us with their intellectual work. We are grateful for the support of WISE11.8 Officers Lynn Futcher, Matt Bishop, Natalia Miloslavskaya, and Erik Moore. Finally, we would like to thank the local organizers for the support. As for the preparation of this volume, we sincerely thank Erika Siebert-Cole and our publisher Springer for their assistance.

June 2019

Lynette Drevin
Marianthi Theocharidou

Organization

Wise12 Conference Chair

Lynn Futcher	Nelson Mandela University, South Africa

WISE12 Program Chair

Lynette Drevin	North-West University, South Africa

WISE12 Conference Secretariat

Matt Bishop	University of California, Davis, USA

WISE12 Publications Chair

Marianthi Theocharidou	European Commission, Joint Research Centre, Italy

WISE12 Local and Logistics Chair

Natalia Miloslavskaya	National Research Nuclear University MEPhI, Russia

WISE12 Web Chair

Erik Moore	Regis University, Colorado, USA

Program Committee

Maria Bada	University of Cambridge, UK
Matt Bishop	University of California, Davis, USA
Jun Dai	California State University, Sacramento, USA
Melissa Dark	Purdue University, USA
Lynette Drevin	North-West University, South Africa
Steven Furnell	Plymouth University, UK
Lynn Futcher	Nelson Mandela Metropolitan University, South Africa
Ram Herkanaidu	Plymouth University, UK
Lech Janczewski	The University of Auckland, New Zealand
Audun Josang	University of Oslo, Norway
Christos Kalloniatis	University of the Aegean, Greece
Sokratis Katsikas	Center for Cyber and Information Security, NTNU, Norway
Basel Katt	Norwegian University of Science and Technology, NTNU, Norway

Siddharth Kaza	Towson University, USA
Andrea Kolberger	University of Applied Sciences, Upper Austria
Elmarie Kritzinger	UNISA, South Africa
Hennie Kruger	North-West University, South Africa
Wai Sze Leung	University of Johannesburg, South Africa
Dan Likarish	Regis University, Colorado, USA
Javier Lopez	University of Malaga, Spain
Edgar Alonso Lopez-Rojas	Norwegian University of Science and Technology, NTNU, Norway
Annlize Marnewick	University of Johannesburg, South Africa
Natalia Miloslavskaya	National Research Nuclear University MEPhI, Russia
Stig Mjolsnes	Norwegian University of Science and Technology, Norway
Erik Moore	Regis University, Colorado, USA
Ida Ngambeki	Purdue University, USA
Jason Nurse	University of Kent, UK
Ruxandra F. Olimid	Norwegian University of Science, Norway and Technology and University of Bucharest, Romania
Jacques Ophoff	University of Cape Town, South Africa
Günther Pernul	Universität Regensburg, Germany
Carlos Rieder	isec ag, Switzerland
Rudi Serfontein	North-West University, South Africa
Chien-Chung Shen	University of Delaware, USA
Marianthi Theocharidou	European Commission, Joint Research Centre, Italy
Alexander Tolstoy	National Research Nuclear University MEPhI, Russia
Ismini Vasileiou	Plymouth University, UK
Sune von Solms	University of Johannesburg, South Africa
Susanne Wetzel	Stevens Institute of Technology, USA
Louise Yngstrom	Stockholm University, Sweden
Sergey Zapechnikov	National Research Nuclear University MEPhI, Russia

Additional Reviewer

Ludwig Englbrecht

Contents

Organisational Aspects

Innovation in Curricula

An Educational Intervention for Teaching Secure Coding Practices

Vuyolwethu Mdunyelwa[1(✉)], Lynn Futcher[1], and Johan van Niekerk[1,2]

[1] Nelson Mandela University, Port Elizabeth, South Africa
{vuyolwethu.mdunyelwa,lynn.futcher,johan.vanniekerk}@mandela.ac.za
[2] Noroff University College, Kristiansand, Norway
johan.vanniekerk@noroff.no

Abstract. Cybersecurity vulnerabilities are typically addressed through the implementation of various cybersecurity controls. These controls can be operational, technical or physical in nature. The focus of this paper is on technical controls with a specific focus on securing web applications. The secure coding practices used in this research are based on OWASP. An initial investigation found that there was a general lack of adherence to these secure coding practices by third year software development students doing their capstone project at a South African University. This research therefore focused on addressing this problem by developing an educational intervention to teach secure coding practices, specifically focusing on the data access layer of web applications developed in the .NET environment. Pre-tests and post-tests were conducted in order to determine the effectiveness of the intervention. Results indicated an increase in both knowledge and behaviour regarding the identified secure coding practices after exposure to the intervention.

Keywords: Educational intervention · Secure coding practices · OWASP · Web application security

1 Introduction

With the recent increase in cyber-related attacks, cybersecurity is becoming a key area of concern for many organisations. Web applications often handle very sensitive data, used for carrying out critical tasks such as banking, online shopping and online tax filing [9]. These applications are trusted by billions of users for performing such daily activities. However, 75% of all attacks on the internet are executed through the application layer of the OSI model [6], and more than 76% of web applications have vulnerabilities [2].

The financial assistance of the National Research Foundation (NRF) towards this research is hereby acknowledged. Opinions expressed and conclusions arrived at, are those of the authors, and are not necessarily to be attributed to the NRF.

Published by Springer Nature Switzerland AG 2019
L. Drevin and M. Theocharidou (Eds.): WISE 2019, IFIP AICT 557, pp. 3–15, 2019.
https://doi.org/10.1007/978-3-030-23451-5_1

Handling risks related to the security of web applications is a major challenge for many organizations. Not surprisingly, Web applications have recently received attention from academia and industry to initiate some defence mechanisms to protect them from security threats [9]. Many of these Web applications have common vulnerabilities which can be easily corrected [18] through introducing secure coding practices.

The secure coding practices used in this research are based on OWASP. An initial investigation found that there was a general lack of adherence to these secure coding practices by third year software development students doing their capstone project at a South African University. This research therefore focused on addressing this problem by developing an educational intervention to teach secure coding practices, specifically focusing on the data access layer of web applications developed in the .NET environment.

The following section highlights the related literature, while Sect. 3 provides the research design. Section 4 presents the educational intervention including both the knowledge and behavioural components. This is followed by Sect. 5 which provides the results of the verification of the educational intervention before concluding in Sect. 6.

2 Related Literature

More than 90,000 vulnerabilities have been recorded in the Symantec comprehensive vulnerability database over the past two decades, from 24,560 vendors representing over 78,900 products. On average, over 340,000 web attacks were blocked from web applications per day in 2014 [2]. Although this improved to 229,000 in 2016 [2], it still remains a serious concern since most attacks are no longer on the networks, but more on the software applications that run on the application layer. If 76% of web applications contain known vulnerabilities, it means that 24% of the scanned web applications do not contain known vulnerabilities. Therefore, it is possible for web applications to avoid known vulnerabilities. Those web applications without known vulnerabilities probably adhere to some form of best practice for secure software development. This is true as some researchers suggest that applying such practices and methodologies can improve security in software application [1,7].

There are various organisations and institutions responsible for developing standards and best practices. These include the National Institute of Standards and Technology (NIST), the International Organizations for Standardization (ISO) and the International Electro-Technical Commission (IEC), the Microsoft Developer Network (MSDN) and the Open Web Application Project (OWASP) which provides best practices for improving security in web applications.

The best practices provided by these organisations were evaluated and OWASP was considered the most relevant for identifying fundamental secure coding practices to be taught to software developers. OWASP is known by many organisations for its Top 10 Vulnerability List (Table 1) that it publishes and updates periodically [4,6,11]. This list focusses on identifying the most serious

Table 1. OWASP top 10 vulnerability list 2017 [15].

Vulnerability	Description
SQL injection	Injection flaws occur when untrusted data is sent to an interpreter as part of a command or query
Broken authentication	This relates to authentication and session management that are often implemented incorrectly. It allows attacks to compromise information, and session tokens or exploit other implementation flaws
Sensitive data exposure	Many web applications and Application Programming Interfaces (APIs) do not properly protect data allowing attackers to steal or modify data
XML external entities	External entities can be used to disclose files using the file Uniform Resource Identifiers (URIs) handler, internal file shares, internal port scanning, remote code execution, and denial of service attacks
Broken access control	Restrictions on what authenticated users are allowed to do are often not properly enforced, allowing attackers to exploit flaws to access unauthorized functionality, or data, such as other users' accounts or change access rights
Secure misconfiguration	This is mostly a result of insecure default configurations, incomplete or ad hoc configurations
Cross-site scripting	Also know as XSS, it allows attackers to execute scripts in the victim's browser which can hijack user sessions, deface web sites, or redirect users to malicious sites
Insecure deserialisation	Insecure deserialisation leads to remote code execution, deserialisation flaws can also be used to perform tasks such as injection attacks, and privilege escalation attacks
Using components with known vulnerabilities	Components including libraries, frameworks and other software modules, run with the same privileges as the application. If a vulnerable component is exploited, such attacks can facilitate serious data loss or server take over
Insufficient logging and monitoring	This allows attacks to further attack systems, maintain persistence, pivot to more systems, and temper, extract, or destroy data

web application security vulnerabilities for many organisations [16]. The Top 10 list changes according to which vulnerability is most dominant at any given time.

The risk posed by each of these vulnerabilities can be reduced by more than one type of control. For the data access layer within .NET, OWASP recommends specific secure coding practices. Table 2 presents the nine secure coding practices (SP1 to SP9) for data access based on OWASP and used in this study. These relate to some of the vulnerabilities shown in Table 1. As an example, parameterised SQL commands (SP1), or the use of stored procedures (SP6), can block SQL injections. Therefore more than one control can reduce a vulnerability.

The secure coding practices shown in Table 2 are referred to using the codes SP1 to SP9 throughout this paper. If one of them is not properly handled, it

Table 2. Secure coding practices. Adapted from [16].

SP	Secure coding practices
SP1	Use parameterised SQL commands for all data access, without exception
SP2	Do not use SQL command with a string made up of a concatenated SQL strings
SP3	Properly validate input fields
SP4	Apply the principle of least privilege when setting up the database of your choice
SP5	When using SQL server, prefer integrated authentication over SQL authentication
SP6	Using stored procedures is the most effective way to counter the SQL injection vulnerability
SP7	Encrypt connection strings
SP8	Connection strings should be based in a configuration file
SP9	Encrypt sensitive data using acceptable encryption algorithms

can be easy for an attacker to access and modify information that is in the database. For example, if the connection string is found in other parts of the application code and not locked in the configuration file, it can be easy for an attacker to access the information using the same connection string to connect to the database. Or, if the expected values in an input field are not whitelisted in a system with concatenated SQL strings, attackers can use characters to manipulate the SQL string in the database and the information would be at risk.

These vulnerabilities cannot be prevented by programmers unless they know the types of flaws that exist in their code [1,3]. Similarly, they cannot implement these security controls unless they are taught how they work [8]. Once software developers have been taught about secure coding practices, it is more likely that they will have the requisite knowledge [5]. However, there has to be some form of compliance instrument to monitor their adherence, since it is known that people with the requisite knowledge do not always behave accordingly. Therefore, an educational intervention that focuses on both knowledge and behaviour was developed and provided to software development students to improve the security of their web applications.

3 Research Design

This research was conducted in the School of Information and Communication Technology at a comprehensive institution in South Africa, offering both degrees and vocational qualifications. In this case, the sample was drawn from students registered for their third year in the National Diploma: Software Development. In South Africa, there are no locally recognised curricular guidelines for computing. Many universities therefore rely on the recommendations provided in global computing curricular publications. The Association of Computing Machinery (ACM) Information Technology curricular guidelines have been used to model IT qualifications. The IT2008 and the more recent IT2017 curricular guidelines require students in computing and engineering disciplines to engage in a capstone project during their final year of study [12,13]. Since the diploma is a three year qualification, students are required to complete a capstone project in their third year of study. These capstone projects take place over a full year of study. According to the ACM IT curricular guidelines, capstone projects should typically adhere to the following [12,13]:

- Project groups of 3 to 5 students;
- Based on a real-world problem;
- Must be integrative;
- Students should have completed most of the curriculum before attempting the project.

Students registered for the diploma are introduced to programming and business application systems development. Therefore, most of their capstone projects focus on developing applications for solving real world problems using business applications. When students choose the capstone projects, many of them focus on web, mobile or gaming applications, while a few develop desktop applications. Although students are taught specifically to develop software in a Windows environment using the .NET framework, students may develop their capstone projects in the programming language of their choice. Most project students choose web applications in the .NET development environment as this is where their skills lie.

This research focused on two aspects relating to secure coding practices, namely knowledge and behavioural compliance of the students and involved four main phases:

- **Phase 1** was the first phase for this research which started off by analysing students' behaviour relating to secure coding practices. This was done by conducting a code review on previously completed third year capstone projects, which were developed in the .NET environment. The results for this behavioural analysis indicated low levels of compliance to the identified secure coding practices.
- **Phase 2** addressed the knowledge assessment phase for this research, which assessed students' knowledge relating to secure coding practices. This was achieved using a questionnaire, which served as a pre-test for this study. Results from the pre-test indicated that students lacked knowledge relating to secure coding practices. Therefore, students lacked in both the knowledge and behavioural aspects.
- **Phase 3** comprised of an educational intervention for addressing both the knowledge and behavioural aspects, which students lacked in Phase 1 and 2. In terms of the knowledge aspect, students were provided with online lessons relating to secure coding practices to work through; in terms of the behavioural aspect, students were given a checklist to check their application code against the listed secure coding practices.

- **Phase 4** involved the verification of the educational intervention for this research. The first part of this phase was the knowledge verification (Phase 4A), and the second part was the behavioural verification (Phase 4B).

The results for Phase 1 and 2 were published in the 2017 Human Aspects in Information Security and Assurance (HAISA) conference [14]. The focus of this paper is therefore on Phases 3 and 4. The following section describes the educational intervention (Phase 3), while Phase 4 (A and B) are discussed in Sect. 5.

4 Educational Intervention

The educational intervention was split into two parts, where the first part focused on the knowledge, and the second part focused on the behaviour of students relating to secure coding practices. Owing to the lack of knowledge on the part of the students, the researcher realised the need to create a knowledge component that could assist students in acquiring the requisite knowledge regarding secure coding practices. The need to address behavioural compliance was also realised since it is known that having knowledge does not necessarily ensure that people would behave accordingly [17]. Both the knowledge and behavioural components of this research were designed using the identified secure coding practices in Table 2.

4.1 Knowledge Component

The knowledge component for this research took the form of a blended learning course, called the Web Application Security Course, that students worked through to improve their knowledge regarding secure coding practices.

Design of the Knowledge Component. The knowledge component for this research included online lessons that the researcher designed using the identified secure coding practices. For each of the secure coding practices, their importance and the security implications if they were ignored were explained. The online learning platform that was used to design the lessons was the *Moodle Learning Management System* that runs on the university's website. Moodle is a learning management system used by educators to create effective blended learning material for students in various higher educational institutions. Moodle has been adopted by many institutions for its cost effectiveness, its ability to expand with increased student populations, and its ability to meet the needs of institutions, students and educators [10]. Figure 1 provides an overview of the process followed by the students when completing the online lessons on Moodle.

The lessons took the form of interactive Microsoft PowerPoint slides, which were converted to videos, for students to work through. Each secure coding practice was addressed in a single lesson. After completing each lesson, the students were required to take a quiz, which allowed them to reflect on the content of the

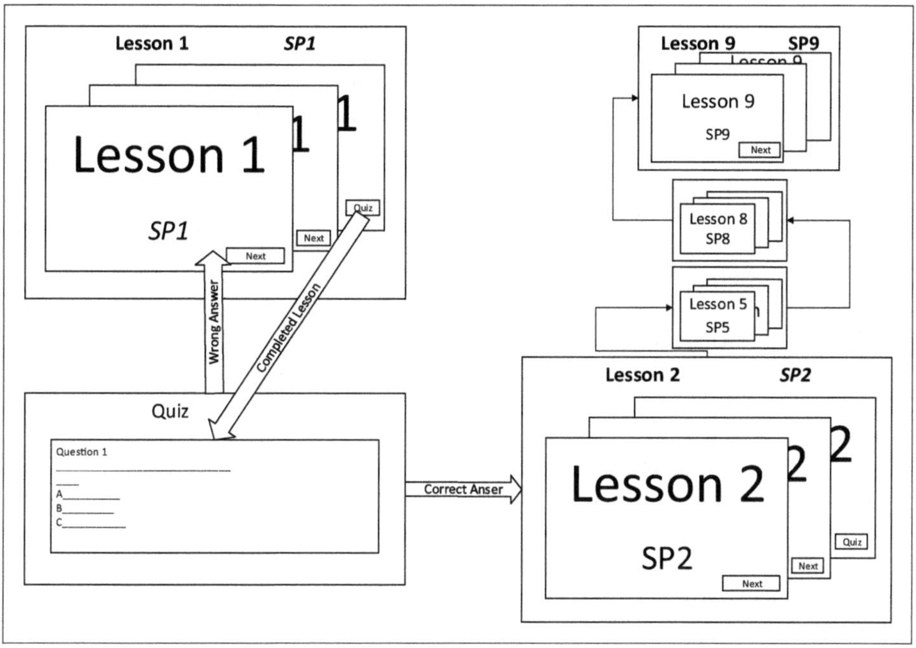

Fig. 1. Lesson content process flow.

lesson. The quiz had four questions assigned to each lesson. The students had to answer only one randomly generated quiz question before continuing to the next lesson. If the student selected the incorrect answer, they were required to work through the lesson again, and if they selected an incorrect answer once again, a different question would be randomly generated. Alternatively, if they selected the correct answer, they were allowed to continue to the next lesson.

A brief overview of each secure coding practice (SP1 to SP9) as listed in Table 2, within the knowledge component follows:

- SP1 (Using Parameterised SQL commands): The content for this secure coding practice firstly provides the background relating to parameterised SQL commands in order to equip students with the necessary information relating to this secure coding practice. The remainder of the lesson shows the students how parameterised SQL commands can be implemented in their code, and why it is necessary to use them.
- SP2 (Concatenated SQL strings): Content for this secure coding practice begins by introducing what is meant by concatenated SQL strings. The lesson proceeds by showing how programmers make use of concatenated SQL strings and the negative implications of using them. This lesson also provides a way in which to avoid using concatenated SQL strings, which is by means of parameterised SQL commands.

- SP3 (Input validation): The content for this secure coding practice begins by discussing validation in general. It also highlights the various types of validation, such as blacklisting and whitelisting, and why they are important. The content also provides suggestions on what to use when dealing with validation, for example, ASP .NET Regular Expressions to tell input fields which values to accept.
- SP4 (Principle of Least Privilege): This secure coding practice content explains what the Principle of Least Privilege is and why it is important when developing web applications. This content also provides a scenario where the use of this secure coding practice is shown and how it can be implemented.
- SP5 (Authentication): The content of this secure coding practice was addressed by means of a video adapted from YouTube. The video was embedded in the slides and distributed as a single lesson to the students to listen to and to watch.
- SP6 (Using Stored Procedures): The content for this secure coding practice focusses on how stored procedures are used and why they are important, providing examples on how they should be implemented in a web application.
- SP7 + SP8 (Connection strings): These two secure coding practices both deal with connection strings, and have been addressed collectively in the same lesson. The content first provides detail about the importance of connection strings, and how they should be handled when developing web applications, providing detail on how to implement both the secure coding practices.
- SP9 (Encryption): For this secure coding practice, an analogy is used to explain the concept of encryption to the students. The lesson further explains the analogy to clarify the concepts for the students. Since OWASP provides recommendations relating to acceptable encryption algorithms, the content for this lesson also emphasises the use of the encryption algorithms recommended by OWASP when developing web applications.

All the lessons were followed by a quiz question to check students' understanding of the content contained in the lesson they had worked on. The results for the short content quizzes were not recorded, since answers were simply used to ensure that students do not move to the next lesson without understanding the content in the previous lesson.

Administering the Knowledge Component. The Web Application Security lessons were prepared by the researcher and distributed to the students on Moodle. The students were permitted to work through the lessons as often as they wanted. During a lecture, the researcher explained the process that the students needed to follow when completing the online content. Most students worked through the content in the computer laboratories at the university as soon as it was made active and available to them. A total of 120 students completed the online lessons. The students had to work through all the lessons, since they were required to take a quiz which served as a Post-test (Phase 4A) for which marks were recorded.

4.2 Behavioural Compliance Monitoring Instrument

Although it is possible for a student to have the requisite knowledge and not perform accordingly when developing their web applications, it is most unlikely for them to behave accordingly when they do not have the requisite knowledge. Therefore, it was deemed necessary to firstly educate the students on secure coding practices and then to monitor their adherence to these practices. This section provides details on how the behaviour of students was monitored when developing their web applications as part of their third year capstone projects.

Design of Behavioural Compliance Instrument. The behavioural compliance instrument took the form of a checklist as seen in Table 3. The code review checklist for this research was adapted from the secure coding practices in Table 2 and was provided to the students electronically via Moodle.

Table 3. Code review checklist.

SP	Questions
SP1	Do they make use of parameterised SQL commands for all data access? *Yes/No (Number of Instances)*
SP2	Do they make use of concatenated strings in the queries? *Yes (Number of Instances)/No*
SP3	Are all input fields validated? *Input Properly Validated/Input not Properly Validated/No Validation*
SP4	Do they make use of the Principle of Least Privilege when setting up their databases? *Yes/No*
SP5	Do they use integrated authentication or do they use SQL authentication? *Integrated Authentication/SQL Authentication*
SP6	Do they use stored procedures for their queries? *Yes/No/Inconsistent Use of Stored Procedures and Queries*
SP7	Do they encrypt their connection strings? *Yes/No*
SP8	Does the connection string only appear once in the web.config file? *Yes/No*
SP9	Is all the sensitive data being encrypted using the OWASP recommended methods? *Encrypted Using Acceptable Method/No Encryption/Encrypted Not using Acceptable Method*

Conducting the Behavioural Compliance Instrument. During a lecture the researcher explained to the students how they should go about using the checklist to review their capstone projects. They were required to check all web forms accessing the data access layer against the secure coding practices for SP1 to SP9 using the checklist provided in Table 3. Having worked through the knowledge component, as discussed in Sect. 4.1, the students should have acquired the requisite knowledge relating to the secure coding practices that should be implemented in their web applications.

Since most students worked in groups when developing their web applications, they were also required to conduct a peer code review on each other's web forms using the checklist provided. The peer code review helped the students to double check whether they had really adhered to the secure coding practices as indicated in their own code reviews. Feedback from the students was positive and most students found the checklist helpful for their code and to ensure compliance to the secure coding practices.

5 Effectiveness of the Educational Intervention

Once students had completed the educational intervention, it was necessary to determine its effectiveness. The knowledge component of the educational intervention was responsible for providing students with knowledge regarding secure coding practices. Having completed the online course, the students were expected to implement the learnt secure coding practices in their capstone projects, showing behavioural compliance.

The verification of the knowledge component was achieved through an online quiz distributed to the students through the Moodle site as discussed in Sect. 5.1. Verification of the behavioural compliance component took the form of a code review by the researcher on the students' capstone projects as discussed in Sect. 5.2.

5.1 Knowledge Verification

The setup for the post-test questionnaire was such that students were only allowed to work through the post-test after they had completed the lessons in the knowledge component of the educational intervention, referred to as the Web Application Security Course. The 113 students who completed the post-test were only allowed to work through the post-test once. The results for the post-test questionnaire were automatically recorded on the Moodle site, where the researcher was able to export the data to an Excel spreadsheet for analysis. A comparison of the knowledge pre- and post-test is shown in Table 4.

Table 4. Knowledge assessment and verification results (Pre-test vs Post-test).

Phases	SP1	SP2	SP3	SP4	SP5	SP6	SP7	SP8	SP9
Phase 2	74%	36%	30%	58%	26%	39%	20%	3%	1%
Phase 4A	95%	95%	89%	91%	91%	77%	93%	88%	83%
Variance	**21%**	**59%**	**59%**	**33%**	**65%**	**38%**	**73%**	**85%**	**82%**

Table 4 shows the results for Phase 2, Knowledge Assessment (pre-test), and Phase 4A, Knowledge Verification (post-test). There was a substantial improvement in the students' knowledge as indicated in the second row, Phase 4A. Students' knowledge has improved in all of the secure coding practices (SP1 to SP9), as seen in the variances. SP2, SP3, SP5 and SP7 showed reasonable improvements, while SP8 and SP9 showed the highest improvements with variances above 80%. As mentioned previously, knowledge acquisition does not guarantee a change in behaviour. In order to monitor the adherence of the students to these secure coding practices when developing their web applications behavioural compliance monitoring was required.

5.2 Behavioural Verification

The behavioural verification instrument used was the same checklist used in Phases 1 and 3 as shown in Table 3. The checklist was used by the researcher to conduct a code review on the third year capstone projects.

The code review was conducted by the researcher before the final submission of the software development projects. The researcher first informed the students about the code review process scheduled to take place during a session in the computer laboratory. Students filled in their group names and were required to be in the computer laboratory in order for their projects to be reviewed. The code review was conducted during the students' practical sessions. For each of the capstone projects, the researcher reviewed five web forms per project, which connected to the database and were related to the capstone projects' main functionality. 17 groups were present for the code review, and they were all reviewed successfully, in the presence of the students who belonged to the group being reviewed. Table 5 shows the results from the behavioural analysis for the students before and after exposure to the educational intervention.

Table 5. Behavioural verification results (Phase 1 and 4B).

Phases	SP1	SP2	SP3	SP4	SP5	SP6	SP7	SP8	SP9
Phase 1	86%	84%	77%	60%	N/A	38%	N/A	68%	31%
Phase 4B	96%	96%	100%	91%	N/A	96%	N/A	100%	100%
Variance	**10%**	**12%**	**23%**	**31%**	**N/A**	**58%**	**N/A**	**32%**	**69%**

As can be seen from the results in Table 5, there was an improvement in students' adherence to secure coding practices after the educational intervention, with most capstone project groups having adhered to all the secure coding practices. Although SP5 and SP7 were recommended by OWASP, they were not required by the capstone projects from which the sample for this research was drawn. All averages per secure coding practice were between 90% and 100%, with SP3, SP8, and SP9 showing 100% compliance. SP6 and SP9 showed the largest improvements of 58%(SP6) and 69%(SP9) respectively, while SP3, SP4 and SP8 showed good improvements of between 20% and 35%.

6 Conclusion

The results of this study indicate that students' adherence to secure coding practices can be positively impacted through a formal educational intervention. However, it is important that such an intervention addresses both the knowledge and behaviour of students since having the requisite knowledge does not ensure compliance. It is for this reason that a behavioural compliance monitoring instrument formed part of the study. This is a step towards educating students in secure application development which is essential in addressing the many security vulnerabilities existing in Web applications today.

Limitations of this study do exist. Firstly, this study addressed only the identified secure coding practices which were determined from OWASP. Secondly, the identified secure coding practices only focused on the data access layer of Web applications developed in the .NET environment. Future research could investigate similar interventions within various other application development contexts.

7 Ethical Considerations

This research project adhered to all ethical requirements of the Nelson Mandela University and obtained ethics approval from the university research committee (REF H15-ENG-ITE-009).

References

1. Bishop, M., Dai, J., Dark, M., Ngambeki, I., Nico, P., Zhu, M.: Evaluating secure programming knowledge. In: Bishop, M., Futcher, L., Miloslavskaya, N., Theocharidou, M. (eds.) WISE 2017. IAICT, vol. 503, pp. 51–62. Springer, Cham (2017). https://doi.org/10.1007/978-3-319-58553-6_5
2. Chandrasekar, K., Cleary, G., Cox, O., Gorman, B.O.: Internet security threat report. Technical report, Symantec, April 2017. https://www.symantec.com/security-center/threat-report
3. Chi, H., Jones, E.L., Brown, J.: Teaching secure coding practices to STEM students. In: Proceedings of the 2013 on InfoSecCD 2013 Information Security Curriculum Development Conference - InfoSecCD 2013, pp. 42–48 (2013). https://doi.org/10.1145/2528908.2528911. http://dl.acm.org/citation.cfm?doid=2528908.2528911
4. Chung, S., et al.: What approaches work best for teaching secure coding practices? In: 2014 HUIC Education & STEM Conference (2014)
5. Conklin, A., White, G.: A graduate level assessment course: a model for safe vulnerability assessments. In: Proceedings of the 9th Colloquium for Information Systems Security Education (2005)

6. Customs Solutions Group: A CISO's guide to application security. Technical report, Customs Solutions Group (2012). http://h30528.www3.hp.com/Security/CISOGuideToApplicationSecurity.pdf
7. Dark, M., Ngambeki, I., Bishop, M., Belcher, S.: Teach the hands, train the mind ... a secure programming clinic! In: Proceeding of the 19th Colloquium for Information System Security Education (2015)
8. Dark, M., Stuart, L., Ngambeki, I., Bishop, M.: Effect of the secure programming clinic on learners' secure programming practices. J. Colloquium Inf. Syst. Secur. Educ. **4**, 18–18 (2016)
9. Deepa, G., Thilagam, P.S.: Securing web applications from injection and logic vulnerabilities: approaches and challenges. Inf. Softw. Technol. **74**, 160–180 (2016). https://doi.org/10.1016/j.infsof.2016.02.005
10. Florian, T.P., Zimmerman, J.P.: Understanding by design, moodle, and blended learning: a secondary school case study. MERLOT J. Online Learn. Teach. **11**(1), 120–128 (2015)
11. Li, X., Xue, Y.: A survey on server-side approaches to securing web applications. ACM Comput. Surv. (CSUR) **46**(4), 54 (2014)
12. Lunt, B., Sabin, M., Hala, A., Impagliazzo, J., Zhang, M.: Information technology curricula 2017. Technical report, Association for Computing Machinery (ACM). IEEE Computer Society (2017)
13. Lunt, B.M., Ekstrom, J.J., Lawson, E.: Curriculum guidelines for undergraduate degree programs in information technology. Technical report, Association for Computing Machinery (ACM). IEEE Computer Society (2008)
14. Mdunyelwa, V.S., Niekerk, J.F.V., Futcher, L.A.: Secure coding practices in the software development capstone projects. In: Proceedings of the Eleventh International Symposium on Human Aspects of Information Security & Assurance, HAISA 2017, Adelaide, Australia, 28–30 November 2017, pp. 282–291 (2017). http://www.cscan.org/openaccess/?paperid=353
15. OWASP: OWASP Top 10 (2017). https://www.owasp.org/index.php/Top_10-2017_Top_10
16. OWASP: The OWASP Foundation (2017). https://www.owasp.org/index.php/Main_Page
17. Vroom, C., Von Solms, R.: Towards information security behavioural compliance. Comput. Secur. **23**(3), 191–198 (2004)
18. Zhu, J., Xie, J., Lipford, H.R., Chu, B.: Supporting secure programming in web applications through interactive static analysis. J. Adv. Res. **5**(4), 449–462 (2014). https://doi.org/10.1016/j.jare.2013.11.006

Learning Principles and the Secure Programming Clinic

Matt Bishop[1(✉)], Melissa Dark[2], Lynn Futcher[3], Johan Van Niekerk[3,4], Ida Ngambeki[2], Somdutta Bose[1], and Minghua Zhu[1]

[1] University of California at Davis, Davis, CA, USA
{mabishop,sombose,mhzhu}@ucdavis.edu
[2] Purdue University, West Lafayette, IN, USA
{dark,ingambek}@purdue.edu
[3] Center for Research in Information and Cyber Security, Nelson Mandela University, Port Elizabeth, South Africa
{lynn.futcher,johan.vanniekerk}@mandela.ac.za
[4] Noroff University College, Oslo, Norway
johan.vanniekerk@noroff.no

Abstract. Several academic institutions have run a clinic on robust and secure programming. Each time a clinic was run, it was associated with a specific class. Using pre- and post-class evaluation instruments, it is clear that the effect of the secure programming clinic on students' understanding of secure programming was generally positive. However, in some instances the clinic was underutilized, and in other cases it could not be run at other institutions. The goal of this paper is to examine the structure of the clinic in light of five basic learning principles, and provide information about when a clinic will not improve students' understanding, and when it will. We validate this by examining an instance of the secure programming clinic, and show how the learning principles explain the improvement in student grades, or lack thereof. From this, we draw conclusions about ways to make the clinic more effective, and when it will not be effective.

Keywords: Secure programming clinic · Learning principles · Robust programming

1 Introduction

The problem of nonsecure code is widely recognized as a major source of security problems. Indeed, of the vulnerabilities in the U.S. National Vulnerability Database in the last 5 years, over 19,000 are identified as injection and buffer overflow vulnerabilities, exemplars of poor programming practices [14]. Some, such as Heartbleed, have impacts throughout the Internet [7]. Industries, government, and many other organizations want programmers who can write secure, robust code. The problem is how to teach this material.

Published by Springer Nature Switzerland AG 2019
L. Drevin and M. Theocharidou (Eds.): WISE 2019, IFIP AICT 557, pp. 16–29, 2019.
https://doi.org/10.1007/978-3-030-23451-5_2

Computer-related majors, and many other majors, teach programming. Introductory classes typically teach good programming style, error checking, and other aspects of programming summarized by the word "robust". Being introductory, their focus is not on security as such, but simply on producing good programmers who understand both the strengths and limitations of the language they learn. Future classes expect the students to apply what they have been taught, and rather than focusing on style and robustness, the emphasis is upon correctness. Hence style and robustness is a minimal part of the grade, if they are included at all, giving students the impression that security and quality of programming is less important than required functionality. Students have no reason to apply what they learned in introductory programming. Further, advanced security issues such as programming to avoid race conditions is not taught in introductory classes, so the students lack knowledge of all the aspects of secure coding. The atrophying of this practice, and the lack of knowledge, leads to programmers who do not write robust, secure code.

This problem is exacerbated by the richness of the current curricular guidelines for computer science programs. The ACM Computing Curricula [23] is laden with more material than can be taught in a typical major program, so faculty and program developers choose which parts to emphasize. Given this, creating a required class on secure programming would require something else to be dropped from the curriculum. Further, most faculty do not know all the aspects of secure coding, so many institutions would need to find the instructors for these courses. Thus, few schools have any courses on secure programming, let alone required ones.

An alternative to additional classes is the Secure Programming Clinic [2,3]. This clinic works analogously to an English writing clinic, and is discussed in detail in Sect. 3, below. Like any other aspect of education, its success depends upon a host of factors. The contribution of this paper is to use results from running several instances of this clinic, and basic educational principles, to identify characteristics of an environment in which the Secure Programming Clinic will enable students and instructors to ensure that students program in a robust and secure style, and that instructors who are not experts in this can have the clinic provide feedback about submitted programs that the faculty can take into account when assigning grades. The paper is structured as a Case Study according to guidelines for such studies provided by [6]. The next section provides a brief overview of the case study's layout and how it reflects in the structure of the remainder of this paper.

2 Methodology

The following structure is often used for the presentation of Case Study research [6]:

- Entry vignette
- Introduction
- Description of the case and its context

- Development of issues
- Detail about the selected issues
- Lessons Learned and Assertions
- Closing vignette

In the context of this paper, the abstract and introduction to the paper respectively serves as the case study's entry vignette and introduction. Section 3 describes the Secure Coding Clinics and serves as a description of the case and its context. The context is further supported by Sect. 4, which provides a review of relevant literature relating to the teaching of secure programming. The issues of concern in this paper are the identified educational principles, and how these were used in past secure programming clinics. These principles are identified in Sect. 5 and the relevance/adherence of the three variations of past clinics to the learning principles are mapped in Sect. 6 which elaborates on the selected issues of concern for this case study. These issues will be used to inform the authors' design intention for future secure programming clinics, which will be presented in the form of lessons learned in Sect. 6.2.

The closing vignette will take the form of our concluding remarks

3 Description of the Secure Programming Clinics

The basic form of a secure programming clinic is a physical or logical space where clinicians are available to students. As students complete homework assignments and other programs, they bring them to the clinic. The clinicians review the programs, and point out examples of code that create security problems or, more generally, are non-robust. They do not identify all such problems, but instead simply point out examples. They do not examine the program for correctness or whether it meets the requirements of an assignment. The students, on their own, correct the problems. The clinicians do not check that the program meets the requirements of the assignment; indeed, the clinic is not associated with any class, and is available on a drop-in basis. In this way, it resembles a writing clinic. Students can bring papers to the clinic, where clinicians will review the grammar and structure of the paper and offer suggestions on how to improve both. They do not examine the content for accuracy or credibility; they simply look at the form.

Several variations of the clinic are possible.

The first major set of variations comes from associating the clinic with a particular class. Here are possible approaches, any combination of which may meet the goals:

1. The instructor may apportion some part of the program grade to robustness. The clinicians would then assist by grading that part of the homework, and providing an appropriate score. The class graders would then grade the program with respect to the assignment's requirements.
2. After #1, the instructor can have the students correct the robustness problems, and then regrade that portion, giving the student some percentage of the points they corrected.

3. The clinicians can act as assistant instructors, helping the students develop threat models for how an attacker might use their program to violate desired security properties. As "security" is defined in terms of requirements, the threat model is critical to knowing the types of security problems that might arise. On the other hand, robustness issues are independent of threats, in the sense that they are common to all threats.

The functions of the clinic can be extended beyond simply reviewing programs. It can also provide information to help the students fix the problems. This typically requires collecting examples of poor programming and how to fix, or (better) avoid, them. It can also provide remote assistance, where the clinicians are not at the institutions. There is a salutary effect for this. If some of the clinicians are volunteers who work in the software industry or for government agencies, their presence and activities will convey the importance that future employers place in high-quality code. This provides incentives for students to learn the material.

The clinic can also be shared among universities. One implementation of the clinic provides a common shared appointment calendar, so students from any of the academic institutions could sign up for appointments even when the local clinicians were not available. The clinicians from the institutions coordinated their times so that one was always available during the day. Were this to be extended internationally, clinicians would probably be available for most of the evening and night (when many students of computer science and related disciplines develop their programs).

The above discussion provides insight into the specific secure programming clinic format of concern to this paper. However, for the sake of comprehensiveness, the next section will briefly highlight other such approaches, and challenges, relating to the teaching of secure programming.

4 Teaching Secure Programming

Secure programming is about writing secure code. The focus of many programming courses, however, is to write code that works with a lack of focus on writing code securely. A developer's unintentional ignorance of known vulnerabilities and insecure coding practices can generate insecure software. Besides the potential financial loss, the successful exploitation of insecure software can impact the confidentiality, integrity and availability (CIA) of critical information. Undetected exploitation can also lead to the embedding of malicious software within an organization, giving the malicious attacker the ability and potential to attack any time [18]. Secure programming should therefore include the basic principles of robust coding to guard against unexpected inputs and events [15].

The challenges of teaching and integrating secure programming into computing curricula have been around for many years, and some of these challenges which are still evident today [13]. These include:

- Lack of faculty buy-in
- Competition with other topics for inclusion into the curriculum
- Computing curricula already full
- Failure of students to grasp other important programming concepts
- Lack of secure programming expertise of faculty members

Much research has been conducted to address some of these challenges. A recent study [21] investigates a Java proof-of-concept plug-in for Eclipse, ESIDE (Educational Security in the IDE), that provides vulnerability warnings and secure programming education in the IDE while students write code. It works by scanning a selected project for code patterns that match predefined heuristic rules of security vulnerabilities. In this way, secure programming knowledge can be introduced early and reinforced throughout a students' education. Generally, ESIDE was found to increase students' awareness and knowledge of secure programming. However, almost no students actually modified their code to mitigate the detected vulnerabilities as they were most concerned with completing functionality and did not want to impact that functionality with additional security-oriented code. In addition, carefully timing the introduction of concepts and skills as well as incentivising such learning is important [21].

ESIDE was compared to the Secure Programming Clinic by running each approach with two separate groups of students, one group assigned to ESIDE and the other to the clinic [21]. Each group of students were asked to report on how likely they would use the recommended changes in their code during the session. The likelihood results for the Secure Programming Clinic were significantly better than for ESIDE. However, the clearest difference between the clinic and ESIDE were the number of specific vulnerabilities covered. Where ESIDE marked on average 42 lines of code per participant, the technical assistants running the clinic pointed out approximately two specific lines of code per participant.

One response to the need to teach students to program more securely was to introduce a serious game for teaching secure coding practices and principles to novice programmers [1]. Initial findings showed the game to be usable and engaging, with the majority of students being able to make clear correlations between the game levels and corresponding security concepts. Similarly, constructing secure coding duels [24] in Code Hunt, a high-impact serious gaming platform released by Microsoft Research, was proposed to instill gaming aspects into the education and training of secure coding. Secure coding duels proposed in this work are coding duels that are carefully designed to train players' secure coding skills, such as sufficient input validation and access control. Using serious games for teaching secure coding could alleviate some of the challenges faced by faculty members in this regard.

Furthermore, scorecards and checklists provide a consistent means of evaluation and assessment [22]. They describe the use of security checklists and scorecards which provide a quantifiable list of security criteria to aid in writing secure code and further reinforce security principles. Checklists distributed to students included:

- Sample code of errors to look for;
- Examples of correct ways of writing code; and
- Security mantras including a list of principles that form the basis for the checklist, for example: "All Input is Evil!"

Regardless of the approach used to teach secure programming, such approaches should take into account recognized learning principles, as discussed in Sect. 5, to ensure that learning takes place.

5 Learning Principles

Systematic studies of human behaviour, including studies of how people learn, is a relatively new field of scientific enquiry [17]. However, despite the youth of this field, many studies have already been dedicated to investigating how learning takes place. During such studies, researchers strive to identify recurring patterns in the data and to make generalizations based on these patterns. Such generalizations lead to the formulation of *learning principles* and *learning theories.* Learning principles identify the factors that influences learning. For example, the *principle* that a behaviour which is rewarded in some way is more likely to re-occur in future than one which is not followed by a reward. A learning *theory* on the other hand aims to provide an explanation of the underlying mechanisms that are involved in learning. Thus, whilst a learning principle presents *what* factors are important, a learning theory would explain *why* those factors are important [17].

Learning *principles* do not change much over time, however, learning *theories* have continually changed as understanding of human behaviour evolved [17]. Due to the fact that learning principles are less changeable, and thus more 'future proof' than learning theories, this research will seek to identify learning *principles* that could be useful in the secure coding clinics, but will avoid subscribing to any specific learning *theory.*

Educational literature provides many such learning principles. These principles have been identified, and their impact verified, in a variety of ways. One such approach is the field of brain compatible education. This educational approach stems from a combination of neuroscience and educational psychology and was first made possible by advances in brain imaging during the 1990s [12].

Brain-compatible, or brain-based, learning is not a formalised education approach or 'recipe for teachers', instead it provides a "set of principles and a base of knowledge and skills upon which we can make better decisions about the learning process" [9, p. xiii]. Brain research has shown that humans literally grow new dendrites and neural connections every time they learn something. Knowing which educational activities are the most effective in stimulating such growth allows educational practitioners to create material that leverages the way the brain naturally learns [10]. For the purpose of this research, it is not necessary to understand how these natural learning processes work. One only needs to understand that these principles were verified as being effective in promoting real learning.

No single complete list of such principles exists. However, many principles are presented and discussed in the literature [4,5,8,9,11,16,19,20]. The list presented in Table 1 contains a subset of principles from those used in literature. The principles included in Table 1 were restricted to those the authors specifically deemed most relevant to the context of the Secure Programming Clinic. Relevant principles from literature were reworded and consolidated in cases where there was significant overlap in meaning between those used in the literature and the context for use in this study. Table 1 thus presents the authors' adaption of these principles. The following discussion briefly elaborates on each of the listed principles:

- LP1 - According to [8,9,11] there is no long term retention without rehearsal. The brain would prune new neural growth if it is not reinforced by being used. It is vital to repeat lessons taught more than once, otherwise students would be likely to forget these lessons. One should also allow enough time for students to assimilate any new concepts. Several studies [4,8,11] explains that the brain will reconsolidate new neural growth for several weeks after learning using both conscious and unconscious (sleep) processes to decide how to incorporate knowledge into existing neural structures.
- LP2 - If the new knowledge is too advanced for the target audience, learning might be inhibited because the learners feel threatened instead of challenged by the content [4,5,8,9]. Furthermore, new knowledge can only be assimilated if it builds upon prior knowledge, since novel patterns can only form as extensions of existing patterns [5,11,19,20].
- LP3 - The process of learning consists of the brain recognizing patterns [4,5, 8,9]. For these patterns to form the learners need to recognize and connect patterns by themselves [5,9,11,19]. This process works best if the learners experience these patterns in contexts that are relevant to themselves [5,9] and their real-life experiences [11].
- LP4 - Humans naturally learn in social settings and through interaction with others [4,8]. Collaboration with others enhances learning [11].
- LP5 - Rehearsal will make learning permanent, however, this does not guarantee the rehearsed learning is in fact correct. Practice should be accompanied by *feedback* that is constant, consistent, and specific to ensure that practice that is permanent is also correct [8,16]. The effect of feedback is also amplified if it is immediate [5,9].

6 Mapping of Clinics to Selected Learning Principles

We begin by examining the instances of the secure programming clinic that have been run, and how they reflect the learning principles. We then discuss how the clinic might be improved by mapping the principles into various forms of the clinic.

Table 1. Learning principles

Principle#	Description
LP1	Lessons must be repeated at suitable intervals
LP2	Lessons must build upon the pre-existing knowledge of the target audience and must be of an appropriate level of difficulty
LP3	Learning happens through the recognition of patterns. To recognize new patterns, learning must be actively, personally, and specifically experienced in a context the learner can relate to
LP4	Learning is enhanced through collaboration and interaction with others
LP5	Immediate feedback amplifies learning

6.1 Experimental Secure Programming Clinics

The University of California at Davis, the California Polytechnic State University at San Luis Obispo, the California State University at Sacramento, and Purdue University Northwest have run the Secure Programming Clinic over the past 4 years. These instances of the clinic were tied to particular classes such as networking, operating systems, computer security, and introductory programming classes. The methodology was the same in all instances.

At the beginning of the term, students were asked to fill out an evaluation form that tested how much they knew about secure programming. They received class credit for beginning the questionnaire, and could indicate if they declined to proceed after giving their name and student ID (so they could get credit). At the end of the class, they filled out a similar questionnaire. The results of the two questionnaires were compared to see how their knowledge of, and ability to practice, secure programming changed. During the class, for each programming assignment, students could go to the clinic before submitting the assignment, and modify their programs based on the clinician's feedback. When assignments were submitted, they were given to the clinicians to check for the robustness and quality of the programming; graders assigned to the class graded the submitted programs for correctness. Then the instructor combined the results to give the program a grade. When the assignments were returned, students were told they could correct the robustness and security problems, and get back a large percentage of the points deducted for this (usually 75% or 80% of the points). They had a week to do this and resubmit the assignment. The clinicians would then review the changes, compare them with the original programs, and inform the instructor about the changes. The instructor would change the grade accordingly.

Institutional Review Boards (IRBs) at all institutions examined the experimental protocols to ensure they complied with federal and state law, and with the institutions' own rules about gathering and retaining student data. At the University of California at Davis, the principle investigator of the project was also the instructor, which the UC Davis IRB saw as a conflict of interest. To keep students anonymous to the instructor, student information (name and student identification number) was coded with a 4-digit number, and all work relating to that student's interaction with the clinic was recorded using that 4-digit number. During the term, the clinicians kept track of each student's 4-digit number, and any analyses had the student names and other identifying information redacted and replaced by the 4-digit number. When assignments were graded, the clinicians were given everyone's grade. This way, the instructor had no access to a particular student's pre- and post-questionnaires, nor to any information recorded about grade improvement.

Data on students' clinic usage and secure programming scores were collected in 2017 in one class (see Table 2). Of 42 students enrolled, 36 visited the clinic and 6 did not. Of the 36 students who visited the clinic, 14 students visited the clinic before the assignment was due, which were called "proactive" clinic users. Five visited the clinic before and after the assignment was due; they were called "consistent" users. Seventeen only visited the clinic after the initial secure programming assignment was submitted and graded; they were called "reactive"" users.

The average score for 12 of these 14 students on the secure programming assignment was 77% and the standard deviation was 4%. These students did not submit their assignment for a regrade. Two of the 12 proactive students (students who visited the clinic before the assignment was due) submitted their original assignment, received a grade, and then made changes to their assignment and submitted their assignments for regrade. These two students differ notably. The first student received an initial score of 9% and did not gain any additional points when he/she submitted the assignment for regrade. The second student scored 78% on the initial assignment and 91% on the assignment that was submitted for regrade.

Table 2. Statistics from the secure programming clinic.

		Initial clinic	Grade		Clinic	Regrade	
	n	Visit	Mean	Stdev	Revisit	Mean	Stdev
Proactive; no regrade	12	Yes	77%	22%	No	N/A	N/A
Proactive; regrade	2	Yes	44%	28%	No	50%[a]	41%
Consistent; no regrade	2	Yes	34%	22%	Yes	N/A	N/A
Consistent; regrade	3	Yes	23%	10%	Yes	77%	19%
Reactive; no regrade	0	No	N/A	N/A	No	N/A	N/A
Reactive; regrade	17	No	21%	17%	Yes	70%	10%
Never; no regrade	0	No	N/A	N/A	No	N/A	N/A
Never; regrade	6	No	23%	98%	No	48%	16%

[a] These data are anomalous. There were only two students in the group. One student scored 91% on the regrade and the other student remained at a score of 9%.

When the learning results of the Secure Programming Clinic are interpreted in the context of the 5 learning principles, there are several interesting findings. In the context of individual student learning, the principles are intersectional. For example, while lessons must be repeated at suitable intervals, what makes an interval "suitable" is partly contingent upon the pre-existing knowledge of the target audience, which is comprised of every student. Thus, pre-existing knowledge levels and learning trajectories vary. Another intersection is between LP1 and LP5. Immediate feedback (LP5) signals to learners the need for additional practice (LP1). When the learning setting provides for additional practice (LP1), at an appropriate level of difficulty (LP2) and supported through interaction with others (LP4), learning is supported.

Interpreted in the context of the principles, the 12 proactive clinic users who did not submit their assignments for regrade, visited the clinic. They then used the specific and timely feedback they were given to practice more secure programming. They submitted the assignment for feedback, and received timely positive feedback via their scores. This signals to the student that they are on track. In the case of the proactive student who received a high score and chose to make modifications to his/her assignment and submit for regrade, the clinic afforded the use of specific and timely feedback (LP5) in support of rehearsal and mastery (LP1 and LP2). In the case of the proactive student who received an initial score of 9% and did NOT improve, there are two considerations. If the student does not care about learning, then most instructional attempts at intervention will fail. However, if the student wants to learn, but is failing, then it would be important to incentivize the student to visit the clinic again. Provided there is desire to learn, the deficiency is likely due to prior knowledge (LP2) and/or lack of active, personally relevant experiences that afford pattern formation (LP3). In this case, the clinic should provide suitable diagnostics.

The 5 students who visited the clinic before the assignment was due and then after receiving an initial grade and before the reworked assignment was due are also interesting. Three of the five received a score of 23% on the robustness of their code for the assignment. It would seem as if the clinic was marginally useful for these three students before they did the assignment, especially if you compare them to the 12 proactive clinic users who scored 77% on the first assignment submission after visiting the clinic. Upon receiving their grade and then revisiting the clinic, these three students raised their grade to 77%. For these students, the value of the clinic demonstrates all of the learning principles. The clinic provided a venue for these students to repeat the exercises. The students seem to have acquired useful knowledge through this rehearsal, even though the new knowledge had to be built on wrong performance. Unlike their 12 peers in the proactive group who were able to attend the clinic, get useful information and submit the homework and earn a high grade, these students attended the clinic, got the proactive information, applied it incorrectly (LP2), received a poor grade (LP5), reattended the clinic (LP2, 3 and 4), learned about the same secure programming practices in the context of marginal performance (LP1, 2), and then succeeded. This is very encouraging.

The 17 students who were reactive users of the clinic are also interesting. Upon receiving an initial grade (mean score for this group was 21%, standard deviation 17%), learners had knowledge of what they did not know. The specific and timely feedback (LP5) acted as a spur to motivate students to use the clinic. The feedback was diagnostic in that it showed students exactly where their thinking was deficient, thereby allowing practice and rehearsal in correcting their insecure programming practices (LP1). In order for these students to continue expanding their secure programming practices, the clinic should support multiple classes, so that lessons are repeated (LP1), in a manner that subsequent knowledge builds on prior knowledge (LP2), culminating in the formation of patterns (LP3). When this is the case, learners will have robust knowledge of robust programming practices.

6.2 Discussion and Lessons Learned

The preceding section shows how important the principles are to the clinic's success. Here we discuss more general lessons learned.

Principle LP2 suggests that students build on pre-existing knowledge to learn, and LP3 says students learn by recognizing patterns. In the instance of the secure programming clinic for an introductory programming class in C, few students availed themselves of the clinic even though they were offered the chance to resubmit work, as described above. The problem was that the students were struggling to learn the language and techniques. Although all were supposed to have programmed before, none had used C, C++, or Java, and so concepts like pointers were new to them. They also had not mastered recursion and other basics. Hence they had no pre-existing knowledge of many features of C, and so they were unable to build on that pre-existing knowledge. Further, concepts of security were too difficult, so the clinic focused on robustness (avoiding buffer overflows, checking input, and so forth). Even these basics required the students to recognize patterns in programming, and they simply did not have the background for this.

The clinics discussed above were tied to specific classes. The students who went consistently (that is, before the assignment was due and again after the grading) showed the greatest improvement. This accords with learning principle LP1, that learning must be repeated at suitable intervals. Were the clinic not tied to specific classes, and were faculty to have their students use the clinic, this finding suggests that students would improve their robust and secure programming skills.

The structure of the clinic had the clinicians interacting directly with the students, sometimes in person privately, sometimes in a group, and sometimes using remote technology such as Skype. They gave immediate feedback by identifying examples of robustness and security problems in the students' programs, and discussing them, and approaches to possible solutions, with the students. The students then had not only to figure out the best solution and implement it, but they also had to analyze their program looking for other instances of that type of problem, because the clinicians did not point out all the problems. The goal was to give the students the skills to find the problems themselves, and learn how to avoid programming them in the future. This is an application of LP5, immediate feedback amplifying learning. Its success is shown by the marked increase in scores for the consistent and reactive students' programs.

The clinic provided students interaction with others (the clinicians). Although no formal statistics were gathered, the clinicians thought the group sessions were better because the students would explain problems to one another and therefore learn from their peers as well as from the clinician. This is an application of LP4, that collaboration and interaction with others enhances learning.

Several lessons from this mapping are apparent:

- The secure programming clinic will not work well with beginners or those who have little programming experience.
- The secure programming clinic will benefit students the most if it is available throughout the students' educational career, and they are required to use it in all classes that require programming (except introductory programming classes).
- The secure programming clinic must be tuned to the experience and background of the students, individually when possible, or taking into account the educational environment of the students when not.
- The secure programming clinic should hold group meetings as well as individual consulting sessions.

7 Conclusion

The secure programming clinic was developed to assist students in learning to write robust, secure programs, and to reinforce this throughout their schooling. A key question is to determine the conditions under which it will work well, and under which it will not work well. The research presented above, and its interpretation in light of the educational principles, provide general answers.

An interesting question would be to determine how to tailor the secure programming clinic to take advantage of specific educational environments. As an example, the clinic would probably be instantiated differently in South Africa than in the U.S. due to the differences in the structure of the academic programs. How to take those differences into account, to make the clinic maximally effective, is ripe for study. Similarly, could the clinic be adapted to a short, week-long course designed to teach programming intensively, and if so, how would the clinic operate to provide support after the course? Any analysis or development of these clinics must examine how to apply the principles in light of the environmental constraints.

Acknowledgements. This material is based upon work supported by the U.S. National Science Foundation under Grant Number DGE-1303211 to the University of California at Davis and Grant Number DGE-1303048 to Purdue University. Any opinions, findings, and conclusions or recommendations expressed in this material are those of the author(s) and do not necessarily reflect the views of the U.S. National Science Foundation, the University of California at Davis, and Purdue University.

References

1. Adamo-Villaani, N., Oania, M., Cooper, S.: Using a serious game approach to teach secure coding in introductory programming: development and initial findings. J. Educ. Technol. Syst. **41**(2), 107–131 (2012). https://doi.org/10.2190/ET.41.2.b
2. Bishop, M.: A clinic for 'secure' programming. IEEE Secur. Priv. **8**(2), 54–56 (2010). https://doi.org/10.1109/MSP.2010.62
3. Bishop, M., Orvis, B.J.: A clinic to teach good programming practices. In: Proceedings of the 10th Colloquium on Information Systems Security Education, pp. 168–174, June 2006. https://www.cisse.info/resources/archives/file/68-s05p05-2006?tmpl=component
4. Caine, R.N., Caine, G.: Making Connections: Teaching and the Human Brain. Association for Supervision and Curriculum Development, Alexandria (1991)
5. Craig, D.I.: Brain-compatible learning: principles and applications in athletic training. J. Athl. Train. **38**(4), 342–349 (2003). https://www.ncbi.nlm.nih.gov/pmc/articles/PMC314395/
6. Creswell, J.W.: Qualitative Inquiry and Research Design: Choosing Among Five Approaches, 3rd edn. SAGE Publications, Thousand Oaks (2012)
7. Durumeric, Z., et al.: The matter of Heartbleed. In: Proceedings of the 2014 Conference on Internet Measurement Conference, IMC 2014, pp. 475–488, November 2014. https://doi.org/10.1145/2663716.2663755
8. Fogarty, R.: Brain-Compatible Classrooms, 3rd edn. Corwin, Thousand Oaks (2009)
9. Jensen, E.: Brain-Based Learning: The New Paradigm of Teaching, 2nd edn. Corwin, Thousand Oaks (2008)
10. Lombardi, J.: Beyond learning styles: brain-based research and English language learners. Clear. House: J. Educ. Strat. Issues Ideas **81**(5), 219–222 (2008). https://doi.org/10.3200/TCHS.81.5.219-222
11. Materna, L.E.: Jump-Start the Adult Learner: How to Engage and Motivate Adults Using Brain-Compatible Strategies. Corwin, Thousand Oaks (2007)
12. McGeehan, J.: Brian-compatible learning. Green Teach. **64**, 7–13 (2001). http://www.bbbforlearning.com/uploads/1/0/4/4/10446722/brain-compatablelearning.pdf
13. Nance, K., Hay, B., Bishop, M.: Secure coding education: are we making progress? In: Proceedings of the 16th Colloquium for Information Systems Security Education, pp. 83–88 (2012). https://www.cisse.info/resources/archives/file/299-p13-2012?tmpl=component
14. National Institute of Standards and Technology: National vulnerability database. https://nvd.nist.gov
15. Ngambeki, I., Dark, M., Bishop, M., Belcher, S.: Teach the hands, train the mind ... a secure programming clinic. In: Proceedings of the 19th Colloquium for Information System Security Education, pp. 1–15, June 2015. https://www.cisse.info/resources/archives/file/359-p10?tmpl=component
16. van Niekerk, J., Webb, P.: The effectiveness of brain-compatible blended learning material in the teaching of programming logic. Comput. Educ. **103**, 16–27 (2016). https://doi.org/10.1016/j.compedu.2016.09.008, https://www.sciencedirect.com/science/article/pii/S036013151630166X
17. Ormrod, J.E.: Human Learning, 6th edn. Pearson Education, Boston (2011)

18. Marpaung, J.A.P., Sain, M., Lee, H.-J.: Survey on malware evasion techniques: state of the art and challenges. In: Proceedings of the 14th International Conference on Advanced Communication Technology, pp. 744–749, February 2012. https://ieeexplore.ieee.org/abstract/document/6174775
19. Smilkstein, R.: We're Born to Learn: Using the Brain's Natural Learning Process to Create Today's Curriculum, 2nd edn. Corwin, Thousand Oaks (2011)
20. Sousa, D.A.: How the Brain Learns, 5th edn. Corwin, Thousand Oaks (2016)
21. Tabassum, M., Watson, S., Richter, L.H.: Comparing educational approaches to secure programming: tool vs. TA. In: Proceedings of the 13th Symposium on Usable Privacy and Security, SOUPS 2017. USENIX Association, Berkeley (2017). https://www.usenix.org/conference/soups2017/workshop-program/wsiw2017/tabassum
22. Taylor, B., Azadegan, S.: Using security checklists and scorecards in CS curriculum. In: Proceedings of the 11th Colloquium for Information Systems Security Education, pp. 82–87 (2007). https://www.cisse.info/resources/archives/file/85-s05p01-2007?tmpl=component
23. The Joint Task Force on Computing Curricula: Computing curricula 2001 computer science. J. Educ. Resour. Comput. **1**(3Es), Fall 2001. https://doi.org/10.1145/384274.384275
24. Xie, T., Bishop, J., Tillmann, N., de Halleux, J.: Gamifying software security education and training via secure coding duels in code hunt. In: Proceedings of the 2015 Symposium and Bootcamp on the Science of Security, HotSoS 2015, pp. 26:1–26:2. ACM, New York (2015). https://doi.org/10.1145/2746194.2746220

Introducing Research into the Undergraduate Curriculum in Cybersecurity

Dimitrios Damopoulos and Susanne Wetzel(✉)

Department of Computer Science, Stevens Institute of Technology,
Castle Point on Hudson, Hoboken, NJ 07030, USA
{ddamopou,swetzel}@stevens.edu

Abstract. In this paper, we describe a new approach for introducing a research experience based on real-world research problems into the two semester Senior Design course sequence of the B.S. in Cybersecurity program at Stevens Institute of Technology as part of the INSuRE consortium. We discuss the necessity of such a research experience in the context of the ever-changing nature of Cybersecurity in that attacks seen and countermeasures developed today may already be different and outdated tomorrow. We also detail the insights gained, challenges encountered, and lessons learned in order to provide the community with the necessary means to use this as a model to implement a research experience as part of other undergraduate Cybersecurity degree programs.

Keywords: Research · Cybersecurity · Bachelor degree · Senior design course sequence

1 Introduction

In the recent past, an increasing number of four-year institutions in the United States started dedicated undergraduate programs in Cybersecurity. In the past, degree programs focused on Cybersecurity were mostly available on the graduate level—often building on undergraduate degrees in computing, engineering, or business—or Cybersecurity was offered as a possible concentration in the context of other traditional undergraduate degree programs—most prominently in Computer Science, Computer Engineering, Mathematics, or Business.

The main benefit of a dedicated undergraduate degree program in Cybersecurity is in that it allows for a greater focus on Cybersecurity content—both in terms of depth and breadth. Consequently, students have more opportunities and options to select a focus within Cybersecurity to pursue their specific interests. Generally, this approach allows for a more comprehensive education in Cybersecurity and is thus assumed to better prepare students for a career in Cybersecurity—already by means of an undergraduate degree. This is particularly important considering the fact that in the US the majority of students pursuing an advanced degree in computing-focused fields are non-domestic

Published by Springer Nature Switzerland AG 2019
L. Drevin and M. Theocharidou (Eds.): WISE 2019, IFIP AICT 557, pp. 30–42, 2019.
https://doi.org/10.1007/978-3-030-23451-5_3

students [2,10]. Furthermore, there is a widely reported workforce shortage in Cybersecurity—and providing a comprehensive education only at the graduate level seems unlikely to be sufficient to address this issue [7,9].

In designing an undergraduate degree program in Cybersecurity, the challenge is not only to find the right balance between depth and breadth in terms of covering the various areas in Cybersecurity but to also ensure that the intrinsic characteristics of the field are properly covered and taught as part of the curriculum. Most importantly, unlike other fields in Science, Technology, Engineering and Mathematics (STEM), Cybersecurity is characterized by the fact that anything and everything may change at an every-increasing pace. Every day brings new challenges and attacks that often require the swift development of novel solutions and countermeasures in order to ensure suitable security guarantees for any and all services, applications, operations, and infrastructure in today's cyber-driven world.

It is in this context that this paper describes an implementation of the so-called Information Security Research and Education (INSuRE) program [4] as part of the required two semester Senior Design course sequence in the B.S. in Cybersecurity program at Stevens Institute of Technology [1]. This paper argues that the INSuRE effort—which exposes the students to a real-world research experience—provides an ideal means to teach the skills necessary in order for them to succeed as Cybersecurity professionals. In particular, through INSuRE students gain a unique educational experience which is team-based (recognizing that most Cybersecurity efforts are carried out by teams), multi-/cross-disciplinary (as Cybersecurity generally draws upon many different disciplines that must be properly integrated in order to enable the development of suitable solutions), multi-institutional (as Cybersecurity problems tend to span across multiple organizations), as well as research-oriented and time-scaled (as devising responses to new and ever-changing vulnerabilities and attacks is typically very time-critical) [4,14,15].

Previously, INSuRE was mostly offered on the graduate level, typically in the context of a one semester elective course. A few institutions, including Stevens, also worked with teams comprised of both graduate and undergraduate students. Furthermore, Dakota State University did a pilot where teams of undergraduate students were paid a stipend instead of earning course credits for their participation in INSuRE [3]. Stevens was the first to carry out INSuRE with teams comprised of all undergraduate students for a duration of two consecutive semesters in the context of a required Senior Design course sequence. Before that, it was not known whether it is feasible to introduce and carry out this kind of research experience in the context of a required two semester sequence on the undergraduate level in an effective manner.

Outline: The remainder of the paper is organized as follows: We first provide a brief overview of the INSuRE program in general (Sect. 2) and then detail its novel implementation in the context of a required two semester Senior Design course sequence (Sect. 3). This is followed by a discussion of lessons learned and challenges encountered (Sect. 4).

2 INSuRE

The INSuRE research collaborative is a self-organizing, cooperative, multi-disciplinary, multi-institutional, and multi-level research collaboration of National Centers of Academic Excellence in Cyber Defense Research (CAE-R) and Cyber Defense Education (CAE-CDE) universities [4,5,14,15] that "cooperate to engage students in solving applied Cybersecurity research problems". The Center of Academic Excellence in Cyber Defense Research designation was launched in 2008 with the purpose to increase the understanding of "robust Cyber Defense technology, policy, and practices that will enable our nation to effectively prevent or respond to a catastrophic cyber event" [6]. The CAE-R designation recognizes universities for their institutional excellence in Cybersecurity research. The vision for the program was to "establish a process that will present opportunities for Cyber Defense research centers to drill deeper into much needed solutions to securing the global information grid and provide NSA, DHS, and other federal agencies with insight into academic Cyber Defense programs that can support advanced academic research and development capabilities" [6]. However, until INSuRE was launched, these government agencies did not have an effective means to tap into the expertise within the CAE-Rs—except for working with some faculty or institutions on an individual basis.

Starting with one university and one government agency in Fall 2012, INSuRE has since grown into a collaboration of 20+ universities (holding the CAE-R or CAE-CDE designations) with many government agencies and labs (on both the federal and local levels)—which suggest the real-world research problems in Cybersecurity (of national interest and need) and provide technical oversight to the student teams. Over the years, the INSuRE partners have worked on more than 100+ distinct research problems resulting in more than 150 project reports, involving hundreds of students across the participating universities—many of whom have subsequently been hired into government jobs. The effort has resulted in refereed conference publications and published data sets (e.g., [11–13]).

Since the beginning, Purdue University has been the central point and coordinating entity of INSuRE. All participating universities follow a common schedule (possibly with minor local adjustments due to the institutions' semester schedule). The coordinating faculty at Purdue solicit research problems from the participating government agencies and labs and make them centrally accessible to all participating universities. In turn, universities locally recruit students to participate. Throughout the semesters, there are various milestones that are coordinated across all universities:

Bids: The first major milestone that all students have to complete is the bidding on a number of the contributed research problems. In particular, all students are asked to review the descriptions that the Technical Directors provided for the research problems they contributed. For at least two research problems the students are interested in, they are then asked to write and submit a brief (two-to-three paragraph) statement on why they are interested in this problem, what excites them about the problem, what they see as possible directions for their project, and why they feel they are qualified to carry out the project. The INSuRE coordinator reviews the bids submitted by all students from all the participating institutions and assigns the students to research problems. In doing so, the coordinator seeks to strive a balance of covering as many research problems and Technical Directors as possible while recognizing the student's interests and preferences as best as possible. Also, teams are typically formed at a participating institution—while teams across institutions are possible and have been done.

Project Proposal: Once project teams have been formed, the teams prepare a project proposal that outlines the team's ideas, directions, milestones, distribution of work, etc. for their project to address the assigned research problem. This also includes an initial literature review. Typically, the teams are in close contact with the Technical Director who contributed the research problem while preparing the project proposal. Oftentimes, Technical Directors phrase the descriptions of their research problems in such a fashion that many different directions and deliverables for a project are possible. The purpose is to allow the students to develop their own ideas and shape their project. Once completed, the Technical Director reviews the project proposal—possibly asking for changes or additions as needed. Once the Technical Director approves the project proposal, the team starts working on the project, executing its plan.

Midterm Deliverables: About half way through the semester, each team prepares a report and a slide deck documenting the current status of their projects. All reports and slide decks are shared with everyone (i.e., all participating institutions and Technical Directors) through the common project platform. In addition, all teams are scheduled to give a midterm presentation—facilitated through WebEx sessions (arranged for by the coordinators at Purdue University). Any participating institution, their teams and students, as well as all Technical Directors may participate in these WebEx sessions. These open sessions provide everyone with a unique learning opportunity on a large variety of projects on current topics (including their state-of-the-art, open issues, results achieved, etc.)—almost like a conference in Cybersecurity that is covering topics across the entire spectrum.

End of the Semester Deliverables: Similar to the Midterm Deliverables, the teams prepare reports and slide decks to comprehensively document their results at the end of the semester. Once again, these documents are shared with everyone and the respective final presentations are facilitated through WebEx.

All offline interactions and data sharing are handled through a central platform—referred to as INSuREHub [4,14,15]. While the coordinators maintain the central components (including the uploading of the research problem sets, semester schedules, etc.), each institution has a dedicated space on INSuREHub where deliverables are uploaded and can be accessed not only by the Technical Directors co-supervising the projects but the INSuRE community at large.

It is important to note that it is not unusual for a Technical Director to offer the same research problem for multiple semesters as a single semester might not be enough time for a team to comprehensively address all facets of a specific research problem. Teams who are assigned to a research problem that has been offered and worked on before have access (through the INSuREHub) to the previous deliverables of these teams (i.e., Project Proposals, Midterm and End of the Semester Deliverables) and may use these as a jump-off point for their own projects. Consequently, there have been research problems that have been worked on for multiple semesters and have seen contributions from various teams leading to a wealth of directions and results over time [15].

In addition to the milestones that are the same across all participating INSuRE institutions, there may be additional ones that individual institutions implement. For example, many (including Stevens) also require the following:

Weekly Dashboards: Each week, the teams are required to submit a two-page slide deck that reviews the status of the project. In particular, as part of their slide deck, the teams discuss the progress they have made during the past week, whether they have encountered any challenges, or whether they have any questions. In addition, each team member reviews what s/he worked on, what s/he individually contributed and delivered to the project, and what s/he is planning in terms of both activities and deliverables for the coming week. The teams also present these dashboards in class—where they also demo the code, review submitted deliverables, and field questions from the instructors and other classmates. The Weekly Dashboards are made available to the Technical Directors in order to keep them updated on the projects. The dashboards also serve as input and basis for the regularly scheduled meetings with the Technical Directors.

Regular Check-in with Technical Directors: Regular meetings (e.g., conference calls) are scheduled with the Technical Directors—ideally during the weekly class time(s). As part of these meetings, the students report on their progress, ask questions, and provide the Technical Directors with the opportunity to give input and shape the projects as needed and desired.

3 Structure of INSuRE in the Context of Senior Design

In implementing INSuRE in the context of a two semester Senior Design course sequence during the Senior year of our B.S. in Cybersecurity degree program at Stevens Institute of Technology [1], we had to make some adjustments to the typical deliverables when offering INSuRE as a single course for one semester only (as described above). In particular, this pertains to defining effective means to connect the two semesters—especially regarding the typical beginning of the semester elements such as the Bids and Project Proposal which are not necessary for the second semester. Instead, we included a milestone to connect back with the Technical Directors and added a Project Realignment milestone:

Project Status Updates: Instead of the Midterm and End of the Semester Deliverables, we adjusted the two semester schedule to include a total of three

Project Status Update milestones, coinciding with the Midterm and End of the Semester Deliverables of the first semester and the Midterm Deliverables of the second semester. For both the second and the third updates, we require that these status updates build on the previous update and that the respective slide decks and reports are updated and extended on correspondingly to properly reflect the project progress since the last status update. Similarly, with each status update we request that the timeline and deliverables going forward are adjusted as needed.

Project Realignment: During the second semester of the two semester sequence of the project, we have adjusted the schedule replacing the Bids and the Project Proposal with a Project Realignment milestone. In most cases, this goes hand in hand with the next newly introduced milestone, namely the facilitating—if possible—of an in-person meeting with the Technical Director. Typically, the Project Realignment milestone is scheduled after such in-person meetings with the Technical Directors and after the first few class meetings have been completed in order to give the students enough time to discuss matters and plan the second semester (including other milestones, deliverables, and assignments of responsibilities to team members) accordingly.

Project Meeting with Technical Director: We were fortunate that we were awarded a grant to support the development and introduction of INSuRE in the context of the Senior Design course sequence of our B.S. in Cybersecurity program at Stevens. In particular, the grant included funding to hold in-person meetings of the teams with the Technical Directors of their project. We arranged for the meetings to take place either right before or at the very beginning of the second semester—thus constituting an integral part of the overall realignment process of the project. Depending on the schedules of the Technical Directors, the meetings typically lasted 2–4 hours and included demonstrations and presentations by the teams, as well as in-depth discussions with the Technical Directors on the progress made during the past semester and plans for the semester ahead.

Optional Extra-credit Assignments: It is not unusual for students to ask for extra-credit assignments in order to boost their grades. To facilitate such requests and yet make it fair to all students in the class, we have designed a set of assignments that all students can take advantage of. In particular, in the first semester we offered a group assignment for the teams to start early with the planning for the second semester of the two semester Senior Design course sequence. In addition, we gave individual team members the opportunity to work on the project over the break in between the two semesters and earn extra-credit for doing so in both semesters (for planning the work to be done at the end of the first semester and reporting on the completed work at the beginning of the second semester).

Grading: Most of the deliverables were graded on a per team basis. The only exception was the Weekly Dashboards where the weekly deliverables and planning include a major individual grading component. This was done on purpose in order to give each team member the opportunity to show his/her individual contributions and distinguish himself/herself beyond the team's performance.

Program Context: Stevens Institute of Technology was one of the first institutions in the US to offer a dedicated degree program in Cybersecurity on the undergraduate level. The program was approved in 2006 and had its first class graduating in 2011.

The B.S. in Cybersecurity program at Stevens [1] includes strong core requirements in Computer Science and Mathematics as well as an extensive set of courses covering a broad spectrum of Cybersecurity aspects (including Cryptography, Privacy, System Security, and Law). In addition, students may select electives from a wide range of Computer Science or Cybersecurity courses.

The two semester Senior Design course sequence at Stevens is to be "the culmination of the undergraduate experience, where knowledge gained in the classroom is applied to a major design project" [8]. In the past, Cybersecurity majors completed their Senior Design course sequence together with the Computer Science majors. However, many Cybersecurity majors expressed great frustration and dissatisfaction as the typical Computer Science Senior Design projects had too little Cybersecurity content. Instead, their efforts had to mostly focus on software development aspects. In order to address this shortcoming, we decided to offer a dedicated Senior Design course sequence for our Cybersecurity majors. The goal was to allow the Cybersecurity majors to apply the Cybersecurity knowledge, skills, and abilities they had acquired in their course work in the context of a comprehensive, challenging, real-world Cybersecurity project. We feel that implementing the Senior Design course sequence as part of INSuRE is especially well-suited to meet this goal.

4 Discussion: Challenges Encountered and Lessons Learned

In the past, Stevens offered INSuRE in the more traditional setting as it is to be found across most of the institutions participating in the consortium over the years. Specifically, the course was offered as an elective course (either as independent study course or special topics course) with some/all team members pursuing a Cybersecurity degree program or concentration in a computing-focused degree program on the graduate level (for more details see [4,14,15]). Consequently, there are two major differences to the newly implemented Senior Design sequence in the context of INSuRE:

Elective vs. Required Course(s): For elective courses, students typically choose courses that best meet their expectations—typically including factors such as their own experience, interest in the topic, anticipated workload, instructor, timing, etc. In general, students taking the elective have made a deliberate decision to take the course. This is very different in case of a required course where students have no choice but complete the course in order to meet graduation requirements. In turn, it means that a required course will include a cross-cutting spectrum of students (w.r.t. strengths, weaknesses, and proficiency).

Undergraduate vs. Graduate Students: Typically, graduate students are more advanced, have more experience, or more generally are more mature. While not a must, these traits at the very least can prove very beneficial when working in a team, dealing with the unknowns and challenges of a research problem, and working under tight time constraints.

In this context we now discuss challenges we have encountered and lessons learned in offering the two semester course sequence for the past two academic years. When possible, we indicate changes we introduced for the second teaching in response to the challenges encountered in teaching the sequence for the first time. For some of the challenges we have not yet introduced any countermeasures as they may need more investigation or implementing solutions may also require some non-trivial changes to the Stevens' B.S. in Cybersecurity curriculum [1].

Typical Student Work Pattern: Many of today's (undergraduate) degree programs in the US seem to be structured such that students can succeed by solely focusing on and working towards the typical course deliverables that come with a (hard) deadline—many of which are now scoped such that students can still complete them rather last minute if they just put in some major effort right before such a deadline. This holds true especially for homeworks and in some cases even exams. This pattern constitutes a major challenge in the context of this Senior Design course sequence.

Specifically, such a research-oriented implementation of the Senior Design course sequence requires that all students in the team consistently work on the project every week. Last minute power work does not prove effective and does not lead to the progress necessary and expected—especially also by the Technical Directors. It proves extremely challenging to get the students to change their work pattern—even though multiple measures have been introduced to at least enforce some of it. This includes that the students must develop a timeline as part of the Project Proposal—which they are required to adjust for each Status Update and as part of the Project Realignment milestone. Furthermore, the Weekly Dashboards are meant to instill some level of regular accountability—forcing the students to report on the work they have completed in the past week and plan ahead for the coming week. Still, we have continuously experienced that students deviate from these plans—especially at times where they have major deliverables or milestones in other classes (e.g., homeworks or midterm/final exams). Students seem to think that there is enough flexibility in this Senior design course sequence that allows them to make up for working less one week by putting in more time during a subsequent week. Clearly, the students underestimate ripple effects and the dependency as well as impact on other team members.

We have experienced that holding the students accountable to the deliverables they have committed to for certain dates (e.g., by deducting points for not meeting them in time) can lead to a lot of tension and complaints. Students tend to do things their way, i.e., the way they have done it in the past and continue to successfully do it for other courses. While some express their dissatisfaction openly, others only do so in the course assessment at the conclusion of the term.

Senior Design Sequence in the Curriculum: Related to the previous matter is the fact that the two semester Senior Design course sequence merely accounts for one of the five three-credit courses that the students are scheduled to take during each semester of their Senior year[1]. Consequently, there is a natural limit on the amount of time that the students can realistically spend working on their Senior Design project. While the expected time commitment outside of the classroom is 6–9 hours per week for a three credit course, in reality students devote a decreasing amount of time on a course with an increasing number of courses they are enrolled in. Given the experience of the first teaching of the two semester sequence with the *"I did not spend much time on the project because it was a busy week with other classes"*, for the second teaching we increased the focus on the Weekly Dashboards seeking to hold the students more accountable to the timelines they have committed to.

Research Methods: Most of the undergraduate students have no major experience in project work other than software development at a small scale or based on typical textbook problems. Furthermore, the main goto source in case of questions is Wikipedia. Even when provided with research papers along with instructions on how to search for papers they cite and papers they are cited by in order to get a comprehensive picture of the topic, by and large the students seem to lack the patience to do so. Also, we experienced a tremendous resistance to thoroughly studying the papers and documenting findings through brief write-ups that can be reviewed by the whole team. Instead of spending some time to comprehensively explore a topic and available resources, we noticed that students would rather just revert to trying things out or coding something up quickly (possibly also to demonstrate activity and produce some results). At this point we can only speculate what the reason is for this—possibly attesting it also to how students have been conditioned—i.e., regurgitate materials instead of making them transfer knowledge to unknown problems.

Once again, we used the Weekly Dashboards during the second teaching of the two semester course sequence in order to force some change in behavior. Specifically, we made the students report on the papers they have read and make them submit short summaries that also discuss what other literature they found based on what they read and what needs to be reviewed next. Similarly, we have used the Weekly Dashboards and the class time where students present their progress to challenge the rapid prototyping and development directions the students prefer to take. In some cases we have even stepped in and not allowed the students to focus on coding until they finished at least some basic specification or mathematical description of the underlying problem.

[1] It is important to note that many of our students elect to overload during their Junior and Senior years—pursuing both a Bachelor and Masters degree program in parallel. Such an increased workload just further exacerbates the problem at hand in terms of time commitment and time management.

As students progressed through the two semester course sequence, we noticed that students acquired more of a critical thinking and adopted a more structured approach.

Expectations of Student, Faculty, and Technical Directors Interactions and Commitments: Having Technical Directors from government agencies and labs suggest real-world research problems and co-supervise the teams (together with the faculty at the respective institutions) is a unique opportunity for the students and faculty alike. All parties can benefit tremendously from the interactions alone. However, we learned that this can also bring about challenges and friction. First and foremost, it is important for all to understand that it is a two semester commitment. We learned that it is important to explicitly address this at the beginning of the first semester. Furthermore, it is important to align expectations. While some Technical Directors (especially those from government labs) may have extensive experience with summer interns, we have come to realize that it is important to manage expectations with regard to experience (which is different when working with undergraduate students versus graduate students) as well as the time commitment (a full-time intern versus a senior who is carrying a full load of classes and only one of which is the research-based Senior Design course sequence).

In turn, students are used to faculty being rather readily available—if not for an in-person meeting then at least by email. However, this is not necessarily the case for Technical Directors as participating in INSuRE is something that many of them do in addition to their usual job responsibilities. Consequently, it has proven rather challenging at times to manage requests for meetings and such. In particular, scheduling a meeting outside of the weekly class time by itself is a non-trivial challenge as individual team members typically have different class schedules and thus finding a common meeting time that works for the whole team, faculty advisors, and the Technical Director alike is generally extremely difficult.

Lastly, it is important to recognize that different Technical Directors not only have different backgrounds but also have different styles in overseeing projects. Some prefer to be hands-off and let the teams find their way—as a fresh set of minds may discover a promising and successful avenue that may lead to great results. Others are very hands-on and expect to see things done in a specific manner. As faculty we thus sometimes have to mediate matters accordingly.

Problem Selection: Another critical element is the selecting of a suitable research problem for the undergraduate student teams to work on for two semesters. It is a tradeoff between too easy (possibly mostly software development focused) versus too technically challenging (possibly even to the extent that the undergraduate students simply do not yet have the necessary background and the topic is too technical in order for the students to quickly get to the level necessary to successfully master the project). Similarly, it is necessary to pick a research problem that allows for a project that is comprehensive enough to span a sequence of two semesters. In turn, if the problem is too extensive, the challenge is to carve out a piece of suitable size that can be accomplished and mastered in two semesters. In addition, there might be research problems that are so tightly defined that students do not have much room to develop their own ideas. In contrast, there may be problems that are so generally phrased that while the students may find them interesting, they do not know where to start and what to aim for. Overall, the right scoping is a major challenge. For the second teaching, we pre-selected some problems for which the students were allowed to submit bids. We are not sure yet whether we will continue with this kind of an approach in the future. While it was easier for students to master the bid phase, it is possible that some students would have better liked some of the other research problems.

Orthogonal to the above is an observation we made after the bid phase for the second teaching. While we had students bid on research problems enthusiastically, some then were stunned when they were actually assigned to these problems. When asked why this came as a surprise, it became apparent that the students had underestimated that stating interest could result in them being assigned to the problem. Or more generally, it seemed that some students did not fully grasp the magnitude and importance of the problem selection at the onset and its impact not just for a short period of time (say days or weeks as in case of deliverables in other classes) but that instead this constitutes a long lasting commitment for a full academic year.

In general, in both years we have learned a lot and anticipate to continue to learn more in future years. We expect that for some of the encountered problems and challenges we will find good solutions over time that will then manifest themselves in rules and directions. For others, we expect that we will need to cope with them as they appear.

5 Conclusion and Future Work

Implementing INSuRE in the context of a two semester Senior Design course sequence has been exciting, challenging, and rewarding at the same time. Some of the challenges faced in the first two years were unexpected. Some of the changes introduced after the first year paid off, others still have to be reassessed. We expect that further adjustments and changes will be made based on the teaching of the two semester course sequence in its second year. For sure, we plan to explore different options of identifying potential projects (from the set of all offered projects) for our students to choose from.

Generally speaking, the experience of the past two years provides a positive answer to the question raised above as to whether it is feasible to introduce and carry out this kind of research experience in the context of a required two semester sequence on the undergraduate level in an effective manner. First, there are research problems contributed as part of INSuRE that can be carried out by undergraduate student teams over a sequence of two semester. Second, the contributed research problems are non-trivial thus requiring the students to apply a wide range of knowledge, skills, and abilities they have acquired throughout their course work. Third, it is possible for undergraduate students to make substantial progress and develop exciting new approaches to challenging research problems.

In particular, over the past two years, our teams successfully carried out a number of projects. For example, for the research problem of devising effective countermeasures to phishing, one of our teams developed a new approach based on visual similarity testing. The team implemented a browser plug-in, a back-end testing tool, and carried out user studies to better understand user behavior in the context of phishing. Another team worked on the research problem of designing effective counter drone mechanisms. Specifically, the team worked on classifying drones based on characteristics found in the 802.11 traffic of drone networks.

Questions we cannot answer to date include whether teams with (some) graduate students would have been able to develop better solutions (faster), whether two semester projects generally result in more comprehensive solutions than those of one semester projects, etc. In order to answer such questions one would have to break with some key principles of INSuRE. In particular, it would be necessary to assign various kinds of student teams (one semester vs. two semester, all undergraduate vs. all graduate vs. mixed teams) to the same research problem, forcing them to pursue the same approach to allow for the comparability of results. Most likely it would also be necessary to do this for a variety of research problems in order to ensure that the results are not specific to a particular research problem.

Going forward, we intend to carry out a comparative study (w.r.t. effectiveness, difficulties, challenges, and success) with other educational systems which introduce research components into the curriculum in other ways. For example in Germany, students pursuing a Bachelor degree in Cybersecurity or Computer Science at a university are typically required to write a Bachelor thesis. The time frames allotted to complete this requirement vary—in some cases it is three months in others it is up to six months. While working on their thesis, students typically are not enrolled in classes and instead can focus all their time and efforts on the project. Yet, a Bachelor thesis is typically completed on an individual basis. Also, earlier in their studies, students are often required to complete a seminar course in which they may already be introduced to some research methods—in particular in conducting a thorough literature search for a specific topic. We would like to investigate similarities and differences in terms of challenges and opportunities. Questions we seek to answer include: Does working in a group when first being introduced to research make things easier or more difficult? Would increasing the number of credits for the Senior Design courses (and thus decreasing the number of other courses that students would take in parallel) improve the quality and outcomes of the projects? How beneficial is it to expose students to some research methods earlier in their studies—e.g., through a seminar course where students are exposed to current research and are required to conduct a literature search?

Acknowledgements. The authors thank the INSuRE consortium—and in particular Melissa Dark and John Springer from Purdue University—for their continued support and guidance.

In part, this work was supported by the CAE Cybersecurity Workforce Education Grant # H98230-17-1-0342. Some of this work was carried out while Susanne Wetzel was serving as Program Director for the Secure and Trustworthy Cyberspace Program at the National Science Foundation[2].

References

1. B.S. in Cybersecurity at Stevens Institute of Technology. https://www.stevens.edu/schaefer-school-engineering-science/departments/computer-science/undergraduate-programs/cybersecurity
2. Foreign Students and Graduate STEM Enrollment. https://www.insidehighered.com/quicktakes/2017/10/11/foreign-students-and-graduate-stem-enrollment
3. INSuRE at Dakota State University. http://dsu.edu/news/dsu-announces-insure-scholarship-recipients
4. INSuRE Project. http://www.insurehub.org/
5. National Centers of Academic Excellence in Cyber Defense. https://www.nsa.gov/resources/educators/centers-academic-excellence/cyber-defense/
6. National Centers of Academic Excellence in Cyber Defense Research. https://www.nsa.gov/news-features/press-room/Article/1631722/nsa-and-dhs-announce-the-first-designees-of-the-national-centers-of-academic-ex/
7. New Data Shows Expansion in Cybersecurity Worker Shortage. https://www.nist.gov/news-events/news/2018/06/new-data-shows-expansion-cybersecurity-worker-shortage
8. Senior Design at Stevens Institute of Technology. https://www.stevens.edu/academics/undergraduate-studies/senior-capstone-projects
9. US Lawmakers Introduce Bill to Fight Cybersecurity Workforce Shortage. https://www.zdnet.com/article/us-lawmakers-introduce-bill-to-fight-cybersecurity-workforce-shortage/
10. Why are American Graduate Programs in Math, Statistics and CS Dominated by International Students? https://www.quora.com/Why-are-American-graduate-programs-in-math-statistics-and-CS-dominated-by-international-students
11. Alabi, O., Beckman, J., Dark, M., Springer, J.: Toward a data spillage prevention process in hadoop using data provenance. In: Proceedings of the 2015 Workshop on Changing Landscapes in HPC Security (CLHS) (2015)
12. Alves, T., Das, R., Morris, T.: Virtualization of industrial control system testbeds for cybersecurity. In: Proceedings of the 2nd Annual Industrial Control System Security Workshop (ICSS) (2016)
13. Narayanan, S.N., Mittal, S., Joshi, A.: OBD Securealert: An Anomaly Detection System for Vehicles. In: Proceedings of IEEE Workshop on Smart Service Systems (SmartSys) (2016)
14. Sherman, A.T., et al.: INSuRE: Collaborating Centers of Academic Excellence Engage Students in Cybersecurity Research. IEEE Secur. Priv. **15**(4), 72–78 (2017)
15. Sherman, A.T., et al.: The INSuRE Project: CAE-Rs Collaborate to Engage Students in Cybersecurity Research. CoRR, abs/1703.08859 (2017)

[2] Any opinion, findings, and conclusions or recommendations expressed in this material are those of the author(s) and do not necessarily reflect the views of the National Science Foundation.

Training

A Short-Cycle Framework Approach to Integrating Psychometric Feedback and Data Analytics to Rapid Cyber Defense

Erik L. Moore(✉), Steven P. Fulton, Roberta A. Mancuso, Tristen K. Amador, and Daniel M. Likarish(✉)

Regis University, Denver, CO, USA
{emoore, sfulton, rmancuso, tamador, dlikaris}@regis.edu

Abstract. Following earlier research in demonstrating the significance of behavioral analysis in cyber defense, the authors developed a framework to incorporating multi-disciplinary datasets along a common timeline to increase incident response feedback for coaching. Currently this framework is being introduced in the state of Colorado, USA as a part of a joint government, industry and academic partnership. Upon project initiation, the feedback cycle had been a minimum of several months from observation to feedback. Presented here is a new framework that can shorten the cycle of psychometric feedback to multiple times in one training day. This Short-Cycle Framework, gathering psychometric and cyber data to provide direct feedback to cyber defense team leaders, was conceived when Regis University's psychometric evaluators observed a real multi-agency cyber defense response. The authors realized the psychometric data can be used in live cyber defense incidents alongside things like network firewall traffic analysis as the cyber defenders provide relief for organizations under active cyber attack. This work presents the context in which the framework was developed, the characteristics of the framework, and suggestions for further research. The framework implements a specific set of short-term state indicators based on well-known personality trait and state models. The coaching cycle was scripted to shorten the delay between observation and feedback so that it can be more useful in both training and live incident response.

Keywords: Psychometric analysis · Cyber defense · Myers-Briggs · Parker Team Player Survey · National Guard · Feedback · Training · Multi-agency · Short-Cycle Framework · Cyber incident response

1 Introduction

Beginning in 2013, Regis University has hosted joint training exercises of multiple Colorado state and local government cybersecurity teams, Colorado based public utilities and cybersecurity focused industry leaders. The University has hosted biannual large (over 100 participants from adjoining states) and smaller joint training exercises that the authors recognized the personal individual member, team cohesion and incident responses community growth and maturation leading up to recognition of a

Published by Springer Nature Switzerland AG 2019
L. Drevin and M. Theocharidou (Eds.): WISE 2019, IFIP AICT 557, pp. 45–58, 2019.
https://doi.org/10.1007/978-3-030-23451-5_4

dynamic self-sustaining Collaborative Training and Response Community (CTRC). We also have witnessed the individual professional development of team members, for instance after hours cyber range practice, 7/24 threat awareness and analysis, regional and national group exercises. Since May of 2016, these exercises have also included psychometric analysts with expertise in personality trait preferences and role diversity to guide the cybersecurity teams toward better team interaction, leadership efficacy, and self-awareness for individual participants, which ultimately benefits the team. The observations and analysis outlined here have occurred at numerous events, providing feedback to leadership and to individual team members based on observed training and incident response behavior.

The leadership of the joint training had completed their initial roadmap of exercises, including technical, incident response practice, and relationships. They recognized the need to improve team performance using additional methods and began looking for a next set of methods to enhance response capabilities. A Regis-based member of the joint training leadership realized that behavioral psychology and health care faculty may be able to add significant value to enhancing cybersecurity team performance. The entire joint training leadership agreed and invited Regis faculty specializing in these fields to perform an initial unstructured observation and present initial ideas on what strategies they might use to enhance cybersecurity team performance.

The authors on the Regis social and health sciences faculty, Mancuso and Amador, were authorized by the joint training leadership to support the training as psychometric analysts. Their operations indicated two areas of opportunity for team enhancement, awareness of behavior types for the individuals and team interaction awareness to support leadership coaching. They recommended Myers Briggs Type Indicator (MBTI) psychometric tool for individuals. For leadership coaching support they recommended the Parker Team Player Survey (PTPS). These tools were selected because they have been extensively tested and utilized with a variety of populations, including those working in crisis management [1] and those working in technical positions [2]. One of the authors, R. Mancuso, had significant experience in using the MBTI to determine team-based efficacy, including certification in the method, so the deployment of psychometric analysts could happen fairly rapidly based on that existing capacity.

During a cyber defense exercise in May 2017, Regis faculty performed psychometric analysis on surveys and observations to create the first coherent baseline data set that combined psychometric data with pre-existing performance measures for cyber defense operations. Thus, the digital behaviors recorded in network firewalls and first-person journaling of participants was interpreted in concert with general psychometric analysis of the training exercise. An actual cyber defense incident occurred in February 2018 where the psychometric evaluators were invited to observe in real time. The framework presented here is based on the baseline data from the May 2017 exercise and the February 2018 cyber defense incident.

2 The Cyber Defense Incident Response

Because of an existing relationship between Regis University and the Colorado National Guard, Defense Cyber Operations (CONG-DCO), select faculty were invited to observe the February 2018 cyber defense incident response activity. The CONG-DCO received a request from the Office of the Governor of the State of Colorado to provide urgent support to the Colorado Department of Transportation in the face of an active intelligent and persistent cyber threat. This was the first time that any National Guard unit within the US had been dispatched to support a state agency in cyber defense activities. This engagement provided the psychometric analysts opportunity to directly observe behavior while the team was under the stress of a real cyber defense incident and engaging in the larger interaction with the chain of command, collaborating teams, and the staff they were supporting. The value of this opportunity was immediately recognized by both the cyber defense experts and the psychometric analysts. Observations could provide leadership coaching multiple times during a live event in support of improving actual cyber defense capabilities. Since then, members of the cyber security training team and the psychometric analysts have collaborated on developing a new "Short-Cycle Framework." This framework is an integration of psychometric and other team performance indicators that provides along a single timeline to provide feedback to the cyber security team during training exercises and real incident response.

When the CONG-DCO was deployed as part of a state response, they embed as a member of a multi-agency response team. These multi-agency response teams are made of individuals who are members of separate institutions with significantly different institutional practices and social norms. These include government IT Departments, National Guard soldiers, and corporate technical staff. Recognizing the personality types and behaviors rapidly may facilitate adaptation to more rapid convergence on threat identification, vulnerability mitigation, and recovery solutioning.

Several questions drove the authors' development work. "Can a Short-Cycle Framework of multiple psychometric and cyber defense indicators help cyber defense team leadership better recognize individual personality and team dynamics for coaching opportunities that can enhance team performance?" Follow-up questions of interest are, "Can psychometric indicators help team leadership move from intuitive to analytical response, overcoming the vulnerabilities of intuitive thinking often exploited by social engineering and psychologically designed attack strategies?" "Can psychometric-based intervention strategies shorten the delay between a single team member's awareness of an exploit, and the team's mitigation of that exploit?" In order to provide a context in which these questions could be effectively answered, the authors added a layer of preparation for both cyber defense training exercises and cyber defense incidents.

3 Event Preparation for Exercises and Cyber Defense Incident Response

In order for the psychometric analysis to be effectively framed during either a cyber defense training exercise or response incident, significant preparation is necessary. Up-front baseline assessments of each team member needs to be established using the

Myers-Briggs Type Indicator and the Parker Team Player Survey and then a focused set of during-event assessments will continue during both cyber defense exercise opportunities and incident response. This established a set of traits against which the psychometric analysts could assess certain variable psychometric states along a combined timeline of cyber defense activities and events within the timeline that the CONG-DCO experienced, either in an exercise or during an incident. The state data is used in both training and incident response to generate short-cycle coaching for team members.

The authors have initiated a traditional pace of psychometric data feedback to cyber defense team leaders where data is analyzed between events. Currently, the sample size is small and the delay in feedback is the months between exercises. Following a March 2019 cyber exercise, we expect the increase in data gathering rate should improve data reliability. In addition, the Short-Cycle Framework is being applied to a broader range of cyber defense exercises including student competitions. Earlier work in the behavioral analysis of teams in cyber defense suggests that team dynamics is significant in relation to outcomes [3]. This impact of team interaction within cyber defense is similar to that observed in exercises like competitive challenge [4].

The technology infrastructure necessary to facilitate a cyber defense training exercise with live active networks are broadly known [5]. Usually all parties involved in the exercise meet at a single facility using a specialized network that simulates the Internet, an adversary network, a network to be defended along with business systems that must sustain services under attack. This can be a competitive challenge between multiple teams or a single-team exercise. These simulate defensive operations like defending a hospital, public utility, or government agency that is under attack where the trainees are brought in to defend the institution and facilitate recovery to normal operations.

The preparation required for an actual cyber defense incident response does not include the same level of network infrastructure as a training exercise. Typically, the cyber defense response team brings in laptops, switches, flip charts, and other resources necessary to establish an incident response center and forensic base of operations embedded within the large, possibly compromised, operations network of the institution that is under attack.

4 A New Model Through Which to Understand Types of Data for Both Exercises and Cyber Defense Incidents

The Myers-Briggs Type Indicator surveys were provided through a web interface by distributing a link to participants approximately six weeks prior to the May 8, 2017 training session. The analysts reviewed 7 completed MBTI surveys from team members before the May 8th training session. The Parker Team Player Survey was provided to participants on the day of the training session. The analysts reviewed 13 completed PTPS surveys. The team was provided by the Colorado National Guard and consisted of active cyber defenders selected by their leadership. The surveys of this team provided a baseline of self-awareness so that members would be more aware of their behavior. The Parker Team Player Survey has behavioral traits that set a baseline and adaptive behaviors that can be observed in real time. The psychometric analysts identified adaptive behavior options as deliverable feedback with coaching support scripts in near real time. This came to be known among the group as the Short-Cycle Framework for psychometric coaching feedback.

The types of data gathered by the authors to enable the Short-Cycle Framework fall into baseline data (MBTI and PTPS traits), established before exercise scenarios and cyber defense incidents, and ongoing data (PTPS adaptive behaviors) that is gathered with different frequencies throughout the event. This all could then be plotted on the same timeline with traditional cybersecurity training metrics listed below and described in detail in later sections.

- Personality Trait Assessments
  - Myers-Briggs Type Indicator (MBTI)
  - Parker Team Player Survey (PTPS)
  - Adaptive Behavior Scale
  - 14-Item Resilience Scale
- Ongoing Data
  - Personality State Assessments
    Team Cohesion Assessment Scale
    Observed PTPS
  - Digital Observations through System and Event, Information Management (SIEM) Network and Log Traffic Data from devices like Firewalls, Server Logs, and Switch Flow Traffic
  - Digital Service Scoring Engine - tracking business digital system state over time of the defended services.
  - Red Team Journaling - presents the active attack and often intentionality
  - "CEO" Injects - provides the timelines of directives issued by a mock CEO

Psychometric state analysis like "Team Cohesion" during events makes ongoing relationship dynamics and causal events of behavior clearer. This is why data were aggregated into a single timeline. To meaningfully address this, the team is developing a set of scripted feedback messages for particular psychometric states that can be evaluated for efficacy as more event data are collected. More detailed explanations of

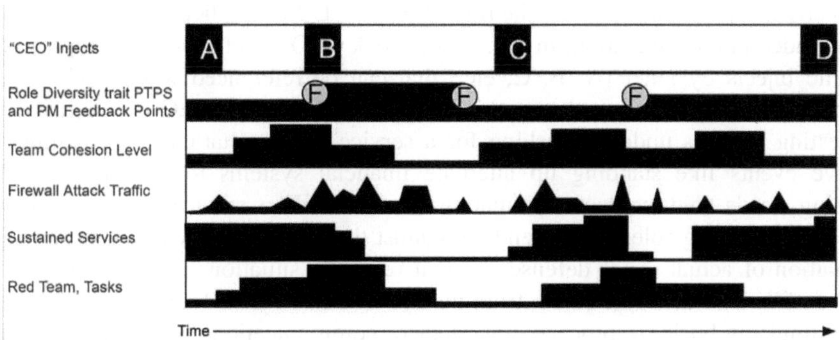

Fig. 1. Short-cycle framework, a simulated set of metrics across cyber defense and team psychometric indicators set in parallel on a timeline to rapidly analyze cyber event causes in relation to ongoing psychometric measurement of the team.

data types, such as the author's use of Parker Team Player Survey components applied as states to the Short-Cycle Framework are provided in later sections. In Fig. 1, the second line of data from the top, they are represented along a single timeline by a circled "F" to facilitate cross-reference as analysis occurs.

5 Cyber Defense Exercise Scenario

Cyber Defense Exercise scenarios are to provide realism and context for success in terms of business scenario, technical infrastructure, and the situation in which the intervention occurred. While scenarios can range from public utilities infrastructure like water dam controls, and electrical grids, it is best to create a scenario from recent cyber defense incidents in order to maintain relevance. An example presented here to provide context was used in the CONG-DCO training exercise in May 2018.

5.1 Scenario Description

A fictitious financial department is in the middle of migrating from local to regional corporate control. With uncontrolled growth and change in governance the department had significant loss of focus on its cybersecurity infrastructure. A major cyber exploitation has occurred with an advanced, persistent threat that is disrupting the department operations. The CONG-DCO are asked to provide defensive intervention against the cyber attack. Primary goals are to identify compromised systems and remove exploits and vulnerabilities. They are responsible for defending the computer system and supporting the internal audit team. Concurrently they must maintain internal and external business services. The department has significant cloud-based service offerings.

5.2 Exercise - CEO Injects

A key control factor was implementing a realistic cybersecurity exercise simulating the behavior of leaders. In the exercise these simulated as a set of directives injected into the scenario by a trainer playing the role of mock CEO of the fictitious organization to be defended in the simulation. In Fig. 1, the mock CEO injects line at the top identifies specific injects by letter (A, B, C, etc.) that can be referenced when evaluating the impact of each inject across the combined timeline. The mock CEO injects range from requesting a status update or asking for a service to be restarted, to sometimes disruptive events like standing up alternate financial systems to sustain a business' ongoing needs mid-incident. Simulating the demand to service institutional needs instead of focusing solely on defending against the red team provides a more realistic simulation of actual cyber defense incident response situations. Another purpose the CEO fulfills is to accept requests from the cyber defense team training in the exercise. This simulates business process, governance, communications, and leadership interaction at the highest level.

6 Cyber Defense Exercise Data Gathered Prior to the CDOT Incident

6.1 Security Incident and Event Management Data

The advantage of a Security Incident and Event Management system (SIEM) for training teams and for the psychometric evaluations is that the logs may be analyzed in real time. A SIEM is a coordinated set of services that aggregate the ongoing digital logs of network and computer devices into a single database. An analytical engine provides alerts, automated responses, and visualizations that guide live security team members as they respond to threats.

In a cyber defense exercise, the Red Team, a team acting as an in-scenario adversary, journals their attack exploits and that journal is confirmed by traffic analysis of the SIEM data. The trainees see the alerts from the SIEM and respond. In a live incident, the attack data presented in the SIEM would be perpetrated by a malicious actor potentially from anywhere in the world. See Fig. 2 for how the types of data vary between a training scenario and a real cyber defense incident.

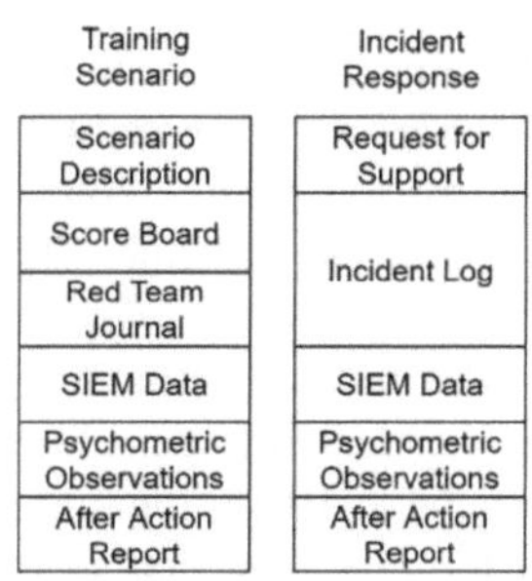

Fig. 2. The exercise scenario and incident response data differ in that more external data can be reviewed independently regarding the threat actor and external services.

Figure 3 indicates digital traffic events as they occur as reported by the SIEM based on known potential indicators of compromise (IoC) as published by the relevant SIEM manufacturers published standards and customized alerts. The vertical scale is each type of IoC events per minute.

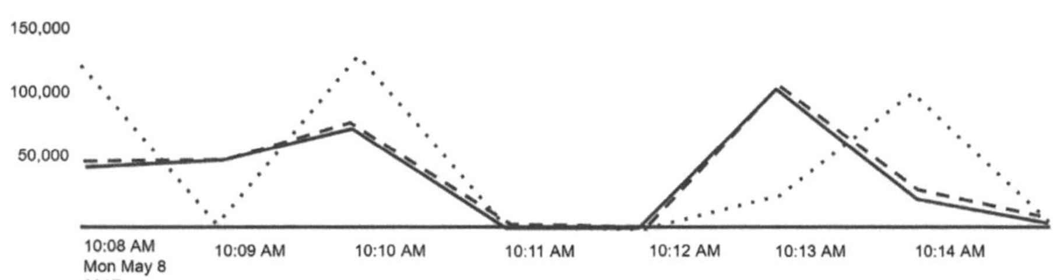

Fig. 3. Illustrates the rough format in which data is presented from the SIEM.

Focusing on the particular data isolated in Fig. 3 graphed are three example indicators of compromise:

Dotted Line: ASA-6-302014 - A TCP connection between two hosts was deleted.
Dashed Line: ASA-6-106100 - The ASA might generate message 106100, indicating that the packet was permitted; however, the packet is later correctly dropped because of no matching connection.
Solid Line: ASA-6-302013 - A TCP connection slot between two hosts was created.

Each of these IoC events has immediate potential impact for the cyber defense teams, and through comparison with other data, each cyber security team's ability to respond can be analyzed. While the timespan represented in the samples is very short, full-day event data would be collected to lay in comparison to the other forms of data like team journaling, psychometric analysis observations, etc. This information is graphed in the 4th line of Fig. 1 in order to determine both impact of digital traffic events on team behavior, and the effects of control efforts by the cybersecurity team on digital traffic.

Using the Splunk tool to analyze the SIEM IoC data, a Colorado School of Mines (CSM) analyst interpreted the data from the Regis University Security exercise held on May 8th, 2017. The CSM analyst identified common penetration techniques utilized by the Red Team and common techniques used by the Blue teams to protect their payloads. In addition to running queries to generate statistics and identify patterns, the CSM team upon review also constructed the line graph visualizations using the Splunk capabilities to develop a more abstracted timeline. This would become the basis of a multifactor timeline presented below.

The CSM team was able to identify the actual firewall used in the exercise which led to the discovery of the syslog codes and opened up a new realm of analysis. They identified the top log codes from the 8–10 am log and created several visualizations to show high-level appearance of the top logs relative to the rest as well as over time. They further analyzed data related to each of the fixed red team IP addresses and listed, described and commented on the top ASA codes. While not presented here, these data are important as an interpretation of red team activity.

6.2 Security Incident and Event Management Data

The Red Team is the attacking team in a cyber defense exercise to simulate what an attacker might be doing to trigger an actual incident response operation. Events on the Red Team Journal, Table 1, can indicate the intentionality of their activities in addition to specific attacks that can be recorded as a journal entry as they engage in training scenario attacks. This provides excellent capabilities to cross reference in the device logs, in the defensive team's behavior, and in relation to whether full recovered status of the network was achieved.

Number of red team tasks per minute are plotted in Fig. 1, line 6, in order to indicate their impact on both service levels and team behavior.

Table 1. Sample journaling performed during exercises by the "Red" cyber attack team playing the role of a malicious perpetrator.

Time started	Time ended	Action
10:05		Scanned domain controller using nmap
10:15		Remote desktop login of DC
10:20	10:30	Blocked internet access
10:24		DNS service, cha ged scope to give 4 Ips only
10:34		Removed 192.168.111.10 from DHCP scope User Network and added 192.168.111.12
10:35		Removed WiFI network from DHCP address 192.168.113.1
10:40		Changed password for Blue 8 and Blue 7 to xxx and Blue 3 to xxx
10:43		Lost connection to DC, tried to RDP but could not
10:59		Disabled MAIL from AD
11:10	1:11	Remote desktop to Cyclos DB server, and closed out active windows, got kicked out at 11:11

6.3 Services Availability - Scenario Scoring Engine Data

The scoring engine provides a real-time indicator to cyber defense exercise organizers and is analogous to availability dashboards present in network operations centers. If a service like a web server is up, it will indicate an up arrow in real time. If that service has been disrupted, its arrow will display as down. This is represented in Fig. 1, line 5, to enable assessment of impact of red team activities, and the cybersecurity team's ability to respond fully to a service interruption. The timeline is designed so that it can become possible to analyze the duration of response times from IoC to service recovery in relation to team resilience.

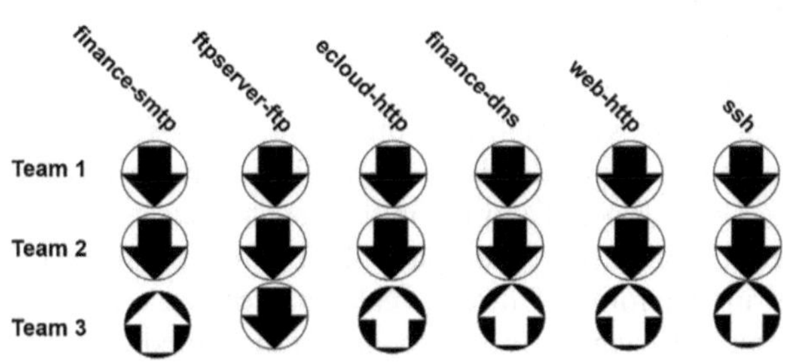

Fig. 4. Service availability scoring engine indicates whether a business service is up or down by simulating the user and checking for success.

Figure 4 represents a sample scoring engine to illustrate how multiple teams can be tracked over time for various network system services. The scoring engine is a key tool in determining the effectiveness of cyber defense teams as they train against a particular scenario, in a competitive challenge, or in a technical walk-through. In this particular case, a single team consisting of 13 members was tracked over time and had access to this scoring engine to determine their performance as they worked to restore services.

7 Identifying and Infusing Personality Trait Preferences and Role Diversity in Cyber Security Teams

Our model utilizes both trait and state measures as central psychosocial factors in cyber security teams. The trait measures that comprise our initial psychometric evaluation will enable us to calculate a predicted effectiveness score for each team. Based on that score, we can develop scripts with prescribed feedback to enhance team performance.

Work in cybersecurity incident response human factors covers several related areas that each add value and provide context for the work presented and complementary value to the work presented here. For instance, Oltramari [6] focuses on the risk associated with trusting individuals. This human factors work highlights the importance of expectations of behavior as they affect the team performance through cohesion of purpose. As Pfleeger and Caputo notes [7], since 2010 there has been a significant effort to align the efforts of behavioral science and cybersecurity to encourage empirical studies to enhance the socio-technical systems that enable cybersecurity. The work presented in this paper follows along that thread, working to develop a systematic process that can generate measurable results in training and incident response events.

For the initial psychometric evaluation (before the cyber defense exercise or incident occurs) the psychometric evaluators identify personality trait preferences by administering the Myers-Briggs Type Indicator [8] and role diversity utilizing the Parker Team Player Survey [9]. Two additional trait assessments that we believe will be useful in predicting cyber security team performance are Adaptive Behavior [10] and the 14-item Resilience Scale [11]. Measures of resilience will be used to develop scripts to support leadership in coaching and can also be used as the basis for future skill development. All of these measures have been shown to be largely stable over time as suggested in referenced material. The 14-item Resilience Scale is plotted in the graph in Fig. 1 on the third line so that it may be cross-referenced to indicate if other events have affected team resilience.

We predict that teams with high trait preference diversity and high role diversity who self-report as being very adaptive and resilient may be more effective at cyber incident response. Using scores from the initial psychometric evaluation as a baseline, we can categorize teams into one of four quartiles by their predicted effectiveness score. Coaching injects in the form of direct, real-time feedback to team leaders can be tailored and scripted for each team in response to their predicted effectiveness score.

Personality state assessments will be used to provide real-time observer assessments of team performance. We propose to assess team cohesion and observed role diversity at three points during the cyber defense exercise in order to gauge the effect of the coaching injects. Team cohesion is measured using a modified Crew Cohesion Assessment Scale [12]. This is coupled with a modified PTPS that can assess observed role diversity. Both are completed by faculty observers following each coaching inject.

Below is a sample paragraph of the psychometric evaluators' assessment of cyber security team members' scores on the Parker Team Player Survey, our measure of role diversity. After uncovering Contributors, Collaborators and Communicators, an example finding was:

- Evaluation 1: There were no Challengers in the team.
- Evaluation 2: These results indicate that the group is predominantly task and goal oriented, but does not excel at process or at questioning that process.

These examples represent general statements within the context of instruments and frameworks like the Myers Briggs Type Indicator [8] and the Parker Team Player Survey [9]. These examples suggest scripts for coaching and are a demonstration of process functionality. Once process is confirmed as functionally able to generate actionable findings in this study, observations and indicators will later be tracked over multiple exercises and adjusted and new constructs may be identified. Over time we expect to identify and differentiate different individual and team characteristics that suggest higher levels of capability in cyber defense training and incident response.

8 Live Response Incident Log and After-Action Report

The Incident Response Log is a compilation of observations entered by incident responders while working through the incident. Specifically, it is a real-time journal of observations and record of actions taken. Often in a digital form it will include malicious file names, system configuration settings, and commands used. In relation to cyber defense exercises it is analogous to a team journal. Also, the journal documents when a service goes down and when it is restored from the perspective of the cyber defense team. The scoring engine provides an alternate means of confirmation.

After action reports occur in both cyber defense exercises and incident response. They are based on journaling and include later analysis intended to determine how things could have been done better, how successful it was, what follow-up items might be valuable, etc. The after-action report is initiated immediately after the incident with a live debrief of all participating members. This is formalized into a document with follow up items. The report is used to inform next steps on defense, revision of cyber defense exercises scenarios, and research on open-ended questions to enhance the capabilities of the trainers and the incident response teams.

9 Strategy for Relating Data

Cyber Defense Team Leads and the exercise designers use the new data from the Short-Cycle Framework to address two development challenges: (1) exercise designers need to increase the relevance of exercise to live incident response by comparing data across incident response and exercise and improve future cyber defense exercises and, (2) during a cyber defense incident or exercise, the team leads need to leverage the full set of new data to better coach their teams to enhance performance.

The authors have spent several years analyzing data pulled from exercises. The technical sets of analysis such as firewall and red team journaling were used to compare exercises to incident response and enhancing performance from session to session. The authors recognized though that key indicators of performance were not being gathered in the earlier data sets. Team interaction such as conflict, collaboration, and motivation played a strong part in success, and yet was not being recorded. The following is a list of key functions and strategies that the psychometric analysts use to enrich the interpretation with both new data acquisition and analysis across exercise and incident response.

Psychometric Analysts

- Provide observations, evaluations, and coaching
- Leadership skills and team member participation feedback for individual team members
- One-on-one discussion about personality traits and leadership guidance
- Increase awareness of participant's interaction styles so they can function more effectively in both cyber exercises and incident response.
  - Increase the rapidity of Multi-Agency Incident Response Teams by enhancing team members' cohesion
  - Develop awareness of leadership using feedback that supports coaching
  - Enhance ability to work in groups
  - Increase self-awareness and awareness of others
  - Adapt to team members and situation and demonstrate resiliency leading to quicker response and better collaboration

10 Conclusion and Recommendations

The Short-Cycle Framework, integration of psychometric observations, SIEM network data, and journaling may be applied so that incident response exercises and live incident response are enhanced through the use of psychometric analysis and feedback to team leads.

The authors intend to continue this research by developing a set of prescribed feedback or "scripts" based on the four psychometric evaluations through the quartile states. Then the team intends to evaluate the effectiveness of these types of feedback over time using the proposed method described here. Preparing scripts may allow leaders very early identification of the disruptive effects on team cohesion potentially caused by some social engineering or other types of psychological attack strategies. Because scripts may be delivered digitally and the psychometric analyst observations may not be interactive, video may allow psychometric teams to provide their services to cyber operations teams through networks.

Some of the authors' previous experience suggests that direct feedback from the psychometric analysts to individual team participants may undermine leadership so we recommend using leadership channels to provide coaching. This approach supports the appropriate authority in behavioral adjustments within the broader context of their individual institutional relationships.

A prerequisite to this work needs to be acknowledged for those looking to produce similar processes. Transitive trust between the analytical/academic community and the cyber defense community must be pre-established. A consideration for future research is how to more rapidly build these types of trust relationships that can stand rapidly and at multiple scales.. Should we be successful in this line of research and development of framework structure, we are looking to achieve replicability of approach by baselining the team state and standardizing how scripts are used to provide feedback to team leaders. Over time, the team hopes to use frameworks like this to discover patterns of behavior that represent effective behavior types in relation to the various aspects of different scenarios. Developing a portfolio of scenarios, the team intends to test the predictive capacity of this type of framework in relation to effectiveness of cybersecurity incident response.

Acknowledgements. The authors have presented the context in which the Short-Cycle Framework was developed in conjunction and collaboration with our Regis University interdisciplinary investigators (Computing and Information Sciences, Liberal Studies and Healthcare), state and local Colorado government entities and private industry partners.

The team thanks Riley Miller, a PhD student at Colorado School of Mines department of Computer Science for his independent analysis of the red team attack traffic that was detected in the main firewall during the cyber exercise referred to in this analysis. The cyber defense exercises at Regis University are sponsored by a series of grants from the Department of Defense of the United States of America. Thank you to Rick Cisneros, the project scientist of Regis University, College of Computing and Information Sciences, for his work gathering the network data as Red Team lead and providing exercise infrastructure. Thank you to Robert Moon for gathering the network data and being a red team member along with Nasser Esmail.

References

1. Sample, J.A., Hoffman, J.L.: The MBTI as a management and organizational development tool. J. Psychol. Type **11**, 47–50 (1986)
2. Beyler, J., Schmeck, R.R.: Assessment of individual differences in preferences for holistic-analytic strategies: evaluation of some commonly available instruments. Educ. Psychol. Measur. **52**(3), 709–719 (1992)
3. Hoffman, L.J., Rosenberg, T., Dodge, R., Ragsdale, D.: Exploring a national cybersecurity exercise for universities. IEEE Secur. Priv. **3**(5), 27–33 (2005)
4. Buchler, N., La Fleur, C.G., Hoffman, B., Rajivan, P., Marusich, L., Lightner, L.: Cyber teaming and role specialization in a cyber security defense competition. Front. Psychol. **9** (2018)
5. Dodge, R.C., Ragsdale, D.J., Reynolds, C.: Organization and training of a cyber security team. In: SMC 2003 Conference Proceedings of the 2003 IEEE International Conference on Systems, Man and Cybernetics. Conference Theme-System Security and Assurance (Cat. No. 03CH37483), vol. 5, pp. 4311–4316. IEEE (2003)
6. Oltramari, A., Henshel, D., Caines, M., Hoffman, B.: Towards a human factors ontology for cyber security. In: Proceedings of the Tenth Conference on Sematic Technology for Intelligence, Defense, and Security, Fairfax, VA, USA, pp. 26–33. IEEE Computer Society (2015)
7. Pfleeger, S.L., Caputo, D.D.: Leveraging behavioral science to mitigate cyber security risk. Comput. Secur. **31**(4), 597–611 (2012)

8. Myers, I.B., McCaulley, M.H., Quenk, N.L., Hammer, A.L.: MBTI Manual: A Guide to the Development and Use of the Myers-Briggs Type Indicator, 3rd edn. Consulting Psychologists Press, Palo Alto (2003)
9. Parker, G.M.: Team Player and Team Work: The New Competitive Business Strategy. Jossey-Bass Inc, San-Farncisko (1990)
10. Charbonnier-Voirin, A., Roussel, P.: Adaptive performance: a new scale to measure individual performance in organizations. Can. J. Adm. Sci./Revue Canadienne des Sciences de l'Administration **29**. 280–293 (2012). https://doi.org/10.1002/cjas.232
11. Wagnild, G.M., Young, H.M.: Development and psychometric evaluation of the resilience scale. J. Nurs. Meas. **1**, 165–178 (1993)
12. Mission-Centered Solutions: Crew Cohesion Assessment; Leadership Toolbox Reference. https://www.fireleadership.gov/toolbox/documents/Crew_Cohesion_Assessment.pdf

Identifying Security Requirements Body of Knowledge for the Security Systems Engineer

Suné von Solms[1(✉)] and Annlizé Marnewick[2]

[1] Department of Electrical Engineering Science, University of Johannesburg, Johannesburg, South Africa
svonsolms@uj.ac.za

[2] Postgraduate School of Engineering Management, University of Johannesburg, Johannesburg, South Africa

Abstract. The interconnected nature of Industry 4.0–driven operations and systems is introducing the use of new digitized and connected industrial systems. These new connected environments impact system security, requirements engineers to include elicitation of security requirements as functional requirements. Academia and industry argue that systems engineers are not adequately prepared for the security- related activities required in the specification of secure systems. This paper utilizes a cybersecurity framework to create the body of knowledge related to Security Requirements Engineering for a module in systems engineering. The determined body of knowledge show Risk Management, Laws and Regulations, and Human Factors related to security must be considered in the changing technological landscape. Although not all systems engineers must have expert knowledge in this field, all systems engineers must have fundamental knowledge in security practice and the ability to apply systems thinking.

Keywords: Engineering education · Security · Security requirements engineering · Industry 4.0 · Systems engineering

1 Introduction

In traditional systems design, security considerations of a system were limited to the integration of security added after the completed system was developed [1–3], treating security features as of secondary importance. The Industrial Internet of Things (IIoT) defines the use of new digitized and highly connected systems [4], which require these systems to be designed, developed and managed by engineers while considering the impact and effects of cyberattacks on these systems throughout the whole system [5]. In reaction to these required changes in design, the systems engineering community identified security roles and responsibilities applicable to the entire systems development life cycle for future connected environments [6], namely the secure systems development life cycle (S-SDLC) [5]. Various sources argue that all engineering disciplines must understand and practice security through all phases of the system lifecycle to meet the project's requirements and manage an acceptable level of risk [8, 9].

Published by Springer Nature Switzerland AG 2019
L. Drevin and M. Theocharidou (Eds.): WISE 2019, IFIP AICT 557, pp. 59–71, 2019.
https://doi.org/10.1007/978-3-030-23451-5_5

In systems engineering, a holistic cybersecurity view is required by Systems Engineers (SEs) to design secure systems as the S-SDLC requires the execution of various specialized security tasks, such as security requirements planning which requires the evaluation of functional systems requirements relating to security and translation into technical solutions [11]. Globally, engineering industries are observing that SEs are not adequately prepared to execute many of these tasks, including the incorporation of system security requirements into the system [11, 12]. Therefore, industries require SEs with holistic cybersecurity knowledge and Security Requirements Engineers (SREs) who can conduct the security requirements process, minimizing the risk during systems development lifecycle [8].

In the South African (SA) engineering space, there exists a high demand in cybersecurity engineering professionals. However, throughout academic institutions in SA there are no known comprehensive cybersecurity engineering courses offered, based on their undergraduate and postgraduate syllabus descriptions [9]. In systems engineering, the lack of cybersecurity content or modules in SA engineering education and the need for cybersecurity professionals point toward a gap in cybersecurity knowledge amongst engineers in industry. The need for such a skill requires the addition of security requirements engineering to the education in systems engineering curricula [13]. The aim of this paper is to design a cybersecurity module for systems engineering students focusing on security requirements engineering.

2 The Need for Security Requirements Engineering Education

Engineering industries globally are observing that SEs are not adequately prepared to incorporate system security requirements into the system [12], which constitutes the need for an additional SE who possesses the knowledge, skills and competencies related to security requirements [11]. This includes the consideration of security requirements as an integral part of system requirements to reduce systems weakness [8], treating security requirements as functional requirements and not just non-functional requirements or of secondary importance [14, 15]. However, not all system engineers can be trained to become security experts. Therefore, academia should develop security experts as a path in system engineering, including the SRE [16].

In the paper entitled "Global Perspectives on Cybersecurity Education for 2030: A Case for a Meta-discipline", the authors argue that cybersecurity must be integrated into existing academic disciplines, not simply be developed as separate degree programs [13]. As with a module educating SEs to have a holistic view of cybersecurity, a module must exist in which a SE responsible for requirements engineering must be educated on the security factors influencing requirement engineering. To ensure the development of relevant content for such modules, this research investigates internal and external factors of the cybersecurity and systems engineering fields which can influence and impact the content of a cybersecurity curriculum.

3 Methodology

A preliminary investigation into a basic body of knowledge of a SE cybersecurity module was presented in [10] which provided a baseline for this research. This paper builds on the work done in [10] where a broader spectrum literature was considered to inform a module in SE. The framework described by Knapp et al. [17] was developed to ensure that cybersecurity certifications remain relevant in industry, by identifying factors which professional bodies recognize as important to a relevant certification. These relevant factors are then used to inform a current curriculum to remain relevant to industry requirements.

This framework was adapted to analyze professional certifications to help shape a new cybersecurity module related to SE. The module was validated against the Curriculum Guidelines for Post-Secondary Degree Programs in Cybersecurity (CSEC2017) guidelines. The adapted framework followed is illustrated in Fig. 1 below.

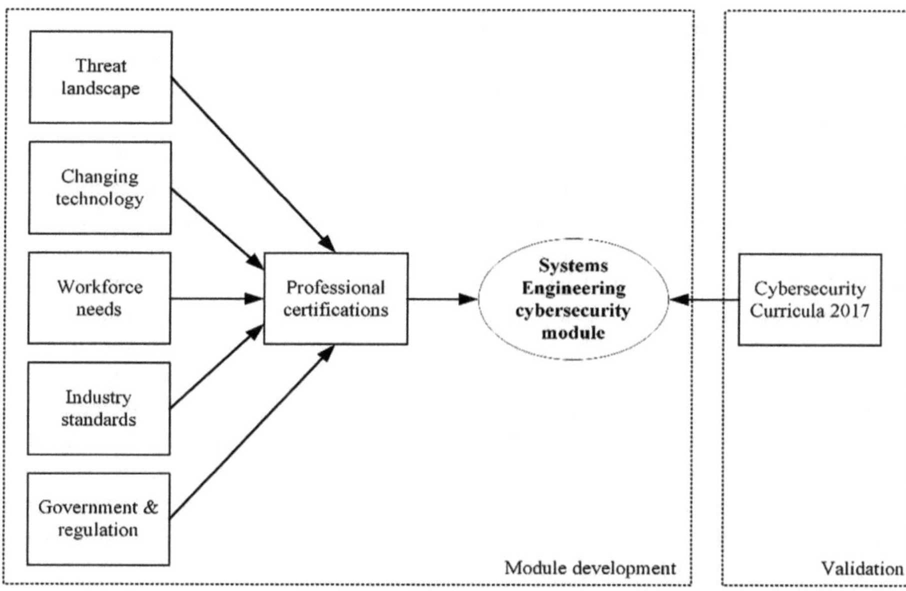

Fig. 1. Methodology for module development [14]

1. Step 1: Review the key input factors that certifying bodies consider relevant, including threat landscape, technology changes, industry standards, workforce needs, and government and regulation as per the framework in [17]. From this review, relevant cybersecurity knowledge and skills are determined.
2. Step 2: Development of a draft SE cybersecurity module from the data collected in Step 1.

3. Step 3: Validate the developed SE cybersecurity module against the CSEC2017 guidelines.

The results of the various steps are discussed in the subsequent sections.

4 Review of Input Factors

To analyze the significant factors that professional certifying bodies consider most important relating to cybersecurity in systems requirement engineering, literature was reviewed to determine specific skills, knowledge and activities relating to security in requirements engineering. The five input factors, shown in Fig. 1, is considered. This is not an exhaustive list and other factors can be considered but is considered comprehensive to provide relevant information for module development [17].

4.1 Threat Landscape

The changing technological landscape constantly gives rise to new threats and risks, like protection of information and information systems and communications and network security [20]. As cybersecurity threats are constantly evolving, it is essential to consider literature discussing any new threats relating to engineering systems and how they should be managed. Traditionally, security requirements were considered as non-functional requirements [11, 14, 15]. Other instances include where security requirements are developed independently from the rest of the requirements engineering activity and hence not integrated into the requirements engineering activities [11]. Generally, this leads to serious design challenges and wide-ranging security vulnerabilities. New requirements must be considered by SEs as part of each system to create innovative solutions to address the new risks. Researchers argue that many security problems can be eliminated through the integration of security with requirements engineering [5, 7, 19]. By conducting security requirements in the early stages of the development process with the system requirements specifications, security threats can be avoided very early in the systems development process as security is adequately planned, acquired, built in, and deployed as an integral part of the system [5, 7, 19].

NIST Special Publication 800-64 - Security Considerations in the System Development Life Cycle [7] comments on the enforcement of security requirements throughout the phases of the life cycle. Nejib and Beyer comment on the importance of systems engineers towards contributing to secure systems [8]. They considered current and evolving policies, guidance, and standards (ISO 15288:2015) regarding security activities in the S-SDLC and provide a framework which identifies the security-related activities applicable to systems engineers. The 5 SE processes related to requirements engineering was identified as important processes which an SRE should implement.

The identified 5 processes will be used as inputs to the cybersecurity module. The output of this investigation yielded the following [8]:

- Elicit Stakeholder Requirements
- Define Stakeholder Security Requirements
- Analyse and Maintain Stakeholder Security Requirements

- Define Systems Security Requirements
- Analyse and Maintain Systems Security Requirements

4.2 Workforce Needs

Von Solms and Marnewick identified that within the S-SDLC, specialized security-related requirement actions relevant to the 5 processes identified in Sect. 4.1 requires the skills of a System Requirements Planner – a position generally filled by a SE [11]. To identify the tasks, skills, knowledge and abilities required by the SE to perform these tasks, the 81 tasks, skills, knowledge and abilities documented in NIST 800-181 relating to this position were investigated. The factors relevant to the requirements engineering process (5 processes identified in Sect. 4.1) were determined.

The output of the analysis is shown in Table 1 below where the NIST code in provided with a shortened description. These 22 identified factors will be used as inputs to the cybersecurity module.

Table 1. Tasks, skills, knowledge and abilities requirements from NIST 800-181 [21]

Code	Table 2 reference code	Code	Table 2 reference code
T0033	Risk assessment & feasibility study	K0012	Requirements analysis
T0039	Functional requirements evaluation	K0038	Data risk management
T0052	Scope definition	K0044	Cybersecurity and privacy
T0062	Requirements development	K0045	Security systems engineering principles
T0127	Integration of security policy & regulation	K0067	SDLC process
T0174	Needs analysis	K0102	SDLC process
T0235	Requirements modelling	K0164	Functionality, quality, and security requirements integration
T0300	User interface requirements		
T0454	Baseline requirements	S0008	System analysis
K0002	Risk management	S0010	Requirements analysis
K0003	Cybersecurity regulation & laws	S0050	Requirements modelling
K0004	Cybersecurity and privacy	S0134	Review and validation
K0005	Cyber threats and vulnerabilities	S0367	Cybersecurity privacy principles application
K0006	Impact analysis	A0064	Translate requirements operational impact
K0008	Operational business domain knowledge	A0123	Cybersecurity privacy principles application

4.3 Changing Technology

Changing technological landscapes, including Industry 4.0 requirements, bring changes to the cybersecurity landscape. The security areas will differ for each new system, so the SRE must be able to elicit the security requirements upfront, impacting the system in development. Salini et al. [19] states that every SRE must have the knowledge related to various types of security requirements and factors which influence requirements. Elicitation of requirements includes considering various non-technical aspects, which includes standards and best practices [11], laws and regulations, as well as knowledge relating to human factors, which can be considered expert knowledge to be used as input to security requirements engineering and threat analysis.

The Cyber Security Body of Knowledge (CyBOK) is one framework developed to provide guidance on the foundational and generally recognized knowledge on cybersecurity [22]. To identify the cybersecurity body of knowledge which applies to the SRE, the 19 top-level knowledge areas (KAs) documented in the CyBOK were evaluated.

The category "Human, Organizational, and Regulatory Aspects" were considered relevant to the SRE as humans, organizations and regulations must be considered when requirements are defined. The output of the analysis is shown in Table 2 below where a unique code in provided with a shortened description. These 3 identified factors will be used as inputs to the cybersecurity module.

Table 2. Cybersecurity knowledge requirements from CyBOK [22]

Code	Table 2 reference code
CyBOK1	Risk management and governance: security management systems and organizational security controls, including standards, best practices, and approaches to risk assessment and mitigation
CyBOK2	Laws and Regulation: International and national statutory and regulatory requirements, compliance obligations, and security ethics, including data protection and developing doctrines on cyber warfare
CyBOK3	Human Factors: Usable security, social and behavioural factors impacting security, security culture and awareness as well as the impact of security controls on user behaviours

4.4 Industry Standards

Industry standard and best practices are considered an important input toward curriculum relevance. Various industry standards and guidelines relating to cybersecurity, including ISO and NIST security frameworks, provides authoritative guidelines, frameworks and procedures to be adopted by industry [17, 23].

Upon the investigation of the eCompetence framework, it was seen that security aspects are only defined in the "Build" function much later in the S-SDLC. This implies that security forms part of the design, but no more detail is provided. Considering security requirements in the eCompetence framework, it was only included in the "Run" phase of the SDLC, implying that security only forms part of the reaction and maintenance processes of a system and not the requirements [24]. A second investigation into the NIST 800-160 [25] framework as well as the INCOSE Systems Engineering Handbook [26] was conducted. These frameworks describe the use of the technical Systems Engineering and Software processes set out in ISO/IEC/IEEE 15288:2015. Nejib et al. mapped the Security Systems Engineering processes described in the NIST 800-160 framework technical processes of ISO/IEC/IEEE 15288:2015, resulting in 27 Security Systems Engineering processes [8]. From these processes, five were related to the Security Requirements phase of the S-SDLC. These five processes were identified in Sect. 4.1, which already formed part of the input factors to the curriculum.

4.5 Government and Regulation

Following the evaluation done on the key input factor of Changing Technology, is was determined that law and regulations must be viewed as stakeholders in the requirements process. When a system is designed, the requirements of these laws and regulation must be integrated into the requirements of the system itself. Kotonya and Sommerville [27] commented on the inputs and outputs of the requirements engineering process and stated that two inputs include Organizational Standards and Regulations [24]. In the same manner, all regulations and standards related to cybersecurity must be included in the Security Requirement Specification process. As stated in Sect. 4.3, knowledge relating to cybersecurity laws and regulations can be considered specialized knowledge and must be considered as an input factor the curriculum design.

5 Module Development

The input factors identified in Sect. 4 is now utilized to design a cybersecurity module for systems engineering students focusing on security requirements engineering. The cybersecurity knowledge, tools and skills identified in Sect. 4 require various levels of understanding by the SRE, ranging from a holistic view regarding systems security to specialized knowledge relating cybersecurity laws and regulations to elicit relevant requirements.

Kossiakoff et al. derived a range of educational components relating to systems engineering development, based on quality work experience and professional certifications [28]. These components include three overhead components, namely engineering process training, systems thinking activities and systems engineering work experience, each consisting of three sub-activities each. Adapting the generalized activities presented in [28] to the field of requirements engineering, the following development activities were identified to use as a guideline in the development of a module for SREs:

- Engineering process training: which include Process Knowledge, Tools and techniques and Skills
- Systems thinking activities which include Security discipline expertise, Problem solving and Holistic view

The evaluation of the threat landscape in Sect. 4.1 identified five engineering processes relating to requirements engineering in the S-SDLC. These processes are viewed in relation to the six engineering development activities listed above to generate a Body of Knowledge (BoK) table, namely the rows and columns of the table, respectively. This BoK table is populated by mapping all the knowledge, skills, abilities and tasks identified in the other sections of Sect. 4 to the six engineering processes and developmental activities. The BoK table is shown in Table 3 below.

Table 3 Body of knowledge for security requirements engineering module

		Stakeholder needs and requirements definition process			System requirements definition process	
		Elicit stakeholder requirements	Define stakeholder security requirements	Analyse and maintain stakeholder security requirements	Define system security requirements	Analyse and maintain system security requirements
Engineering process training	Process knowledge	Needs analysis (T0174) Law and Regulation (CyBOK2)	Functional requirements evaluation (T0039) Scope definition (T0052)		Risk assessment & feasibility study (T0033) Requirements development (T0062)	Integration of security policy & regulation (T0127)
	Tools and techniques			Baseline requirements (T0454)		Requirements modelling (S0050) (T0235)
	Skills			Requirements analysis (K0012 & S0010)		User interface requirements (T0300) System analysis (S0008)
Systems thinking activities	Security discipline expertise	Risk Management (K0002) Cybersecurity regulation & laws (K0003) Cybersecurity and privacy (K0004) Cyber threats and vulnerabilities (K0005) Impact analysis (K0006) Security systems engineering principles (K0045) Local and industry regulation	Security systems engineering principles (K0045)	Security systems engineering principles (K0045) Human Factors (CyBOK3)	Data risk management (K0038) Security systems engineering principles (K0045) Risk Management and Governance (CyBOKl)	Security systems engineering principles (K0045)

(*continued*)

Table 3 (*continued*)

		Stakeholder needs and requirements definition process			System requirements definition process	
		Elicit stakeholder requirements	Define stakeholder security requirements	Analyse and maintain stakeholder security requirements	Define system security requirements	Analyse and maintain system security requirements
	Problem solving	Operational business domain knowledge (K0008) Cybersecurity privacy principles application (A0123 & S0367) Cybersecurity & privacy (K0044)	Cybersecurity privacy principles application (A0123 & S0367)	Translate requirements operational impact (A0064)	Cybersecurity privacy principles application (A0123 & S0367)	Translate requirements operational impact (A0064)
	Holistic view	SDLC process (K0067& K0102)	SDLC process (K0067 & K0102)	Review and validation (S0134)	Functionality, quality, and security requirements integration (K0I64)	Review and validation (S0134)

This populated table provides an overview on the cybersecurity module for SE students. The columns of the BOK table are the five processes related to the Security Requirements phase of the S-SDLC identified in Sects. 4.1 and 4.4. The table is populated with the knowledge, skills, abilities, tasks and requirements identified in Sects. 4.2, 4.3 and 4.5. This table can provide guidance to determine the content of a Security Requirements Engineering module in systems engineering as the codes in the table indicate the topics of interest for each Security Requirements process in the S-SDLC.

Table 3 presents the content for the cybersecurity module for security requirements within a SE curriculum. From the table mapping the systems thinking ability is very important for the future and a lot of focus should be in this area to help teach future students to think in this manner.

6 Module Validation

The CSEC2017 framework provides guidance for education efforts in cybersecurity [18] which offers a sound guideline for the validation of the developed module. The CSEC framework divides the cybersecurity content into 8 KAs and states that the content must be aligned to workforce needs by viewing the work through a disciplinary lens. In the development of a cybersecurity module for SEs, von Solms and Futcher identified systems engineering as the disciplinary lens and determined that 3 of the 8 knowledge areas can be considered too technical for the systems engineering domain

Table 4. Security requirements engineering module outline

		Stakeholder needs & requirements definition process			System requirements definition process	
		Elicit stakeholder requirements	Define stakeholder security requirements	Analyse & maintain stakeholder security requirements	Define system security requirements	Analyse and maintain system security requirements
Software security	Essentials	X	X		X	
	Design	X	X		X	
	Analysis and testing		X		X	
	Ethics	X				
System security	Essentials					X
	System thinking	X	X	X	X	X
	System management	X				X
	System control		X			
	System testing		X		X	
Human security	Essentials	X		X		
	Social engineering	X		X		
	Awareness and understanding	X		X		
	Social & behavioral privacy	X		X		
	Personal privacy & security	X		X		
	Usable security and privacy	X		X		
Organizational security	Essentials	X				
	Risk management	X			X	
	Security governance & policy	X	X		X	
	Cybersecurity planning	X				
	Security program management	X	X			
	Personnel security	X				
	Security operations	X				
Societal security	Essentials	X				
	Cybercrime		X			
	Cyber law	X				
	Cyber Ethics	X				
	Cyber policy	X				
	Privacy	X	X		X	
Systems engineering specialized	Needs analysis	X				
	Requirements tools & modelling					X
	System analysis					X
	Impact analysis	X				
	Security SE principles	X	X	X	X	X
	SSDLC process	X				
	Functionality, quality, and security requirements integration				X	

[10]. Building on this research, the 5 KAs considered in the validation of this developed module are Software, System, Human, Organizational and Societal security.

The five processes which formed the headings of Table 3 columns were used as the divisions for five module units of work. Using the key words of the various knowledge, skills, abilities and tasks included as entries in the Table 3, the CSEC2017 document was investigated and corresponding KAs and knowledge units (KUs) were identified and indicated in Table 4. When a corresponding CSEC2017 KU could not be found, an addition entry was added to Table 4, named "Systems Engineering Specialized".

7 Discussion and Recommendations

From the validation process shown in Table 4, emphasis is placed on five main KAs:

- Systems Thinking: As a SE, the professional must have skill of systems thinking and be able to view a system holistically.
- Risk Management and Governance: The SE must be able to implement and understand risk management of systems and organizational security controls, which requires knowledge of applicable standards, best practices, and approaches. In addition, the new threats that the connected systems introduce must be analysed and risk estimations must be done during requirements phase.
- Security systems engineering principles: The SE responsible for the security requirements engineering needs to have expert knowledge in the security discipline.
- Law and Regulation related to Cybersecurity: All local and international statutory and regulatory requirements, compliance obligations, and security ethics, must be known to elicit security requirements.
- Human Factors: Knowledge relating to human factors and user behaviours and how it impacts security, security culture and awareness must be known by SREs.

These observations support the findings in Table 3 where it was shown that systems thinking skills must be considered in the changing technological landscape. However, the SE must have fundamental expert knowledge in security practice and the ability to apply systems thinking. Security threats will change, and the SE must be able to consider all possible scenarios when specifying requirements. Due to technological changes in systems, this module needs to be developed and used in the training of specialized SEs to prepare them for the changes brought forth by changing technological landscapes.

8 Conclusion

The creation of systems to comply with Industry 4.0 environments and cyberattacks requires the elicitation of security requirements from various sources, including regulations, client needs and human behavioral factors. The elicitation of these security requirements requires a SE who are specialize in the field of security requirements engineering and had specialized knowledge relating to various security aspects which may influence the security requirements of the system.

Engineering education in SA does not include comprehensive cybersecurity modules in systems engineering and does not provide specialized education in the field of security requirements engineering. This paper includes an investigation to determine the BoK for the creation of a module which specializes in security requirements engineering. Input factors from industry were considered to determine the knowledge, skills, abilities and tasks required for security requirements elicitation. The CSEC2017 framework were utilized to validate the educational content to be included in the module. The basic BoK for a security requirement engineering module is presented, which shows that the KAs of Systems Thinking, Risk Management and Governance, Security systems engineering principles, Law and Regulation related to Cybersecurity and Human Factors are the most important for inclusion in the module.

This work will contribute to cybersecurity curriculum design in systems engineering and other specialized systems engineering fields, such as security requirements engineering. This work can also be used as a roadmap for the development of SE modules outside of SA, as it is based on international standards and best practices. However, the laws and regulations relevant to the specific country must be considered.

References

1. Dove, R., Bayuk, J., Wilson, B., Kepchar, K.: INCOSE System Security Engineering Working Group Charter (2016). https://www.incose.org/docs/default-source/wgcharters/systems-security-engineering.pdf?sfvrsn=cc0eb2c6_8
2. Shreyas, D.: Software Engineering for Security: Towards Architecting Secure Software. http://citeseerx.ist.psu.edu/viewdoc/download?doi=10.1.1.3.4064&rep=rep1&type=pdf. Accessed 05 May 2018
3. Haridas, N.: Software Engineering – Security as a Process in the SDLC. SANS Institute InfoSec Reading Room (2007)
4. Kiel, D.: What do we know about "Industry 4.0" so far? In: Proceedings of the International Association for Management of Technology (IAMOT) (2017)
5. Waslo, R., Lewis, T., Hajj, R., Carton, R.: Industry 4.0 and cybersecurity Managing risk in an age of connected production. Deloitte University Press (2017). https://www2.deloitte.com/insights/us/en/focus/industry-4-0/cybersecurity-managing-risk-in-age-of-connected-production.html
6. Nejib, P., Beyer, D., Yakabovicz, E.: Systems security engineering: what every system engineer needs to know. In: INCOSE International Symposium, vol. 27, no. 1, pp. 434–445 (2017)
7. Kissel, R.L., Stine, K.M., Scholl, M.A., Rossman, H., Fahlsing, J., Gulick, J.: Security Considerations in the System Development Life Cycle. NIST (2008)
8. Nejib, P., Beyer, D.: Systems security engineering whose job is it anyway. INSIGHT **19**(2), 47–53 (2016)
9. Tamura, E.: Hewlett Packard Enterprise Leads Transformation of Cyber Defense with "Build it In" and "Stop it Now" (2016). http://www8.hp.com/us/en/hp-news/press-release.html?id=2184147#.WtlU5S6uyUl. Accessed 20 Apr 2018
10. von Solms, S., Futcher, L.: Identifying the cybersecurity body of knowledge for a postgraduate module in systems engineering. In: Drevin, L., Theocharidou, M. (eds.) WISE 2018. IAICT, vol. 531, pp. 121–132. Springer, Cham (2018). https://doi.org/10.1007/978-3-319-99734-6_10

11. von Solms, S., Marnewick, A.: Towards educational guidelines for the security systems engineer. In: Drevin, L., Theocharidou, M. (eds.) WISE 2018. IAICT, vol. 531, pp. 57–68. Springer, Cham (2018). https://doi.org/10.1007/978-3-319-99734-6_5
12. Bayuk, J.: Systems security engineering: a research roadmap. Systems Engineering Research center (2010). https://www.fbiic.gov/public/2010/sep/SERC-2010-TR-005-Security.pdf. Accessed 7 Mar 2019
13. Parrish, A., et al.: Global perspectives on cybersecurity education for 2030: a case for a meta-discipline. In: Proceedings of the Proceedings Companion of the 23rd Annual ACM Conference on Innovation and Technology in Computer Science Education (2018)
14. Bayuk, J.L.: Systems security engineering. IEEE Secur. Priv. **9**(2), 72–74 (2011)
15. Batcheller, A., Fowler, S.C., Cunningham, R., Doyle, D., Jaeger, T., Lindqvist, U.: Building on the success of building security in. IEEE Secur. Priv. **15**(4), 85–87 (2017)
16. Oren, J.C.: What does a systems security engineer do and why do systems engineers care? INSIGHT **16**(2), 16–18 (2013)
17. Knapp, K.J., Maurer, C., Plachkinova, M.: Maintaining a cybersecurity curriculum: professional certifications as valuable guidance. J. Inf. Syst. Educ. **28**(2), 101–113 (2017)
18. Burley, D.L., et al.: Cybersecurity Curricula 2017 (2017)
19. Salini, P., Kanmani, S.: Survey and analysis on security requirements engineering. Comput. Electr. Eng. **38**(6), 1785–1797 (2012)
20. Squires, A., Wade, J., Dominick, P., Gelosh, D.: Building a competency taxonomy to guide experience acceleration of lead program systems engineers. Stevens Institute of Technology HoBoKen NJ School of Systems and Enterprises (2011). Accessed 30 Jan 2019
21. Newhouse, W., Keith, S., Scribner, B., Witte, G.: National Initiative for Cybersecurity Education (NICE) Cybersecurity Workforce Framework. NIST (2017)
22. Rashid, A., et al.: Scoping the cyber security body of knowledge. IEEE Secur. Priv. **16**(3), 96–102 (2018)
23. Backhouse, J., Hsu, C.W., Silva, L.: Circuits of power in creating de jure standards: shaping an international information systems security standard. MIS Q. **30**(Special Issue), 413–438 (2006)
24. European committe for standardization, "European e-Competence framework 3.0" (2016)
25. Ross, R., McEvilley, M., Oren, J.C.: Systems Security Engineering: Considerations for a Multidisciplinary Approach in the Engineering of Trustworthy Secure Systems, vol. 800–160. National Institute of Standards and Technology (2016). Accessed 28 Jan 2019
26. Walden, D.D., Roedler, G.J., Forsberg, K.J., Hamelin, R.D., Shortell, T.M.: INCOSE Systems Engineering Handbook: A Guide for System Life Cycle Processes and Activities. Wiley, Hoboken (2015)
27. Kotonya, G., Sommerville, I.: Requirements Engineering Processes and Techniques. Wiley, Chichester (1998)
28. Kossiakoff, A., Sweet, W.N., Seymour, S.J., Biemer, S.M.: Systems Engineering Principles and Practice, 2nd edn. Wiley, New York (2011)

Andragogy as a Scientific Basis for Training Professionals in Information Security

Alexander Tolstoy and Natalia Miloslavskaya(✉)

The National Research Nuclear University MEPhI (Moscow Engineering Physics Institute), 31 Kashirskoye shosse, Moscow, Russia
{AITolstoj,NGMiloslavskaya}@mephi.ru

Abstract. The paper presents the results of research on the use of the basic provisions of andragogy to improve modern systems of training professionals in a particular professional field (information security). To do this, the characteristics of such systems were determined, the classification of trainees according to the criteria of adulthood was carried out, the possibilities of applying the basic provisions of andragogy to the object (an educational system) and the subject (processes, methods, and technologies of training) of research in the selected area were considered.

Keywords: Andragogy · Pedagogy · Adult learning · Adult education · Information security · Training

1 Introduction

The "andragogy" term most often refers to a sufficiently large area of knowledge relevant to adult education. Its history can be divided into several phases [1, 2]:

Phase 1. The emergence of the "andragogy" term. The term as a part of pedagogy relating to adult education was first used in 1833 by A. Kappa, a German high school teacher. The Kappa's "Plato's educational ideas as pedagogy for individuals and as public education" [3] includes a section entitled "Andragogy or education for men in adulthood" ("Die Androgogik uber Bildung im manlichen Alter"). On 60 pages, the author considers the problems of education, characterizes education in the context of the main values of human life and connects these problems with the training of physicians, soldiers, teachers, speakers, rulers and men as fathers of their families. Using the "andragogy" term, the author does not give its definition and does not talk on its authorship. It should be noted that in most of the subsequent works of his followers the priority of this term's usage is given to Kappa. However, he did not develop the theory of andragogy but justified the practical importance and necessity of education for adults. Over the following decades, the "andragogy" term was almost forgotten. This can be explained by the fact that studies conducted actively in this area in Europe and America had their own history and terminology. Therefore, the new term did not have widespread support.

Phase 2. "Andragogy" was reborn. In 1920, adult education became the subject of active research in Germany. In one of the first published works (Lindeman, 1926)

Published by Springer Nature Switzerland AG 2019
L. Drevin and M. Theocharidou (Eds.): WISE 2019, IFIP AICT 557, pp. 72–85, 2019.
https://doi.org/10.1007/978-3-030-23451-5_6

andragogy was considered as a new direction in science without special justification [4]. Most of the works were related to the study of practical problems of adult education. In most studies, andragogy was reduced to the method of teaching of adults, thereby significantly narrowing its subject and weakening its theoretical foundations. At this phase, the important results include not only the initial stage of disclosure of the "andragogy" concept but also the formation on an interdisciplinary basis of a community of researchers from academic and scientific institutions that have begun to work actively in this area.

Phase 3. Formation of andragogy as a separate science. Studies of andragogy in the 2nd phase remained largely unnoticed until the 50s and 60s of the XXth century when in Europe and the US there was a new interest in the formation and development of andragogy as a scientific discipline related to adult education. These two directions of research can be explained by the fact that the accumulation of research results occurred in different conditions (social, economic, due to the end of the 2nd World war, and even geographical) and was based on different needs in adult education. A comparison of these two approaches on a scientific basis can be found in Savicevic's work [5]. We will not consider in detail the differences of scientific schools of the US and Europe but will focus only on the results of research in andragogy, which can form the scientific basis of the development of training of professionals in information security (IS).

A leading scientific school was formed in the US under the leadership of M. Knowles, who called andragogy an art and science of helping adults in learning and a system of statements on adult learners, which should be applied differentially to different adults depending on the situation [6]. The key element of Knowles's works is the justification of differences between pedagogy and andragogy [7] made on the basis of considering the main characteristics of an adult learner. Further, he formulated the basic principles of andragogy, identified the key factors to be taken into account in the development of programmes for adult education and considered the variety of factors motivating adults to learn. The main results, which were obtained by the Knowles's scientific school, are published in [8]. This monograph was reprinted 7 times (last time in 2011)!

In Europe, studies were on a broad front in Germany, Switzerland, the Netherlands, Yugoslavia, Hungary, Finland, Poland, and Russia [5]. Currently, scientific journals are published with the "andragogy" word in their titles. Departments of Andragogy are operating actively in various universities, which teach disciplines related to andragogy. The International Society for Comparative Adult Education (ISCAE) with a recognized leader J. Reischmann as its President unites the scientific community, which carries out research on adult education.

The results, which are useful for our study, can be highlighted as follows [9, 10].

1. The definition of andragogy was clarified. It refers to an art and science to help adults to learn, as well as to study the theory of education, the processes, and technologies associated with it.
2. The statement of the need for continuous adult education was justified.
3. The requirements for teachers to teach adults were defined. These teachers were called "andragogues" that emphasizes their differences from teachers.

4. The necessity of introducing the "Andragogy" discipline into the curricula of academic training of teachers is substantiated in the assumption that universities' graduates can participate professionally in adult education. The latter is implemented in dozens of universities around the world but not always under the above-mentioned name.

It should be noted that the experience of teaching such a discipline accumulated at universities does not solve the problem of a universal andragogue [11] as his possible follow-up practical activities, which are associated with adult learning, are significantly influenced by specifics of a professional field, to which the adult learner prepares.

This conclusion was the basis for research on the use of the recommendations of andragogy to improve modern systems of training of professionals in a particular professional field (IS). To do this, the characteristics of such systems will be determined, the classification of trainees according to the criteria of adulthood will be carried out, the possibilities of applying the basic provisions of andragogy to the object (educational system) and the subject (processes, methods, and technologies of training) of research in the selected area will be considered in the paper.

2 IS Professional Training Systems

IS professional training systems in different countries have their peculiarities. The following is common among them:

- Professional training is conducted within the systems of higher (academic) (1st stage) and postgraduate additional professional (2nd stage) education;
- The system of higher education usually has two levels: Bachelors and Masters;
- The system of postgraduate additional professional education (APE) is based on the short-term professional refresher courses (RC) for obtaining additional professional competencies and retraining (RT) programmes for developing trainees' competencies related to a new type of their professional activity.

It should be noted that the same features are typical for other professional areas. However, the peculiarity of the IS field is due to the fact that it is constantly changing. This fact leads to the need to correct the content of educational programmes almost every two years that results in the following. It is necessary to adapt constantly the higher education programmes that contradicts the principle of their stability within each curriculum. It increases the APE role, for which it is necessary to develop new educational programmes permanently. If an IS professional wants to meet modern requirements, he must improve constantly his skills through self-education and APE, following the principle of continuous professional learning (learning throughout the whole professional life).

Differences between countries in their IS professional training systems relate to the presence of separate trajectories of academic education and duration of training for individual educational programmes. For example, in the UK [12] it involves the development of the trajectory of academic education, which includes the implementation of the following programmes (Fig. 1):

- For the Bachelor's degree (B), the duration *Tb* of training on which is 3 years. On the timeline on Fig. 1, it corresponds to the time difference (*Tb* = *Tbe*−*To*). Its volume called laboriousness is 360 credits,
- For the integrated Master's degree (M), the duration *Tm* of training on which is 4 years (*Tm* = *Tme*−*To*) with laboriousness of 480 credits,
- For the Master's degree (M), the duration *Tm* of training on which is 1 year with laboriousness of 180 credits.

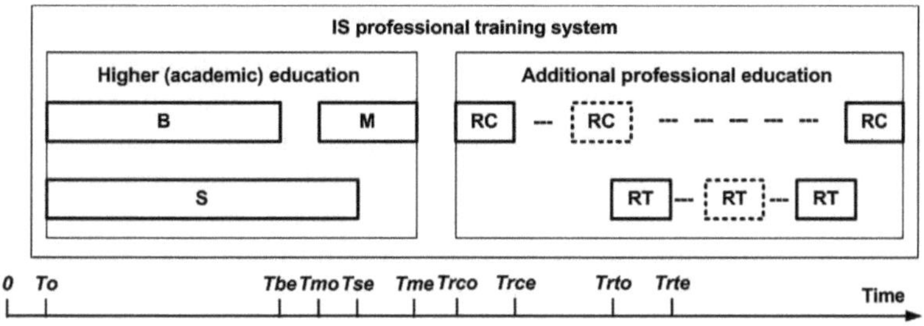

Fig. 1. Structure of the IS professional training system

In the Russian Federation [13], the trajectory of academic Bachelor's and Master's training is also implemented, as well as in-depth engineering education on the basis of so-called Specialitet (S), and additional professional training in the form of RC and RT programmes is traditionally developed (Fig. 1). The implementation of Specialitet programmes forms a separate learning path. In this case, the duration *Tb* of training of Bachelors (B) is 4 years with laboriousness of 480 credits; for Masters (M) *Tm* is 2 years with laboriousness of 240 credits, for Specialists (S) *Ts* it lies in the range of 5–6 years (*Ts* = *Tse*−*To*) with laboriousness of 600–720 credits. The duration of various RC programmes *Trc* is from 16 to 250 academic hours (*Trc* = *Trce*−*Trco*) and of RT programmes *Trt* – from 250 to 1000 h (*Trt* = *Trte*−*Trto*).

It should be noted that regardless of the countries the start of training on Bachelor's and Specialist's degree programmes (*To*) often coincides with the time of graduation from secondary schools (possibly after a period of practical activity). The Master's degree programmes can be implemented immediately after the Bachelor's degree programmes (*Tbe* = *Tmo*) or at some interval related to professional activities (not always in the field of IS). The RC programmes should be held at least every two years (the interval between the end of academic education should not exceed two years). The RT programmes should be associated with a change in the type of professional activity within the field of IS (for example, from operational to organizational and management, or from operational to teaching).

3 Adult Learners: Who Are They?

Consideration of the features of IS professional training systems taking into account the time scale tied to the trainee's age shows that the minimum age of applicants for the Bachelor's and Specialist's degree programmes is 17–18 years, for Master's - 20–22 years and for RC and RT – 22–24 years correspondently. If we take into account the fact that in Russia, for example, a young man 18-years old has the right to participate in elections, form a family and be called up for military service, where he will be entrusted with weapons and may die defending his homeland, trainees in any IS professional training programmes can be considered the adult trainees.

To accept only trainees' age as a basis for defining the adulthood, without taking into account their psycho-physiological properties, is not sufficient. For example, one can also consider the basic life tasks that can be set only by an adult. On this basis, Knowles divided the adults into three groups: 18-30, 30–65 and 65+ years [6]. Adults in each group have their own attitude to their profession, career, family, home, development of personality, use of free time, health, public life, etc. Knowles considered an adult a person "who behaves like an adult, i.e. plays adult roles (employee, spouse, parent, responsible citizen, soldier) – the sociological definition" and "whose self-consciousness is the self-consciousness of an adult – the psychological definition". A person is an adult to the extent that he perceives himself responsible for his life [6].

Thus, an adult refers to a person who performs socially significant productive roles (citizen, employee, family member), has physiological, psychological, social, moral maturity, relative economic independence, life experience and a level of self-awareness sufficient for responsible self-governing behavior.

Based on the idea of an adult, we should rely on these characteristics in his training and expect that he will treat the educational process consciously and responsibly. In addition, since an adult is usually engaged in a specific activity, his need for training will be related to some extent to his main professional activity, as well as the performance of other social roles. So he will pursue specific, practical and real goals. It is also obvious that if usually in conditions of well-established life the adult with well-established social roles decides to study, then he has a strong enough interest (i.e. high motivation) to this. It is determined by the urgent need for training to solve an important life problem. At the same time, he seeks to apply immediately his knowledge, skills, personal qualities and value orientations acquired in the educational process to solve the above problem as soon as possible. In learning activities, an adult learner relies inevitably on his life experience (everyday, professional, social), which often serves as an important source of learning for both himself and his colleagues.

Considering all of the above, we can define an adult learner as a person with five fundamental characteristics that distinguish him from the non-adult learners [14]. He is aware of himself as an increasingly independent, self-governing person. He is gaining more and more life experience (everyday, professional, social), which becomes an important source of training for himself and his colleagues. His readiness to learn (motivation) is determined by his desire to solve his vital problems and achieve specific goals with the help of educational activities. He strives for the immediate implementation of the acquired knowledge, skills, personal qualities, and value orientations. His educational activity is largely due to temporary, spatial, professional, household and social factors (conditions). In this case, if the adult approaches his training consciously, he primarily evaluates his real possibilities and abilities.

Summarizing numerous studies on the definition of human age periods, it can be argued [14] that physiologists, psychologists, sociologists, philosophers and researchers of educational problems have found that a person throughout his life goes through three clearly defined stages with their distinct features. The first stage called "immaturity" is divided conditionally into childhood, adolescence, and youth. According to various expert estimates, it lasts on average up to 20 years. The second stage called "adulthood" lasts from 20 to about 65 years. It is divided into the periods of early adulthood (up to about 35 years), maturity (up to about 50 years) and late adulthood. Finally, after 65 years a period of elderly ("golden" or "third") age comes.

If we apply the description of human adulthood to the modern education system, the following conclusions will be obvious:

1. In the implementation of the Bachelor's and Specialist's degree programmes, the trainee becomes an adult (early adulthood). This process needs help that should correct the trainees' activities.
2. It is necessary to treat training in the Master's degree programmes and APE programmes as adult education (the period of mature and late adulthood).
3. Educational programmes of the appropriate level and their implementation should reflect the characteristics of adult learners.

4 Pedagogy or Andragogy?

The principal features of the andragogical approach to the educational process can be identified by comparing the pedagogical and andragogical learning models [15]. The main differences between these models are presented in Table 1. The table shows that andragogy can be considered as a separate science of adult education, justifying the activities of adult learners and teachers in organizing the educational process.

Like any science, andragogy has its objects (adult educational processes) and subject (patterns of activity of adult learners and teachers while organizing and implementing the educational process) of consideration, as well as its structure, concepts, and terminology. Theoretical statements of andragogy as a science can be formulated and presented in the form of an andragogical learning model (Table 1).

In the previous section, we came to the conclusion that IS professional training must be approached as to the implementation of adult educational processes. Further, we consider the possibility of applying the andragogical model directly to our case.

Table 1. A comparison of the pedagogical and andragogical learning models

Characteristic	Pedagogical model	Andragogical model
Trainee's self-awareness	Feeling of dependence	Awareness of increasing self-government
Trainee's experience	Low value	Rich source of learning
Trainee's readiness to training	Determined by physiological development and social compulsion	Determined by the tasks of personal development and mastering social roles
Application of acquired knowledge	Deferred	Immediate
Orientation in training	On the subject	To solve the problem
The psychological climate of learning	Formal, teacher's authority-oriented, competitive	Informal, based on mutual respect and collaboration
The educational process's planning	By the teacher	Together with the trainees
Identification of training needs	By the teacher	Together with the trainees
Formulation of learning objectives	By the teacher	Together with the trainees
The educational process's construction	The logic of the subject, meaningful units	Depending on the trainee's readiness to learn, problem units
Educational activity	Technology of knowledge transfer	Technology of searching new knowledge on the basis of experience
Assessment	By the teacher	Joint identification of new training needs and evaluation of training programmes

5 Andragogical Approach to the Preparation of Training in the Field of IS

Preparation of training for any programme (including the field of IS) involves the following steps:

1. Definition of goals, objectives and expected learning outcomes.
2. Development of curriculum and syllabus for its components (disciplines, modules).
3. The choice of technologies for the educational process implementation.

4. Determining the curriculum for the training implementation.
5. Formation of the trainees.
6. Formation of the teaching staff.

Let us apply these steps to IS professional training using the adragogical model. In this case, the experience gained in the Russian Federation in the creation and implementation of the system for IS professionals training in general and at the National Research Nuclear University MEPhI (Moscow Engineering Physics Institute) in particular will be taken into account.

5.1 Definition of Goals, Objectives and Expected Learning Outcomes

The learning objectives, the tasks to be addressed to achieve these goals and the expected learning outcomes will be different for different educational programmes in IS.

For the Bachelor's and Specialist's degree programmes in the first years of training (basic training), a pedagogical model is applicable. The second half of training (teaching professional disciplines, Internship) includes the transition to the andragogical model in terms of the formation of trainees' awareness of increasing self-government, the acquisition of modern learning experience and practice of solving problems related to either IS ensuring basic issues (for Bachelors), or practical (engineering) issues (for Specialists).

The andragogical model is fully applicable to the Master's degree programmes and APE programmes. It is assumed that the trainee has a certain level of self-awareness in relation to readiness for training (including on the basis of practical problem solving), understanding of the role of self-management in training, a positive learning experience, and he is ready to apply immediately in practice the knowledge gained.

When defining the goals, objectives and expected learning outcomes, it is also necessary to take into account the qualification requirements formed by the professional community, for example, in the form of a model [16] or professional standards [17].

Thus, the purpose of training will be the formation of certain professional competencies in terms of the development of the learner's understanding that he is an adult (Bachelors and Specialists), or in terms of the implementation of educational processes that take into account the fact that the learners are adults (Masters and APE).

It can be recommended to formulate the goals, objectives and expected learning outcomes for a specific programme in IS in the form of a trainee's model, which should also reflect the characteristics of those entering the training.

5.2 Development of Curriculum and Syllabus for Its Components

A specific curriculum in IS should contain a list of disciplines with an indication of their volume (laboriousness in credits or in academic hours), forms of control of knowledge and place in the schedule of classes (in the curriculum).

The curriculum of any programme contains the following modules (cycles): Basic (General), General professional, Professional, Internship, and Control (current, final).

In accordance with the andragogical model (Table 1), one of the principles of adult education is the joint learner-trainee activity, related to the planning of the educational process, the definition of learning needs and the formulation of learning objectives. This means that the curriculum of a specific educational programme should include all the appropriate forms of individual training:

- Blocks of several elective disciplines. The trainee has the right to choose one of them; after that it becomes mandatory for him. His teacher should help him in choosing such disciplines. Our experience shows that the total laboriousness of these disciplines can reach half of the laboriousness of the Professional module. For example, if the curriculum includes a unit related to ensuring IS of automated systems (ASs), then it can include such disciplines as "IS of Automated Banking Systems", "IS of Automated Control Systems for Technological Processes", "IS of Decision-making AS", etc. This choice can also be ensured by the availability of elective disciplines in both Professional and Basic modules;
- Internship module. The Internship topic is chosen by the trainee and his teacher jointly. Its implementation is controlled by the teacher. For example, the Internship topic may be related to a certain type of professional activity (production, organizational and management, information and analytical, research, teaching);
- Trainee's independent work, the content of which is consistent with his teacher. Its volume (laboriousness) is included in the volume of a particular discipline (up to 50% of its volume) and in the volume of a particular Internship;
- Implementation and protection of a final qualifying work (FQW) with the topic selected by the trainee with his teacher. It is reasonable to involve in the supervision of FQW implementation not only the leading teachers of an educational institution but also the leading employees of the organizations-potential consumers of the graduates trained under the specific programme. The volume of FQW's implementation and protection is defined by the type of training programme.

Syllabus of disciplines from the curriculum are formed on the basis of determining their content (sections, topics), forms of training (contact or classroom work, independent work, monitoring of learning outcomes), the information base (mandatory and additional) and the forms and content of intermediate and final control of knowledge. In the discipline's syllabus, the requirements for the initial educational level of the trainee (for example, the level of knowledge and skills) should be defined and the levels of professional competencies, which should be formed during the discipline's mastering, should be formulated. This information should be consistent with the goals, objectives and expected learning outcomes generated during the phase of training preparation (for example, in the trainee's model).

Disciplines' syllabus of the Professional module in IS should have a practical orientation. Therefore, the acquired professional competencies should include a set of abilities (practical skills) that can be applied not only after graduation from the programme but also in the FQW's implementation. This can be done if the discipline's programme includes laboratory work, practical (case) training, homework followed by public protection of the results of their implementation [13].

Taking into account the peculiarities of adult education, it is possible to allow the development of individual curriculum and disciplines' syllabus, which correspond to the peculiarities of the andragogical model (Table 1).

5.3 The Choice of Technologies for the Educational Process Implementation

When choosing a technology for the implementation of the educational process, it is necessary to take into account not only the features of adult learning but also modern trends in the development of IT and IS areas. The IT development in general and, especially, the formation of information resources on the Internet have made a significant change in educational technology. The use of distance learning technologies (DLT) becomes relevant. The IS professional training is characterized by regular changes in the content of training, the presence of case training and the importance of teacher-trainees contacts. This imposes certain restrictions on the breadth of DLT usage. For example, in the Russian educational standards, there are restrictions on the volume of disciplines that can be implemented using DLT (not more than 25% of the volume of the Professional module), as well as a complete ban on distance learning.

The formation (implementation of Bachelor's and Specialist's degree programmes in IS) and the presence of a trainee's certain level of awareness of increasing self-government and readiness for training (implementation of Master's degree programmes and APE programmes in IS) justifies the high role of the trainee's independent work (discussed in Sect. 5.2) with the support of his teacher in the education process. This form of training allows to implement such element of the anragogical model as of how to apply the technology of searching new knowledge (Table 1). Public protection of the results of independent work in the framework of practical training allows to form a mechanism for joint assessment of the effectiveness of the training programme that also corresponds to the andragogical model.

5.4 Determining the Syllabus for the Training Implementation

When forming the curriculum for implementation of any training programme in IS, it is necessary to consider the following: features of the curriculum; the contact educational forms used (lectures, practical classes -seminars, and laboratory works); teachers' individual consultations; the content of the syllabus of individual disciplines (modules); presence in the curriculum of such forms as independent work and Internship; and the possibility of DLT usage. You should also consider the fact that trainees in senior courses in Bachelor's and Specialist's degree programmes as well as studying in Master's degree programmes very often combine training and work as interns or employees. At the same time, it is necessary to strive to ensure that the place and content of such work correspond to the specifics of the implemented programme.

As a rule, RC programmes are implemented in isolation from practical activities. Therefore, their curriculum is formed within the framework of intensive training in the time interval of 6-8 academic hours per day, 5-6 days per week.

The implementation of RT programmes can be associated with either full or partial separation from practical activities and the use of mixed (part-time) technology. Therefore, it is necessary to design the duration of this training up to 6 months.

5.5 Formation of the Trainees

The trainee decides to study under the Master's degree programme or APE programme in IS guided by the task to improve his skills to a level that is in demand in this labor market. Thus, he shows his readiness for training, which is determined by the tasks of its development. This is fully consistent with the andragogical model.

The trainee decides to study under the Bachelor's or Specialist's degree programme taking into account the peculiarities of his physiological development and under the influence of the social environment. It can include, for example, the pressure of parents' opinion and the prevailing opinion that exists in his information environment, which determines the prospects for the acquisition of professional competencies in IS. Therefore, these trainees can be attributed either to the late stage of immaturity (youth) or to the early stage of adulthood. Training in these programmes should be aimed not only at the formation of certain professional competencies but also to transform him into an adult learner in the view of the andragogical model. The consequence of this may appear in the trainee's opinion that he choose the wrong field of study. The experience gained by the authors in the MEPhI shows that the proportion of trainees who have interrupted their studies can reach several tens of percent.

The solution lies in the introduction of a special system of vocational guidance for the selection of young people on the basis of the formation of a culture of IS (inclusion of disciplines related to the IS basics in the school curriculum), the organization of Olympiads in IS, as well as the introduction of methods of psychophysical testing.

It is very important to connect to this system organizations interested in getting trained professionals of a certain level and specialization. The ideal is the formation of a contingent of trainees within the target order of a particular organization, which can participate in the formation of the goal, objectives and expected learning outcomes, as well as in the development of curricula and harmonization of disciplines' syllabus. It can be useful to send trainees to Internship to these organizations - the future place of work of graduates, as well as the inclusion of representatives of these organizations in the Commission for public protection of the results of their FQWs.

5.6 Formation of the Teaching Staff

The above analysis of the stages of preparation of training programmes in IS has shown that the teacher must have certain specific professional competencies in the field of training programmes in IS. Our studies have shown the lack of information on the existence of current operational systems of teacher training for the implementation of General professional and Professional modules in IS. Most often we are talking about the selection of such teachers. Based on our experience, which is not very different from the experience of other educational centers, we can identify the following main factors that are taken into account in the selection of teachers:

- Practical experience in the field of designing or usage of IS maintenance systems;
- Experience in carrying out research taking into account the specifics of an individual training programme;
- Teaching experience in the framework of similar educational programmes.

Here, the requirements for andragogues can be present only in relation to the teaching experience, and not to the presence of basic education in andragogy (even in relation to the RC in this field).

6 Conclusion

The analysis of the andragogical learning model conducted in conjunction with the consideration of the main stages of preparation for training programmes of academic and additional education in IS allows us to formulate the following conclusions:

1. An important reason for the need to move from the pedagogical to the andragogical model is the presence of factors that determine the attitude to trainees as adults. In this case, the role of the educator (teacher) also changes dramatically.
2. The level of applicability of the andragogical model will be different for different educational programmes.
3. The andragogical model is fully applicable to Master's degree programmes and APE programmes.
4. The andragogical model can be applied for the educational process of Bachelor's and Specialist's degree programmes in the senior courses.

Further research can be aimed at the development of andragogical models of trainees in various training programmes for IS professionals and appropriate models of teachers.

The development of the system of teacher-andragogue training is urgent. Fundamental is the availability of the professional competencies not only in IS relevant to the implementation of specific programmes but professional competencies in andragogy. Training of such teachers is possible in three directions. Firstly, in the framework of the curriculum of the Master's degree programme, which aims to form trainees' professional competencies for two areas of professional activity, for example, organizational and managerial (or project or operational) and teaching. Secondly, conducting RC for teachers with experience in the implementation of specific IS professional training programmes with the inclusion in the curriculum of the RC programme of disciplines on various aspects of andragogy. Thirdly, the implementation of RT programmes for IS specialists (possibly in IT too) with the inclusion in their curricula of a module related to andragogy. In all these cases, it is necessary to develop appropriate training programmes and corresponding methodological support.

The quality of teacher-andragogue training can be controlled if the evaluation system of teachers similar to the system of IS professional certification will be established. The appropriate programmes should be developed to do this.

The features of the results obtained in this research should also be noted. Foremost, they have a novelty in terms of the integrity of the chosen model, based on the andragogical approach. Separate elements of the andragogical model without its designation were used earlier in practical educational activities in the field of IS. However, we are not aware of publications in which the features of the use of the scientific foundations of andragogy in this field were considered. Secondly, the results obtained are systematic in terms of applicability to various educational programmes in the field of IS. Thirdly, the results obtained are universal. They can be applied with a certain correction for the training of professionals in other areas for which the essential features are the need for continuing education and the high dynamics of the development of the subject area (for example, information technology).

Acknowledgement. This work was supported by the MEPhI Academic Excellence Project (agreement with the Ministry of Education and Science of the Russian Federation of August 27, 2013, project no. 02.a03.21.0005).

References

1. Reischmann, J.: Andragogy. History, Meaning, Context, Function. Version 9, September 2004. http://www.andragogy.net. Accessed 14 Feb 2019
2. Kessels, J.: Andragogy. In: Poell, R.F., Rocco, T.S., Roth, G.L. (eds.) The Routledge Companion to Human Resource Development, 1st edn., Chap. 2, pp. 13–20. Routledge, Oxford/New York (2015). http://www.routledge.com/books. Accessed 14 Feb 2019
3. Kapp, A.: Platon's Erziehungslehre, als Pädagogik für die Einzelnen und als Staatspädagogik. Minden and Leipzig, Verlag Ferdinand Eßmann (1833)
4. Lindeman, E.C.: Andragogik: the method of teaching adults. Workers' Education L 4, 38 (1926)
5. Savicevic, D.: Understanding andragogy in Europe and America. In: Reischmann, J., Bron, M., Jelenc, Z. (eds.): Comparative Adult Education 1998, Ljubljana, Slovenian Institute for Adult Education, pp. 97–119 (1999). http://www.iscae.org/ISCAE-Book1999.pdf. Accessed 14 Feb 2019. ISBN 961-6130-27-7
6. Knowles, M.S.: The Modern Practice of Adult Education: Andragogy Versus Pedagogy. Association Press, New York (1970). 1980
7. Knowles, M.S., et al.: Andragogy in Action. Applying Modern Principles of Adult Education. Jossey Bass, San Francisco (1984)
8. Knowles, M.S., Holton, E.F., Swanson, R.A.: The Adult Learner: The Definitive Classic in Adult Education and Human Resource Development, 7th edn. Elsevier, London (2011)
9. Reischmann, J.: Andragogy. In: English, L. (ed.) International Encyclopedia of Adult Education, pp. 58–63. Palgrave Macmillan, London (2005)
10. Popović, K., Reischmann, J.: Andragogik, andragogy and administering graduate programs (2017). http://www.academia.edu/36240364/Andragogik_Andragogy_and_Administering_Graduate_Programs_2017. Accessed 14 Feb 2019
11. Reischmann, J.: Andragogy: because "adult education" is not beneficial to the academic identity! In: 2015 Adult Education in an Interconnected World, DVV International – International Perspectives in Adult Education, vol. 71, pp. 87–97 (2015)
12. Furnell, S., Michael, K., Piper, F., Chris, E., Catherine, H., Ensor, C.: A national certification programme for academic degrees in cyber security. In: Drevin, L., Theocharidou, M. (eds.) WISE 2018. IAICT, vol. 531, pp. 133–145. Springer, Cham (2018). https://doi.org/10.1007/978-3-319-99734-6_11

13. Budzko, V., Miloslavskaya, N., Tolstoy, A.: Forming the abilities of designing information security maintenance systems in the implementation of educational programmes in information security. In: Drevin, L., Theocharidou, M. (eds.) WISE 2018. IAICT, vol. 531, pp. 108–120. Springer, Cham (2018). https://doi.org/10.1007/978-3-319-99734-6_9
14. Zmeev, S.I.: Andragogy: Fundamentals of Theory, History and Technology of Adult Education, Moscow, PER SE (2006). (In Russian)
15. Knowles, M.S.: The Adult Learner: A Neglected Species. 207 p., Houston (1973)
16. State Government Information Security Workforce Development Model: A Best Practice Model and Framework, USA, June 2010. Final Version 1.0
17. Professianal standards in the field of information security. http://azi.ru/. Accessed 14 Feb 2019. (In Russian)

Applications and Cryptography

Light Cryptography

Pascal Lafourcade[1], Takaaki Mizuki[2], Atsuki Nagao[3], and Kazumasa Shinagawa[4,5](✉)

[1] LIMOS, University Clermont Auvergne, CNRS UMR 6158, Aubière, France
[2] Tohoku University, Sendai, Japan
[3] Ochanomizu University, Tokyo, Japan
[4] Tokyo Institute of Technology, Tokyo, Japan
[5] National Institute of Advanced Industrial Science and Technology, Tokyo, Japan
shinagawa.k.aa@m.titech.ac.jp

Abstract. Physical cryptography provides cryptographic protocols using physical objects like cards and envelopes instead of using computers. In this paper, we introduce a new model for physical cryptography, called *light cryptography*. It uses transparent sheets and some properties of light and shadows. We design several secure light cryptographic protocols: one for set-intersection (which can solve the scheduling problem), one for maximum (which can solve the Yao's Millionaires' problem), one for computing the sum of integers. We believe that our protocols using light cryptography are a powerful tool for information security education because they are fairly simple and fun to use.

Keywords: Secure computation · Physical cryptography · Light cryptography · Information security education

1 Introduction

Suppose that a group of friends wishes to hold a party next month, but they have not yet decided the date of the party. They wish to choose a date that suits everyone because they want the presence of everyone. In the usual way to arrange a schedule, each participant must reveal his convenient dates and times to other participants. However, for privacy reasons, some participants do not want to reveal their agendas to other ones because their agendas contain personal information such as professional meetings, personal appointments or hobby schedules.

Secure computation is a cryptographic solution for such a problem [2,9,17]. It enables parties to compute some function of their inputs while only revealing the output value and no information about the input values. It is known that secure computation for any function is possible based on cryptographic assumptions (e.g., the hardness of the enhanced trapdoor permutation [9]) or setup assumptions (e.g., the existence of secure channel [2]). Various secure computation protocols have been proposed following these pioneer works [2,9,17]. Despite

Published by Springer Nature Switzerland AG 2019
L. Drevin and M. Theocharidou (Eds.): WISE 2019, IFIP AICT 557, pp. 89–101, 2019.
https://doi.org/10.1007/978-3-030-23451-5_7

their usefulness, it is difficult for non-experts to understand why they are correct and secure because these protocols often rely on the knowledge of deep mathematics. Moreover, since we cannot check the inside of computers, a program implementing a protocol behaves like a black box from the user's point of view. It is clearly a difficulty to convince the user to trust such a computer-based system.

Physical cryptography is a suitable solution for secure computation to find a common date. The goal is to design a secure computation protocol using physical objects (e.g., cards, boxes, envelopes) instead of using computers. For example, *card-based cryptography* [5,7] is a physical cryptographic model using a deck of cards; information is encoded in a sequence of face-down cards with for example the rule that ♣♡ represents a 0 and ♡♣ represents a 1, and a protocol consists of a list of operations like rearrangement, turning over, and shuffles. Because all computational flows are visible from all parties, it is easy to verify and understand the correctness and the security of protocols without the knowledge of deep mathematics.

Contributions: We introduce a new model for physical cryptography. All previous papers used physical objects like cards or envelopes and the users have to perform some computations. We change the paradigm and use *light* and its properties to compute the results of some functions securely; we naturally call this new approach *light cryptography*. Light cryptography allows us to design physical light cryptographic protocols. It is a secure computation protocol that uses transparent sheets and the properties of light and shadow. The idea comes from *ombromanie* (also known as *shadowgraphy*); this is the art of creating shadow images using hands (e.g., rabbits, birds, old men). The key observation is that it is sometimes difficult to guess the original shape of hands by watching only the printed shadow; thus, it has *one-wayness* in some sense like one-way functions in cryptography: a one-way function f is easy to compute but it is hard to find an input x from the output $y = f(x)$. In light cryptography like in ombromanie, it is hard to find the original shape of hands by giving only the shadow of the hands. We also believe that light and shadows are familiar physics concepts for everyone. Moreover, the correctness and the security of our protocols are easy to understand without the knowledge of deep mathematics.

We first define a model of secure computation based on light cryptography. Then we construct several protocols that use this concept for secure computations. We design a protocol to allow participants to determine a common date without revealing any information about their personal agendas. We also propose a maximum protocol that allows users to compute the maximum of their values in a secure way in order to demonstrate that light cryptography can easily solve the famous Yao's Millionaires' problem [16], where two millionaires want to know which has more money without revealing how much each has. We propose an extension that also gives the identity of the owner of the maximum. Finally, we propose a protocol to compute the sum of some integers.

We also believe that light cryptography can be a powerful tool for information security education which is important but somewhat difficult. Specifically, it is

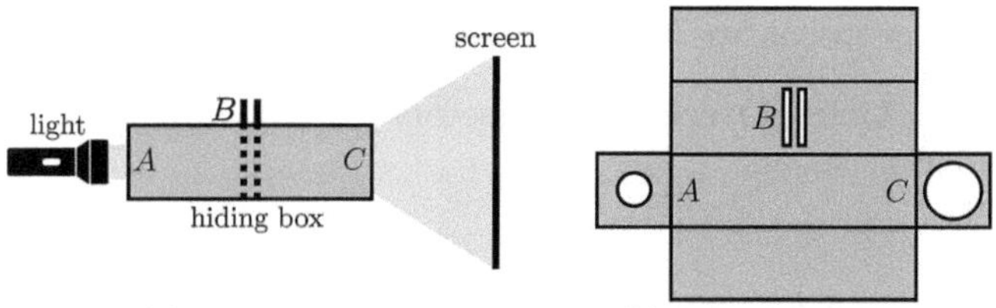

(a) Our system (b) A net of the hiding box

Fig. 1. Illustration of our system

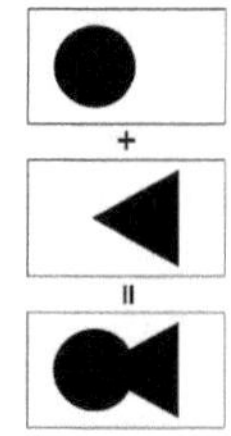

Fig. 2. Shadow addition.

useful for teaching secure computation, which seems to attempt to achieve an impossible (or unbelievable) task at the first glance. Light cryptography is a nice teaching material that gives an intuition that it is possible to do secure computation in some settings. The correctness and the security of protocols are also intuitive for students even who are not familiar with deep mathematics because its computation process is very simple; it just uses light. Moreover, it is suitable to perform our protocols in a classroom because result images can be displayed on a screen.

Related Work: There are many works of physical cryptography based on various physical objects. They are classified by type of input format. The first type of input format is by private actions like private rearrangements; for instance secure computations using a PEZ dispenser [1], a dial lock [11], marbles [8] and a 15 puzzle [12]. The other type of input format, which includes our model, is by submitting encoded objects like a sequence of face-down cards; such examples are secure computation protocols using a deck of cards [3–5, 7, 13], polarizing cards [15], and visual secret sharing schemes [6]. Polarizing cards [15] is based on the property of polarizing plates but the basic strategy to construct protocols is similar to other card-based cryptography [13]. D'Arco and De Prisco [6] proposed a physical cryptographic model, which combines the gate evaluation of secret sharing [10] and visual secret sharing scheme [14], which also uses transparent sheets for computation. While the paper presented a general protocol, it is somewhat complex compared to our protocols due to the gate evaluation from [10].

2 Model of Light Cryptography

In Sect. 2.1, we depict how the principles of light cryptography work. In Sect. 2.2, we define an important operation, *shadow addition*, which is an abstract property of light and shadow. In Sect. 2.3, we formally define *protocols* in our model of light cryptography.

2.1 Overview of Our System

Suppose that n players $P_1, P_2, \ldots, P_n$ having secret inputs $x_1, x_2, \ldots, x_n \in X$, respectively, wish to compute a joint function of their inputs $f(x_1, x_2, \ldots, x_n) \in Y$, where X and Y are a domain and a range of the function, respectively.

Before an execution of a protocol, we have to prepare the following:

- n transparent sheets (e.g., OHP (OverHead Projector) sheets),
- n black pens for transparent sheets,
- a light (e.g., projector),
- a screen,
- a non-transparent box called a *hiding box.*

Figure 1(a) shows an illustration of our system viewing it directly above (when $n = 2$) and Fig. 1(b) shows a blueprint of the hiding box. The hiding box has a number of holes; the hole A is a hole for inputting light, the hole C is a hole for outputting light, and n holes B are used for inserting one transparent sheet per each player P_i.

At the beginning of a protocol, each player P_i has a transparent sheet (which is called an *input sheet*) and a black pen, and he/she writes a black image on the transparent sheet with the black pen according to his/her input x_i. Each player P_i covertly puts the sheet into the i-th hole of holes B of the hiding box. Finally, the hole A of the hiding box is illuminated by the light, and then, an output image corresponding to $f(x_1, x_2, \ldots, x_n)$ is displayed on the screen (see Fig. 1(a)).

2.2 Shadow Addition

Imagine that we have two transparent sheets (e.g., OHP sheets), on each of which black images are drawn. By superimposing them, we have a new image which is the union of two original images. We call it *shadow addition* and denote it by the symbol $+$.

We now formally define this operator. Let U be a set of all black-and-white images of fixed size. The shadow addition $+ : U \times U \rightarrow U$ is defined by $A + B = C$, where $A, B, C \in U$ and the black area of C is the union of the black areas of A and B. Figure 2 shows an example of shadow addition of two images: the input images are a circle and a triangle, and the resulting image is a keyhole. It is easy to observe that the shadow addition satisfies the *commutative law* and the *associative law*, i.e., it holds that $A + B = B + A$ and $A + (B + C) = (A + B) + C$ for any $A, B, C \in U$. We also have the *idempotence* property: $A + A = A$.

2.3 Defining Protocols

Formally, a *light cryptogrpahic protocol* is defined by a 7-tuple (n, U, I, X, Y, g, h), where n is the number of players, U is a set of all black-and-white images of the same size, $I \in U$ is an *initial image* which is drawn on every input sheet, X is the domain of the players' secret inputs, Y is the range of the output, $g : X \rightarrow U$ is an *input function*, and $h : U \rightarrow Y$ is an *output function*. The protocol proceeds as follows:

1. At the beginning of the protocol, each player has a black pen and an input sheet. On the input sheet, the initial image I has already been drawn.

2. According to his/her input $x_i \in X$, each player draws an image $g(x_i)$ on his/her input sheet; the new image is $I'_i = I + g(x_i)$.
3. Each player covertly puts his/her input sheet into a black box in turns.
4. By switching on light, every player knows the union image $I_{\mathsf{result}} \in U$ of their input sheets, where $I_{\mathsf{result}} = I'_1 + I'_2 + \cdots + I'_n$. The output of the protocol is $h(I_{\mathsf{result}}) \in Y$.

Correctness. We say that a protocol correctly computes a function f if for any $x_1, x_2, \ldots, x_n \in X$, the value $h(I_{\mathsf{result}})$ of the output function h for the union image $I_{\mathsf{result}} = I'_1 + I'_2 + \cdots + I'_n$ is equal to $f(x_1, x_2, \ldots, x_n)$, where $I'_i = I + g(x_i)$ for all $i \in \{1, 2, \ldots, n\}$.

Security. A protocol is secure if the output function h restricted on $U_X \subset U$ is injective, where U_X is the set of all images generated by the inputs.

We assume that all players are semi-honest, i.e., they follow the protocol specification, and they cannot see the input sheets in the hiding box even after the computation. In order to achieve such a hiding property, we can use a shredder to destroy the input sheets after the computation. Now let us explain the meaning of the security defined above. Suppose that a protocol Π correctly computes a function f. The security definition requires that for any pair of input-sequences $X = (x_1, x_2, \ldots, x_n), X' = (x'_1, x'_2, \ldots, x'_n) \in X^n$ such that $f(X) = f(X') = y$, the output images I_{result} and I'_{result} induced by X and X', respectively, are the same image, i.e., it holds that $I_{\mathsf{result}} = I'_{\mathsf{result}}$. Otherwise, the output function h is not injective because $h(I_{\mathsf{result}}) = h(I'_{\mathsf{result}}) = y$ holds from the correctness.

Enhancing Security. In our security model, all players are assumed to be semi-honest and they must not see the other players' input sheets. It can be accomplished by shredding the input sheets with a shredder just after the end of the protocol, but occasionally the input sheets may be seen by other players due to a mistake in operation. The idea for hiding the inputs even when such an accident occurs is applying a shuffle to the input sheets before putting them into the hiding box. Specifically, each player puts his own input sheet into an envelope and places it on a public table, and then all players together apply a shuffle on the envelopes in order to hide the order of the input sheets. Of course, when the input sheets are revealed after the computation, even if we applied the shuffle to them, some of input information is leaked. But in this case, an adversary cannot guess the correspondence between the input sheets and the players, while our original model leaks all inputs in the case of such an accident.

3 Set-Intersection (SI) Protocol

Suppose that n friends wish to decide the date of a party next month. They wish to make it a convenient schedule for everyone without revealing the convenient schedule of each participant.

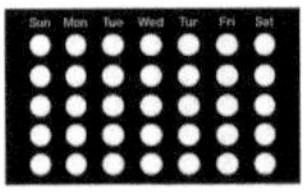

Fig. 3. Input sheet for set-intersection.

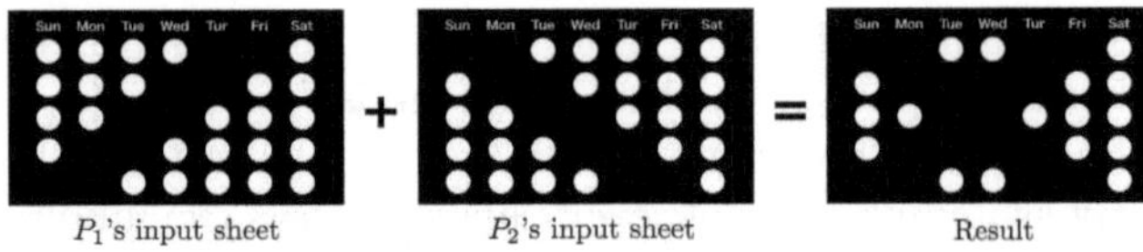

Fig. 4. Example of set intersection.

Our SI Protocol

Let D be a set of possible dates with ℓ elements and assume that each participant P_i has a subset $x_i \subset D$ as input. A set-intersection function for n inputs over D takes n subsets $x_1, x_2, \ldots, x_n \subset D$ and outputs their intersection $x_1 \cap x_2 \cap \cdots \cap x_n$. Our set-intersection protocol is defined by the following tuple $(n, U_{\mathsf{SI}}, I_{\mathsf{SI}}, 2^D, 2^D, g_{\mathsf{SI}}, h_{\mathsf{SI}})$, where :

- The initial image I_{SI} is an image with $|D|$ holes (white circles). Figure 3 shows an example of I_{SI} with 35 holes, i.e, 5 weeks of 7 days, $\ell = 35 = 5 \times 7$.
- U_{SI} is the set of all images of the same size as the initial image I_{SI}.
- The domain and the range are 2^D, i.e., the set of all subsets of D.
- The input function g_{SI} takes an input $x \in 2^D$ and outputs a set of black circles corresponding to $D \setminus x$. For example, if it holds $D \setminus x = \{1, 2, 3\}$, $g_{\mathsf{SI}}(x)$ is the set of three black circles corresponding to $\{1, 2, 3\}$.
- The output function h_{SI} is the inverse function of g'_{SI}, where $g'_{\mathsf{SI}}(x) = g_{\mathsf{SI}}(x) + I_{\mathsf{SI}}$; it returns a set of elements corresponding to white circles.

SI protocol proceeds as follows:

- Each player has a black pen and the input sheet.
- Using a black pen, each player P_i fills a set of holes which corresponds to $D \setminus x_i$. Namely, he/she fills a hole corresponding to d with a black pen if and only if $d \notin x_i$. It means that he/she is not avaible at the date x_i.
- Each player puts his/her input sheet into the hiding box.
- The output is obtained by switching on the light. Namely, lighting holes are a set of holes corresponding to $x_1 \cap x_2 \cap \cdots \cap x_n$.

Figure 4 shows an example execution of our set-intersection protocol for two players. White circles in the input sheet of each of P_1 and P_2 are available dates for the party. The function g_{SI} returns a set of black circles corresponding to unavailable dates. The rightmost image is the resulting image I_{result}, which has a set of white circles corresponding to available dates for both parties.

The correctness holds from the fact that the resulting image I_{result} has a set of holes corresponding to the dates available for all players. The security holds from the fact that each result image is unique for each output value.

Fine-grained Scheduling Protocol

The situation is almost the same as that of set-intersection but now each participant has a yes/no/maybe schedule.

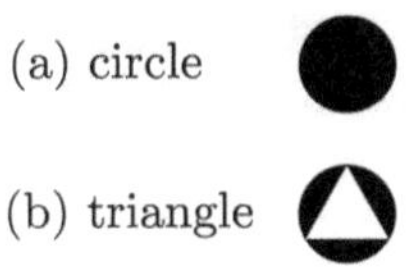

Fig. 5. Input circles.

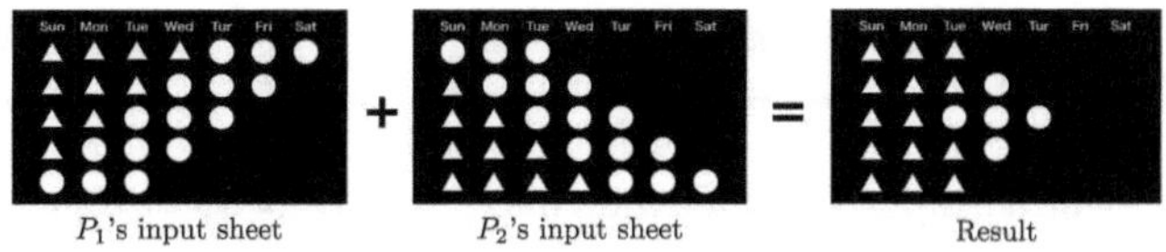

Fig. 6. Execution of fine-grained scheduling protocol.

Let D be the set of possible dates with ℓ elements. Now each P_i has an input $x_i = (x_i^{(1)}, \ldots, x_i^{(\ell)})$ with $x_i^{(j)} \in \{$"yes", "no", "maybe"$\}$. The output function that they wish to compute is $y = (y^{(1)}, \ldots, y^{(\ell)})$ defined as follows:

- $y^{(j)} =$ "yes" if $x_i^{(j)} =$ "yes" for all $i \in \{1, 2, \ldots, n\}$,
- $y^{(j)} =$ "maybe" else if $x_i^{(j)} \in \{$"yes", "maybe"$\}$ for all $i \in \{1, 2, \ldots, n\}$,
- $y^{(j)} =$ "no" otherwise.

Our fine-grained scheduling protocol is defined by $(n, U_{\mathsf{FS}}, I_{\mathsf{FS}}, X, X, g_{\mathsf{FS}}, h_{\mathsf{FS}})$:

- U_{FS} and I_{FS} are the same as U_{SI} and I_{SI} of our set-intersection protocol, respectively.
- The domain and the range are $X = \{$"yes", "no", "maybe"$\}^\ell$, i.e., the list of ℓ elements of "yes"/"no"/"maybe".
- The input function g_{FS} takes an input $x_i = (x_i^{(1)}, x_i^{(2)}, \ldots, x_i^{(\ell)})$ and outputs a set of (at most ℓ) black circles, where at the j-th position, a circle is put if $x_i^{(j)} =$ "no", a circle with triangle is put if $x_i^{(j)} =$ "maybe" (see Fig. 5).
- The output function h_{FS} is the inverse function of g'_{FS}, where $g'_{\mathsf{FS}}(x) = g_{\mathsf{FS}}(x) + I_{\mathsf{FS}}$.

Figure 6 shows an example execution of our fine-grained scheduling protocol for two players when $\ell = 35$. White circles and triangles in the input sheet of P_1 and P_2 are "yes" dates and "maybe" dates for the party. The rightmost image is the resulting image I_{result}.

The correctness and the security hold from a similar observation to the case of our set-intersection protocol.

4 Min/Max Protocol

Suppose that n students wish to know the highest score among all the students in an examination without revealing each score to other students.

Our Max Protocol

Let $\ell \in \mathbb{N}$ be the highest score (e.g., $\ell = 100$) and let $X = \{0, 1, 2, \ldots, \ell\}$ be the input domain. Assume that each student P_i has a score $x_i \in X$ as input. The function they wish to compute is the max (resp. min) function that takes n integers $x_1, x_2, \ldots, x_n \in X$ as input and outputs the maximum number $\max(x_1, x_2, \ldots, x_n) \in X$ (resp. the minimum number $\min(x_1, x_2, \ldots, x_n) \in X$).

Our max protocol is defined by $(n, U_{\max}, I_{\max}, X, X, g_{\max}, h_{\max})$, where:

Fig. 7. Input sheet for min/max.

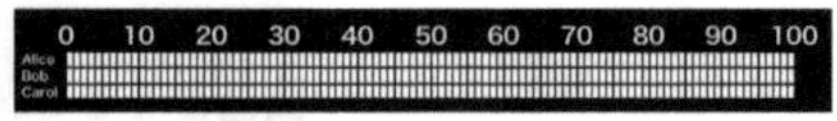

Fig. 8. Input sheet for max with name.

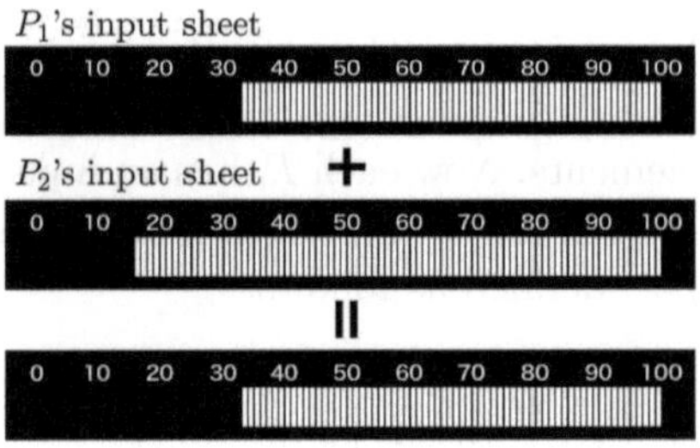

(a) Max protocol when $x_1 = 33$ and $x_2 = 16$

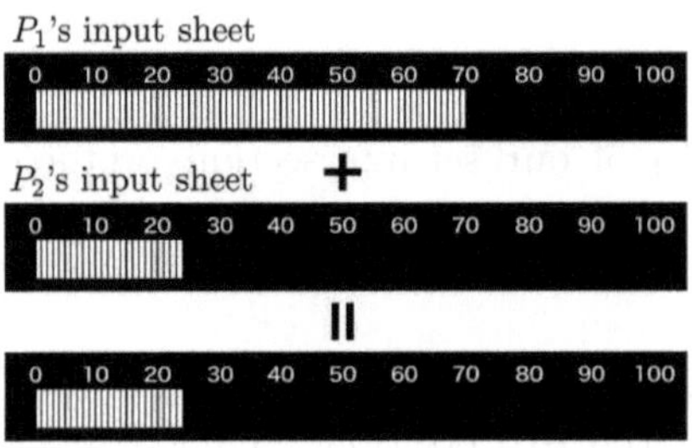

(b) Min protocol when $x_1 = 70$ and $x_2 = 24$

Fig. 9. Executions of max/min protocol.

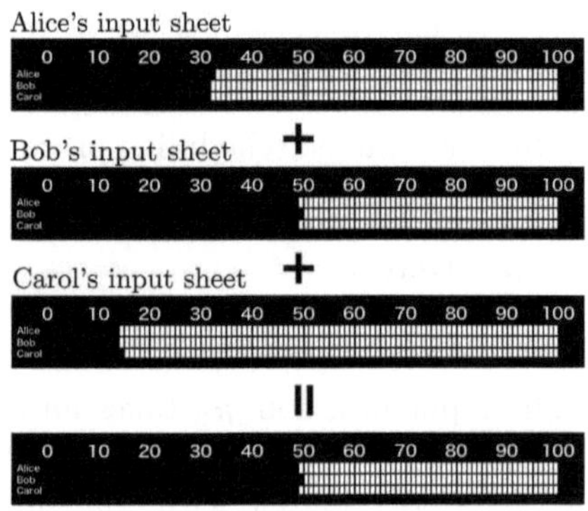

Fig. 10. Execution of max with name protocol when $(x_1, x_2, x_3) = (33, 50, 15)$.

- $U_{\max}$ is the set of all black-and-white images of the same size as the one in Fig. 7.
- The initial image $I_{\max}$ is given in Fig. 7.
- The input function $g_{\max}$ takes an input $x \in X$ and outputs a black rectangle from 0 to x.
- The output function $h_{\max}$ is the inverse function of $g'_{\max}$, where $g'_{\max}(x) = g_{\max}(x) + I_{\max}$; it outputs the value of the scale at the boundary between black and white.

Figure 9 (a) shows an example execution of our max protocol when $x_1 = 33$ and $x_2 = 16$. The function $g_{\max}$ with the input $x_1 = 33$ (resp. $x_2 = 16$) returns a black rectangle from 0 to 33 (resp. 16). Because the output image has a rectangle from 0 to 33, the output value is 33; it is correct because $33 = \max(33, 16)$.

The correctness holds from the above observation. The security holds from the fact that each resulting image is unique for each output value.

Our Min Protocol. Our min protocol is obtained by the analogy with our max protocol. Figure 9 (b) shows an example execution of our min protocol when $x_1 = 70$ and $x_2 = 24$.

Max with Name Protocol

The situation is almost the same as that of max but now there are three students Alice, Bob, and Carol having $x_1, x_2, x_3 \in \{0, 1, \ldots, 100\}$, respectively, and they want to know the owner of the maximum together with the value of maximum.

Let $N = \{A, B, C\}$ be a set of names and suppose that Alice, Bob, and Carol have $(A, x_1), (B, x_2)$, and (C, x_3). The function that they want to compute is $\mathsf{MN} : (N \times X)^n \to 2^N \times X$ that takes the inputs as above and outputs $(S, \max(x_1, x_2, x_3))$, where $S \subset 2^N$ is a set of all names who have the maximum value. For instance, if $x_1 = 10$ and $x_2 = x_3 = 20$, then $S = \{B, C\}$.

Our protocol is defined by $(n, U_{\mathsf{MN}}, I_{\mathsf{MN}}, N \times X, 2^N \times X, g_{\mathsf{MN}}, h_{\mathsf{MN}})$, where:

- U_{MN} is the set of all black-and-white images of the same size as the one in Fig. 8.
- The initial image I_{MN} is given in Fig. 8. There are three lines, each of which corresponds to Alice, Bob, and Carol, respectively.
- The input function g_{MN} is defined as follows: for an input $(\mathsf{name}, x) \in N \times X$, the output $g_{\mathsf{MN}}(\mathsf{name}, x)$ is three black rectangles from 0 to x in the name's line and 0 to $x - 1$ in other two lines.
- The output function h_{MN} is the inverse function of g'_{MN}, where $g'_{\mathsf{MN}} : 2^N \times X \to U_{\mathsf{MN}}$ takes a set $S = \{\mathsf{n}_1, \ldots, \mathsf{n}_k\}$ and $x \in X$ for $k \leq 3$ as input and outputs the union of the images $g_{\mathsf{MN}}(\mathsf{n}_1, x) + \cdots + g_{\mathsf{MN}}(\mathsf{n}_k, x) + I_{\mathsf{MN}}$.

Figure 10 shows an example execution of our max with name protocol when $x_1 = 33$, $x_2 = 50$, and $x_3 = 15$. The function g_{MN} with the input (A, x_1) returns a black rectangle from 0 to 33 in Alice's line and a black rectangle from 0 to 32 in others' lines. Because the output image has a rectangle from 0 to 50 in Bob's line and a rectangle from 0 to 49 in others' lines, the output value is $(\{B\}, 33)$; it is correct because $(\{B\}, 33) = \mathsf{MN}((A, 33), (B, 50), (C, 15))$.

The correctness and the security hold from a similar observation to the case of our max protocol.

5 Extension to Randomized Input

Our model defined in Sect. 2.3 does not allow to use randomness in computation, thus all of our protocols are deterministic. Of course, deterministic is a nice property in order to make protocols simple, but randomness enables us to construct protocols for a larger class of functions. In this section, we extend our model to the randomized input setting.

5.1 Defining Protocols in the Randomized Input Setting

In the randomized input setting, a protocol is defined as in the same in Sect. 2.3 except that the deterministic input function $g(x_i)$ is replaced by a randomized

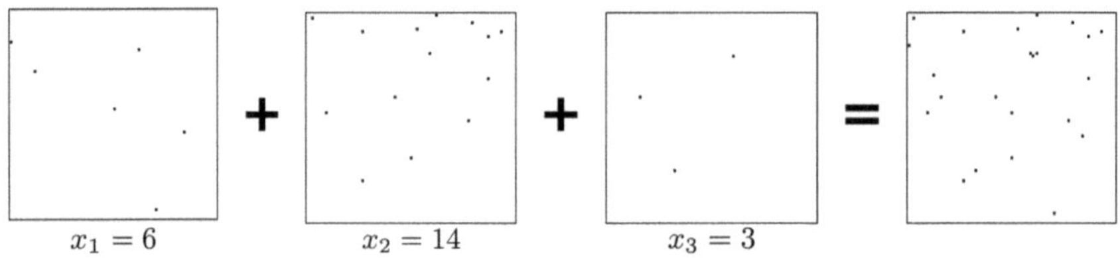

Fig. 11. Example of addition.

input function $g(x_i; r_i)$ that takes a random coin $r_i \in \{0,1\}^*$ together with an input $x_i \in X$. In the following, we define a relaxed variant of correctness and a randomized version of the security.

p-Correctness. A protocol is p-correct if for any $x_1, x_2, \ldots, x_n \in X$, the value $h(I_{\mathsf{result}})$ of the output function h for the union image $I_{\mathsf{result}} = I'_1 + I'_2 + \cdots + I'_n$ is equal to $f(x_1, x_2, \ldots, x_n)$ with a probability of at least p, where $I'_i = I + g(x_i)$ for all $i \in \{1, 2, \ldots, n\}$.

Simulation Security. A protocol is secure if there exists a probabilistic polynomial-time simulator $\mathcal{S}$ such that the following two random variables are equal:

- A random variable I_{result} over U: it is generated honestly when all parties' random tapes are chosen uniformly and independently at random.
- A random variable I_{sim} over U: it is generated by $\mathcal{S}$ given only the output value $f(x_1, x_2, \ldots, x_n)$.

5.2 Addition Protocol

Suppose that n students wish to know the average score among them without revealing each score to other students. Assume that each student P_i has a score $x_i \in \{0, 1, 2 \ldots, \ell\}$ as input. The function they wish to compute is the summation among them $x_1, x_2, \ldots, x_n$. (Note that the average can be obtained from the summation just by dividing by n.)

Our addition protocol is defined by $(n, U_{\mathsf{AD}}, I_{\mathsf{AD}}, X, X, g_{\mathsf{AD}}, h_{\mathsf{AD}})$, where:

- U_{AD} is the set of all square images of a fixed size with $M \times M$ pixels for some integer M.
- The initial image I_{AD} is just a white image.
- The input domain is $X = \{0, 1, \ldots, \ell\}$.
- The input function $g_{\mathsf{AD}}(x; r)$ takes a value $x \in X$ with a random coin r and outputs a set of x pixels chosen uniformly random by the use of r.
- The output function h_{AD} is the inverse function of $g_{\mathsf{AD}}(\cdot, r)$, where r is a fixed value; it just counts the number of pixels.

Figure 11 shows an example execution of our addition protocol when $x_1 = 6$, $x_2 = 14$, and $x_3 = 3$. The function g_{AD} with the input $x_1 = 6$ (resp. $x_2 = 14$ or $x_3 = 3$) returns a set of 6 (resp. 14 or 3) black pixels randomly. The total number of points in the resulting image is 23.

Our addition protocol has $(1-\delta)$-correctness if it holds $\frac{(n\ell)^2}{2M^2} < \delta$.

Proof. Let coll_i be the event that at least one collision exists among $\{P_1, P_2, \cdots, P_i\}$'s input sheets ($i \in \{1, 2, \ldots, n\}$). From a simple observation, we have

$$\Pr[\mathsf{coll}_n] = \Pr[\mathsf{coll}_2] + \Pr[\mathsf{coll}_3 \mid \neg\mathsf{coll}_2] + \Pr[\mathsf{coll}_4 \mid \neg\mathsf{coll}_3] + \cdots + \Pr[\mathsf{coll}_n \mid \neg\mathsf{coll}_{n-1}].$$

For a fixed ℓ points in P_1's sheet, the probability that a P_2's single point colludes one of the P_1's points is exact $\frac{\ell}{M^2}$. By union bound, we have

$$\Pr[\mathsf{coll}_2] \le \frac{\ell^2}{M^2} \quad \text{and} \quad \Pr[\mathsf{coll}_{k+1} \mid \neg\mathsf{coll}_k] \le \frac{k\ell^2}{M^2}.$$

Thus, combining them and the assumption, we have

$$\Pr[\mathsf{coll}_n] \le \frac{\ell^2}{M^2} + \frac{2\ell^2}{M^2} + \cdots + \frac{(n-1)\ell^2}{M^2} \le \frac{(n\ell)^2}{2M^2} < \delta.$$

This completes the proof. □

In order to prove the security, we have to construct a simulator $\mathcal{S}$ that can generate a simulated resulting image I_{sim}. Given an output value $y = x_1 + x_2 + \cdots + x_n$, $\mathcal{S}$ draws a set of random y pixels on the input sheet and sets it as simulated resulting image I_{sim}. Because it is the same distribution as the original resulting image I_{result}, we can conclude that our addition protocol is secure.

Idea for Enhancing Correctness

Using a circle with line "⊘" instead of a pixel "·" improves the probability of the correctness. Now a random coin is used to determine a position of a circle and an angle of the line. If there are L possible angles, then the probability p of the p-correctness is roughly $1 - \frac{\delta}{L}$. (We can not place the center of the circle ⊘ at the edge of input sheets, so the number of possible "positions" is reduced a little. However, this is not a problem because the "angle" effect is much greater.)

6 Conclusion

In this paper, we introduce a new physical cryptography, light cryptography, which uses the property of light. We also give some simple protocols in order to solve some problems that are complex to solve and to understand using classical cryptography. These examples can be explained to non-experts and clearly show the power of our light and shadow model. The next future step is to design more protocols and also to provide practical lecture material for information security education and use it in our cryptography courses.

Acknowledgments. This work was supported in part by JSPS KAKENHI Grant Numbers 17J01169 and 17K00001.

References

1. Balogh, J., Csirik, J.A., Ishai, Y., Kushilevitz, E.: Private computation using a PEZ dispenser. Theor. Comput. Sci. **306**(1–3), 69–84 (2003)
2. Ben-Or, M., Goldwasser, S., Wigderson, A.: Completeness theorems for non-cryptographic fault-tolerant distributed computation (extended abstract). In: Proceedings of the 20th Annual ACM Symposium on Theory of Computing, Chicago, Illinois, USA, 2–4 May 1988, pp. 1–10 (1988)
3. Bultel, X., Dreier, J., Dumas, J., Lafourcade: P.: Physical zero-knowledge proofs for Akari, Takuzu, Kakuro and Kenken. In: 8th International Conference on Fun with Algorithms, FUN 2016, Vol. 49 of LIPIcs, pp. 8:1–8:20 (2016)
4. Bultel, X., et al.: Physical zero-knowledge proof for Makaro. In: Izumi, T., Kuznetsov, P. (eds.) SSS 2018. LNCS, vol. 11201, pp. 111–125. Springer, Cham (2018). https://doi.org/10.1007/978-3-030-03232-6_8
5. Crépeau, C., Kilian, J.: Discreet solitary games. In: Stinson, D.R. (ed.) CRYPTO 1993. LNCS, vol. 773, pp. 319–330. Springer, Heidelberg (1994). https://doi.org/10.1007/3-540-48329-2_27
6. D'Arco, P., Prisco, R.D.: Secure computation without computers. Theor. Comput. Sci. **651**, 11–36 (2016)
7. den Boer, B.: More efficient match-making and satisfiability *the five card trick*. In: Quisquater, J.-J., Vandewalle, J. (eds.) EUROCRYPT 1989. LNCS, vol. 434, pp. 208–217. Springer, Heidelberg (1990). https://doi.org/10.1007/3-540-46885-4_23
8. Dreier, J., Jonker, H., Lafourcade, P.: Secure auctions without cryptography. In: Ferro, A., Luccio, F., Widmayer, P. (eds.) Fun with Algorithms FUN 2014. LNCS, vol. 8496, pp. 158–170. Springer, Cham (2014). https://doi.org/10.1007/978-3-319-07890-8_14
9. Goldreich, O., Micali, S., Wigderson, A.: How to play any mental game or a completeness theorem for protocols with honest majority. In: Proceedings of the 19th Annual ACM Symposium on Theory of Computing, 1987, pp. 218–229 (1987)
10. Kolesnikov, V.: Gate evaluation secret sharing and secure one-round two-party computation. In: Roy, B. (ed.) ASIACRYPT 2005. LNCS, vol. 3788, pp. 136–155. Springer, Heidelberg (2005). https://doi.org/10.1007/11593447_8
11. Mizuki, T., Kugimoto, Y., Sone, H.: Secure multiparty computations using a dial lock. In: Cai, J.-Y., Cooper, S.B., Zhu, H. (eds.) TAMC 2007. LNCS, vol. 4484, pp. 499–510. Springer, Heidelberg (2007). https://doi.org/10.1007/978-3-540-72504-6_45
12. Mizuki, T., Kugimoto, Y., Sone, H.: Secure multiparty computations using the 15 puzzle. In: Dress, A., Xu, Y., Zhu, B. (eds.) COCOA 2007. LNCS, vol. 4616, pp. 255–266. Springer, Heidelberg (2007). https://doi.org/10.1007/978-3-540-73556-4_28
13. Mizuki, T., Sone, H.: Six-card secure AND and four-card secure XOR. In: Deng, X., Hopcroft, J.E., Xue, J. (eds.) FAW 2009. LNCS, vol. 5598, pp. 358–369. Springer, Heidelberg (2009). https://doi.org/10.1007/978-3-642-02270-8_36
14. Naor, M., Shamir, A.: Visual cryptography. In: De Santis, A. (ed.) EUROCRYPT 1994. LNCS, vol. 950, pp. 1–12. Springer, Heidelberg (1995). https://doi.org/10.1007/BFb0053419
15. Shinagawa, K., et al.: Secure computation protocols using polarizing cards. IEICE Trans. **99**(6), 1122–1131 (2016)
16. Yao, A.C.: Protocols for secure computations. In: Proceedings of the 23rd Annual Symposium on Foundations of Computer Science, SFCS 1982, pp. 160–164. IEEE Computer Society, Washington (1982)

17. Yao, A.C.: How to generate and exchange secrets (extended abstract). In: 27th Annual Symposium on Foundations of Computer Science, Toronto, Canada, 27–29 October 1986, pp. 162–167 (1986)

Blockchain and Its Security: Ignore or Insert into Academic Training?

Natalia Miloslavskaya(✉) and Alexander Tolstoy

The National Research Nuclear University MEPhI (Moscow Engineering Physics Institute), 31 Kashirskoye shosse, Moscow, Russia
{NGMiloslavskaya,AITolstoj}@mephi.ru

Abstract. At present, the blockchain technologies (BCT) cause a serious burst of interest of young people in the first place. Not to meet the rising demand and not to pay attention to the BCT during the training means not to be modern. Any educational institution, which doesn't offer courses in the BCT, is going to be left behind as a non-competitive. The paper analyzes a state of the current training in the BCT worldwide, paying special attention to security issues. It also lists standards and books, which can support this training. On these bases, the desired competencies after mastering a full-time BCT course and an exemplary structure of this course are proposed.

Keywords: Blockchain technologies · Security · Academic training · Competencies · Standards · Survey · Educational course structure

1 Introduction

Starting from 2009 with Bitcoin, there are countless publications advertising the "magic" of blockchain (BC) technologies (BCT) and supporting a high level of "hype" around their usage [1]. The BCT for creating verifiable digital records have shown notable success not only in digital currencies but also in financial application domains (like online payments, currency exchanges, money services and transfers, soft and hard wallets, trade finance, markets, microtransactions, investments, brokerage, insurance, etc.), as well in non-financial domains (like digital identity management, authentication and authorization, digital content storage and delivery systems, smart contracts, certification validation systems, application development, real estate, election voting, patient medical records management, distributing the workload for communication system, computer systems that must comply with legal agreements without human intervention, etc.).

If someone will use the "blockchain" word as a search criterion in the IEEE digital library as well as in Scopus and WebofKnowledge databases, many titles will be returned in the reply. For example, the search for 2018 returned 1427 from Scopus, 418 items from WebofKnowledge and 605 from the IEEE digital library (access date 06.11.2018)! But in 10 years the BCT is not well understood as yet, and no single agreed definition of this technology has appeared. Some of the most known BC definitions are quoted below:

Published by Springer Nature Switzerland AG 2019
L. Drevin and M. Theocharidou (Eds.): WISE 2019, IFIP AICT 557, pp. 102–113, 2019.
https://doi.org/10.1007/978-3-030-23451-5_8

- UK Government, 2016: "A distributed ledger technology" [2];
- PriceWaterhouseCoopers, 2016: "A decentralized ledger of all transactions across a peer-to-peer network, where participants can confirm transactions without the need for a certifying authority" [3];
- OpenBlockchain, 2017: "A technology that enables the secure and resilient management of distributed data in combination with data analytics techniques that add scale and flexibility" [4];
- Wilson, 2017: "It is not a "trust machine". By the blockchain protocol, it only reaches consensus about one specific technicality – the order of entries in the ledger, free of bias" [5];
- Nielson, 2017: "A distributed file system that keeps files copies of the participants who agree on the changes by mutual consensus, where the file consists of blocks and every block has a cryptographic signature of the last block, making an immutable record" [6];
- Primechaintech, 2018: "A peer-to-peer network which timestamps records by hashing them into an ongoing chain of hash-based proof-of-work, forming a record that cannot be changed without redoing the proof-of-work" [7].

We define a BC as a secure distributed data structure (database, DB) that maintains without centralized administration and data storage a constantly expanding list of non-editable time-stamped blocks (records) and sets rules about transactions which are tied to these blocks [8].

So far as the BCT cause such a serious burst of interest to them of young people in the first place, not to meet the rising demand and not to pay attention to the BC during the training means not to be modern. Speaking easier, any educational institution, which doesn't offer courses in the BC, is going to be left behind as a non-competitive. That is why the goal of the paper is to analyze a state of the current training in the BCT and to work out on this basis some recommendations for conducting it for security professionals, paying special attention to security issues. To achieve this goal the paper is organized as follows. Survey of the BCT training worldwide is given in Sect. 2. Standards as the basis for the BCT training are discussed in Sect. 3. Section 4 is devoted to books, which can support the BCT training. The desired competencies after mastering a full-time BC course are formulated in Sect. 5. An exemplary structure of the course in the BCT is proposed in Sect. 6.

2 Survey of the BCT Training Worldwide

The efforts to develop individual disciplines (courses) in the BC started a few years ago. The Coinbase Company reviewed BC course catalogs at the top 50 universities [9]. Their study was focused on classes available to undergraduate-level students in the fall 2018 semester or the most recent semester, for which information was available online. We used it to begin our search on the BCT courses worldwide. It was found that 42% of the top 50 universities offer at least one class on BC or cryptocurrency, and 22% offer more than one. These courses are most prominent in the U.S. Only 5 of the 18 international universities on the list (27%) offer at least one class. And only two—

Swiss Federal Institute of Technology Zurich and National University of Singapore—offer more than one.

Our analysis shows that at present the training proposed can be divided into two groups: the first one is designed for distance learning only and the second one for face-to-face full-time (not online) training. The first group is represented by the following universities and companies, providing training in the BCT by means of online, usually paid open courses (on successful completion of these courses, students earn certificates) and even master's degree programmes (like the last item in the list):

On Coursera [https://www.coursera.org]:

- State University of New York and University of Buffalo (USA): the "Blockchain" course covers basics, smart contracts, decentralized applications, and platforms. It includes projects for practicing. Potential students can get a free 7-days trial before deciding to pay for the course. Duration: 4 weeks (w), 3.5 h per week (hpw);
- University of Buffalo: the "Blockchain Basics" course provides a broad overview of the essential BCT concepts – by initially exploring the Bitcoin protocol followed by the Ethereum protocol – to lay the foundation necessary for developing applications and programming (4w-3.5hpw);
- Princeton University (USA): the "Bitcoin and Cryptocurrency Technology" course teaches the basic technical foundations of how the BC works and archives decentralization, dispelling misconceptions and pointing to the future of the BCT. (11w);
- The "IBM Blockchain Foundation for Developers" course teaches software developers with a little or no experience concepts and strategies on building private BC networks for IBM Bluemix. Students can learn how to add code for smart contracts using the chaincode interface from the Hyperledger Project's Fabric. The course includes a lab demo of how assets are transferred to several roles across a network (6w–2hpw);
- ConsenSys Academy: the "Blockchain: Foundations and Use Cases" course consists of several modules, introducing the BCT, Ethereum and different business use cases (5w–2hpw);

On edX [https://www.edx.org]:

- University of California at Berkeley (USA): the "Blockchain Technology" course provides the ideal foundation required to comprehend the BCT. Among other things, it covers distributed systems, alternative consensus mechanisms, fundamental applications and implementations of the BCT (like JP Morgan's Quorum, Ripple, Tendermint, HyperLedger). It is good for both beginners and those at the intermediate level (6w–3–5hpw);
- University of California at Berkeley: the "Bitcoin and Cryptocurrencies" course learns, for example, the basics of smart contracts, the Ethereum platform and how to build decentralized applications (6w–3–5hpw);
- Linux Foundation: the "Blockchain for Business – An Introduction to Hyperledger Technologies" course covers key features of the BCT and the differentiators between various types of Hyperledger projects (10w–3–4hpw);
- Linux Foundation: the "Blockchain: Understanding Its Uses and Implications" course analyzes the concept of transparent ledgers, both public and permissioned,

and focuses on using cryptography to achieve consensus, immutability, and governance of transactions (5w–3–4hpw);
- University of Hong Kong: the "Blockchain and FinTech: Basics, Applications, and Limitations" course discusses the BCT, the differences of the various existing BC platforms, applications best fit the BCT, as well as limitations and the downside of the BC with respect to the protection of criminal activities (6w–3–4hpw);

On Udemy [https://www.udemy.com] (only the first 7 courses with the best scores are represented here):

- The "Blockchain and Bitcoin Fundamentals" course by G. Levy (2.5 h of video, 37 lectures (l), 2 articles(a)) learns all about the fundamentals, including how miners and block hashes work;
- The "The Basics of Blockchain: Ethereum, Bitcoin, & More" course by T. Serres, B. Warburg, Dr. Bull (3.5 h–51 l–4a) gives fundamentals of the BCT;
- The "Blockchain for Business 2018: The New Industrial Revolution" course (6 h-60 l-3a) develops solid fundamental understanding of the inner workings of BC with detailed explanations of mining, decentralized consensus, cryptography, smart contracts and many other important concepts;
- The "Blockchain A-Z™: Learn How To Build Your First Blockchain" course by H. de Ponteves (14.5 h-94 l-9a) learns how to build a BC, create a cryptocurrency and smart contracts;
- The "Ethereum & Solidity: The Complete Developer's Guide" course by S. Grider (24 h-246 l-13a) teaches how to use Ergereum, Solidity and secure Smart Contracts to build applications based on the BC and to use the latest version of Ethereum development tools;
- The "Become a Blockchain Developer with Ethereum & Solidity" course by S. Agrobast (15 h-86 l-4a) learns from the very basics to advanced levels how to develop a distributed application, to unit test them and create a user interface for them, and to use the Truffle build/testing framework;
- The "Build a Blockchain and a Cryptocurrency from Scratch" course by D. J. Katz (6.5 h-71 l-5a) discusses the implementation of the BC, gives understanding of the main concepts like Proof-of-Work, mining, peer-to-peer connections, etc. and how to build your own BC, create a NodeJS application with real-time websocket connections and build an API with NodeJS and Express;

Miscellaneous:

- Royal Melbourne Institute of Technology (Australia): the 8-week, fully online short course in the BCT [https://www.rmit.edu.au/news/all-news/2018/feb/blockchain-strategy-course-students-jobs-future] is designed in partnership with the Accenture company and Stone and Chalk Fintech hub;
- The "Blockchain Developer" two 3-month terms Nanodegree programme [https://www.udacity.com/course/blockchain-developer-nanodegree–nd1309] teaches to work with the Bitcoin and Ethereum protocols, as well as to build smart contracts and projects for real-world application;
- B9Lab ACADEMY [https://academy.b9lab.com], an independent firm in London and Hamburg working in collaboration with private industry and higher education,

provides several online courses in the BCT, consults with businesses who want to make use of it, and performs crucial research on the BCT developments and applications. Students have access to experienced tutors via a dedicated slack channel. Students who complete their studies successfully receive a certificate in the BC, backed up by the Ethereum network;
- University of Nicosia (Cyprus): the first full, 3-semester long Master's degree programme in digital currency offered through distance learning [https://digitalcurrency.unic.ac.cy/about-the-program]. The majority of the courses consist of lectures delivered by the faculty, but in some cases by guest lecturers with academic and business background related to topics covered in courses. Practical exercises, individual and group projects, simulations and case study analyses form an integral part of the programme. One additional note: the UNIC is the first university to accept Bitcoin as payment for tuition.

The second group of face-to-face full-time (not online) courses in represented mostly by American universities having specialized research centers in their structures supporting training in the BCT. They are appeared in the list in alphabetical order, not in any scientific or statistical ranking:

- Cornell University with the support from Cornell's IC3 (Initiative for Cryptocurrencies and Contracts) research organization has created in 2017 the Cornell Blockchain project [https://cornellblockchain.org] to provide education, certification, and application of the BCT for students and corporate clients. Unfortunately, the content of this web site is available only to its members;
- Duke University's Blockchain Lab [http://www.dukeblockchainlab.com] is a specialized, student-led research center designed to bring students and faculty alike up to speed on the newest developments in the BCT through lectures, interest groups, and workshops. On the web site, there are some links to the selected resources for further learning, research, news, etc.;
- Center for Financial Markets and Policy of the Georgetown University' McDonough School of Business [https://finpolicy.georgetown.edu/about] is one of the most notable academic studies in the BC, sponsoring an annual international BC Summit and seminars and publishing white papers and analysis of BC's impact on finance and investment;
- Massachusetts Institute of Technology is one of the world's authorities on the BCT through the Media Lab's Digital Currency Initiative [https://dci.mit.edu], which is working to push the BC development with research projects, papers, and groups while raising awareness of its risks and potential;
- New York University's Stern School of Business has the BCT as an integral part in the FinTech MBA program [http://www.stern.nyu.edu/programs-admissions/full-time-mba/academics/areas-interest/fintech] focused on technology's impact on finance, including analytics, artificial intelligence, and the BC. They offer the "Digital Currencies, Blockchains, and the Financial Services Industry" course in the BC. The first course was offered in 2014;
- Blockchain at Berkeley at the University of California at Berkeley [https://blockchain.berkeley.edu] is a student-led organization, uniting students, alumni, and community members to offer education, research, and consulting in the BCT

and their future uses via workshops, lectures, seminars, and meetings. They offer the 1-semester "Blockchain Fundamentals" course with 1 h of lecture per week and 1 h of interactive discussion. Among their workshops are the following: "What is Blockchain (Introduction to the BC)", "Bitcoin (How a Bitcoin transaction works)", "Ethereum (Introduction to Ethereum)", "Consensus Algorithms (Algorithms, data structures and scripting)", "Smart Contract Security (Programming smart contracts with Ethereum)", "How to Consult (Lessons learnt from the BC)", "Blockchain vs Database (What makes the BC unique)", "Smart Contracts and Business (What makes the BC unique)", and "EVM (Ethereum Virtual Machine)";
- Decentralized Systems Lab of the University of Illinois at Urbana-Champaign [http://decentralize.ece.illinois.edu] is a multidisciplinary research center for educating and extending the academic conversation with research projects and papers, as well as creating the BCT. In 2018, they offered the half-semester "Smart Contracts and Blockchain Security" course (2 credits, slides are available at http://soc1024.ece.illinois.edu/teaching/ece398sc/spring2018/);
- National University of Singapore: the "Blockchain: Embarking on the Journey" [https://academy.smu.edu.sg/blockchain-embarking-journey-1136] is a 1-day course targeted at professionals seeking to gain an understanding of the BCT and their applications in the business world;
- Swiss Federal Institute of Technology Zurich: the "Blockchain and Internet of Things" [http://www.vvz.ethz.ch/lerneinheitPre.do?semkez=2018S&lerneinheitId=122368&lang=en] 1-semester course provides opportunities to gain fundamental understanding of promising new technologies as well as develop creative decentralized solutions for societal challenges using these technologies. During the hackathon, students work in mixed teams on concrete challenges (like climate change, financial instability, energy, or mass migration, etc.) and develop decentralized approaches towards a sustainable, sharing circular economy using BC and Internet of Things (IoT) technologies;
- Financial University under the Government of the Russian Federation: the only one in the world full-time face-to-face Master's degree "Blockchain Technologies and Cryptocurrency" programme (2 years, 120 credits) in the framework of the "Applied Mathematics and Computer Science" direction [http://www.fa.ru/en/admissions/Pages/Master-programs.aspx] started in 2018. Graduates are preparing to use the BCT in various fields of activity, technological support for the secure usage of cryptocurrencies, ensuring cybersecurity in the field of finance using BC and cryptocurrency technologies.

In Russia, PwC Academy conducts the "First touch to Blockchain. Features and application of blockchain technology" 4-h face-to-face master class [https://training.pwc.ru/seminars/workshop-blockchain], introducing the use of the BCT in the financial sector, its purpose, open and closed types, and distinctive advantages. Cryptoacademy [https://cryptocademy.ru] offers several 6-h intensive courses in the BCT. Blockchain Academy [https://block.academy/ru/edu/] has several 1-2-days face-to-face programmes for banks, developers, and investors. The "Blockchain Basics" online course from the Skillbox Company consisting of 10 seminars and 5 assignments is available at [https://skillbox.ru/blockchain]. Luxoft Training [https://www.luxoft-training.ru/kurs/blokcheyn_i_kriptovalyuty.html] teaches the “Blockchain and Cryptocurrencies” 6-h course.

This list can be continued more and more, but from our perspective, it is enough information to define main competencies for those who will master a course in the BCT.

3 Standards as the Basis for the BCT Training

In 2016, the ISO/TC 307 “Blockchain and distributed ledger technologies” has been created for standardization of the BCT and distributed ledger technologies (DLT). This technical committee combines several specialized and working groups, namely “Blockchain and distributed ledger technologies and IT Security techniques”, “Foundations”, “Use cases”, “Security, privacy and identity”, “Smart contracts and their applications”, “Governance of blockchain and distributed ledger technology system” and “Interoperability of blockchain and distributed ledger technology systems”. At present, they just started 10 standards, technical specifications and reports in the BCT and DLT, the majority of which are at the preparatory stage: ISO 22739 Terminology (the first draft is registered – for January 2019); ISO 23244 Overview of privacy and personally identifiable information (PII) protection; ISO 23245 Security risks and vulnerabilities (the first draft is registered – for November 2018); ISO 23246 Overview of identity management using BCT and DLT; ISO 23257 Reference architecture; ISO 23258 Taxonomy and Ontology; ISO 23259 Legally binding smart contracts; ISO 23455 Overview of and interactions between smart contracts in BCT and DLT systems; ISO 23576 Security of digital asset custodians; and ISO 23578 Discovery issues related to interoperability.

The IEEE P2418.1 standard for the framework of BC use, implementation, and interaction in one particular application – IoT – has started in June 2017 with June 2019 as an expected date of draft submission to the IEEE-SA. This framework will include BC tokens, smart contracts, transaction, credentialed network, permissioned and permissionless IoT BC enable decentralized, autonomous peer-to-peer, consumer-to-machine and machine-to-machine communications without the need for a trusted intermediary and address scalability, interoperability, security and privacy challenges with regard to BC in IoT.

The Draft NISTIR 8202 “Blockchain Technology Overview” [1] discusses how the BC works, especially when applying to electronic currency. It shows the BCT’s broader applications (banking, supply chain, insurance, healthcare, trusted timestamping, energy industry) and highlights some of their limitations, concerning the BC control, malicious users, no trust, resource usage, transfer of burden of credential storage to users, and Private/Public Key Infrastructure and identity. This draft defines the high-level components of BC system architecture like transactions, blocks, hashes, forks, etc. It describes how new blocks are added to the BC and how consensus models resolve conflicts among miners. Different BC permission models and their use case examples are introduced. The draft also covers smart contracts and BC platforms in use today. Here we rely on this document as the only one is currently publicly available.

We hope that for the beginning of the next educational year some of these standards will be adopted and published, so they could be used as a basis for the training.

4 Books Support for the BCT Training

As our search has shown, there are a lot of books, which can be taken as the basis for conducting training in the BCT. Here is a list of books published in 2016–2018 and available on the book markets in alphabetic order (with their volumes in pages):

1. Bahga A., Madisetti V. 2017. Blockchain Applications: A Hands-On Approach. 380 p.
2. Bashir I. 2017. Mastering Blockchain: Deeper insights into decentralization, cryptography, Bitcoin, and popular Blockchain frameworks. 542 p.
3. Bashir I. 2018. Mastering Blockchain: Distributed ledger technology, decentralization, and smart contracts explained, 2nd Edition. 658 p.
4. Bishop A. 2018. Blockchain Technology Explained: A Beginner's Guide to Blockchain Technology. 66 p.
5. De Filippi P., Wright A. 2018. Blockchain and the Law: The Rule of Code. 312 p.
6. Drescher D. 2017. Blockchain Basics. 255 p.
7. Ellis R. 2017. Blockchain Maturity: A New Internet. 310 p.
8. Gaur N., Desrosiers L. 2018. Hands-On Blockchain with Hyperledger: Building decentralized applications with Hyperledger Fabric and Composer. 460 p.
9. Hill B., Chopra S. 2018. Blockchain Quick Reference: A guide to exploring decentralized Blockchain application development. 350 p.
10. Kuo Chuen D. L., Deng R. H. 2017. Handbook of Blockchain, Digital Finance, and Inclusion, Volume 2: ChinaTech, Mobile Security, and Distributed Ledger. 514 p.
11. Norman T.A. 2017. Blockchain Technology Explained: The Ultimate Beginner's Guide About Blockchain Wallet, Mining, Bitcoin, Ethereum, Litecoin, Zcash, Monero, Ripple, Dash, IOTA and Smart Contracts. 127 p.
12. Oliver P., Reads C. 2018. Blockchain 101: Distributed Ledger Technology (DLT) (Book 1). 59 p. and Blockchain 101: Forking, Smart Contracts, Scaling, & Permissioned States (Book 2). 47 p.
13. Prusty N. 2018. Blockchain for Enterprise: Build scalable blockchain applications with privacy, interoperability, and permissioned features. 220 p.
14. Richmond T. J. 2017. Blockchain: 2 Books in 1 - The New Ultimate Guide To Understanding and Using Blockchain Technology (Blockchain, Bitcoin, Cryptocurrency). 210 p.
15. Sebastian L. 2018. Blockchain: Two Books - The Complete Edition On The Blockchain Basics, Technology and Its Application in Cryptocurrency and Other Industries That Are Happening Now. 183 p.
16. Vigna P., Casey M. J. 2018. The Truth Machine: The Blockchain and the Future of Everything (2018). 302 p.
17. Xu X., Weber I. 2019. Architecture for Blockchain Applications.

We allocate separately the books devoted to BC and security issues:

1. Gupta R. 2018. Hands-On Cybersecurity with Blockchain: Implement DDoS protection, PKI-based identity, 2FA, and DNS security using Blockchain. 236 p.
2. Karame G., Audroulaki E. 2016. Bitcoin and Blockchain Security. 218 p.
3. Pherr G. 2018. Blockchain and Cybersecurity: How the Blockchain technology can change the face of security in the Internet of Things Era. 30 p.
4. Robinson R.J. 2018. Introduction To Embedded Blockchain Cyber Security. 17 p.
5. Shetty S. and Kamhoua C.A. 2019. Blockchain for Distributed Systems Security.

5 Desired Competencies After Mastering a Full-Time BCT Course

Based on a detailed analysis of all the previously mentioned courses, the content of standards and some of the books listed above, we are ready to formulate what students who have completed full-time semester training on a BCT-related course will know and be able to do.

Upon successful completion of this training, students should:

- Know and understand what the BC is and the terminology used;
- Know where, how and why the BCT can be used in the modern world;
- Know and get a deep understanding of international standards on the BC;
- Know key BC's theoretical principles and practices and understand how they can be applied within an individual business environment;
- Have a deep understanding of how to build a BC (meaning building a blockchain system from scratch);
- Understand BC's security and know its vulnerabilities and security risks.

Besides this, students should master basic BC handling skills and be able to:

- Identify and analyze the challenges and prospects of the BCT and propose or develop systems and services that address them;
- Develop or participate in developing the BCT itself and the things that interact with the BC (like developing a new BC protocol or improving existing one, understanding and being able to apply cryptography used in BC systems, designing a distributed system architecture, innovative systems, and services that complement and extend the existing BC concept);
- Implement requirements of international standards on the BCT;
- Carry out the synthesis and analysis of design projects on distributed ledgers, smart contracts, and applications for the BCT;
- Analyze and compare different BC platforms, as well as select the right BC platform to be applied within an individual business environment;
- Analyze best practices of the BCT applications, specify business opportunities, and apply the BCT-based innovative solutions to address business problems;
- Conduct a security risk assessment for the BCT and propose a set of measures (rules, procedures, practical methods, guidelines, and tools) to mitigate them.

Of course, the given list of knowledge and skills can be taken only a basis. It does not pretend to completeness as every educational institution training on the BCT can broaden it according to the country and its business specific, for example.

6 Exemplary Structure of the Course in the BCT

Based on the above-formulated knowledge and skills, it is possible to determine the structure of a typical full-time 1-semester university course in the BCT for a Master's degree programme as it requires some prerequisites as knowledge in cryptography, networks, information security and so on. The following exemplary detailed structure is proposed for a classical course in the BCT.

Section 1. Introduction

Module 1. Blockchain Technologies in Modern Business Environment

- Introduction to the BC and its ecosystem; History of BC's development (to understand its roots); Problems solved by the BCT (to know their implications and to recognize the potential); The areas of the BCT's application (to know their scope and to see the big picture); BC in the different fields of law (transactional, corporate, commercial); BC regulation and regulatory environment

Module 2. Technologies used by the BCT

- Fundamentals of cryptography (including independent, repeated, combined, sequential and hierarchical hashing and asymmetric cryptography) and crypto programming; Fundamentals of data and databases; Private and public networks; Distributed and centralized system architectures; Peer-to-peer systems and their architecture; Ledger and authorities

Section 2. BC foundation

Module 3. Basics of the BCT

- Introduction of a BC concept; BCT terminology (including the following terms: account, actor, agent, altchain, block, chain, consensus, cryplet = runtime, distributed ledger, immutability, forking, hybrid BC, ledger, main chain, middleware, miner, mining mechanism, node, ordering service, peer, permissioned (dedicated, private) ledger, sidechain, shared ledger, smart contracts, transaction, unpermissioned (permissionless, public) ledger, user, validating mechanism, etc.); BC-related standards (ISO/IEC, NIST, etc.)

Module 4. BC Characteristics and Architecture

- Characteristics of the BC (immutable, append-only, ordered, time-stamped, open, transparent, secure, eventually consistent, interoperable); Architecture of BC networks; Soft and hard forking; Security and privacy protection issues for the BC; Trust and ownership in the BC

Section 3. How the BC works
Module 5. Planning the BC

- Describing and protecting ownership; Storing transaction data; Preparing and distributing ledgers; Adding new transaction; Deciding on trust; BC deployment architecture; Resource management in the BC development

Module 6. BC protocols

- Protocol for transactions; Protocol for peer-to-peer communications; Consensus protocol (proof of work; proof of stake; round robin; ledger conflicts and resolutions); Data storage protocol

Module 7. Maintaining the history of transactions

- Choosing a transaction history; Storing, using, adding the history of transactions; Ordering the transactions; Integrity of the history; Detecting changes in the history

Module 8. Hashes and cryptography in the BC

- Providing hash values for data in the BC; Detecting changes in data; Asymmetric cryptography in the BC for identifying accounts and authorizing transactions; Merkle tree; Cryptographic Changes and Forks

Module 9. Transactions and data storage in the BC

- Creating a new block for inclusion into the BC; Chaining blocks; Verifying and adding transactions; Distributing the data store among peers

Section 4. BC vulnerabilities and limitations and how to overcome them
Module 10. BC vulnerabilities and limitations

- BC control and hidden centrality; The security model utilizing asymmetric cryptography; No trust; Lack of privacy; Resource usage; Limited scalability; High cost; Critical size; Malicious users; Double spending as a problem of distributed peer-to-peer systems of ledgers and how to solve it; Transfer of burden of credential storage to users; Conflicting BC goals: transparency vs. privacy, security vs. speed; Lack of legal acceptance;

Module 11. How to overcome some BC limitations

- Redactable BC by Accenture

Section 5. Using the BC
Module 12. Specific BC use cases

- Finance, digital identity, notary services, voting, manufacturing, IoT, supply chain, security, etc. BC use cases; Detour to the emergence of cryptographic currencies; introduction to BC platforms: Bitcoin, Ethereum, Ripple, etc.; Hyperledger project; Multichain platform; Economical, social, cultural and political implications of the BC;

Module 13. BC research and further development

- Research and development in the BCT;
- Further BC development

Section 6. BC Project

Option 1 – Choose a BC topic from the given content for its detailed discussion
Option 2 – Create a BC business plan for the application area selected
Option 3 – Create a BC for the application area selected

7 Conclusion

After a detailed study of the issue put at the beginning, for us it is obvious that teaching the BCT and their security is the urgent need of today.

The next steps in preparing a course with the proposed structure for teaching in the MEPhI in the framework of the "Business Continuity and Information Security Maintenance" Master's degree programme since the Autumn 2019 semester will include the development of all educational and methodical materials required for its support, a set of laboratory works to acquire the necessary skills and a web site as a tool for coordinating the educational process and providing a teacher-student interaction during it.

Acknowledgement. This work was supported by the MEPhI Academic Excellence Project (agreement with the Ministry of Education and Science of the Russian Federation of August 27, 2013, project no. 02.a03.21.0005).

References

1. Yaga, D., Mell, P., Roby, N., Scarfone, K.: Draft NISTIR 8202 Blockchain Technology Overview (2018). https://csrc.nist.gov/CSRC/media/Publications/nistir/8202/draft/documents/nistir8202-draft.pdf. Accessed 15 Apr 2019
2. PriceWaterhouseCoopers: Making sense of bitcoin, cryptocurrency, and blockchain (2016). https://www.pwc.com/us/en/financial-services/fintech/bitcoin-blockchain-cryptocurrency.html. Accessed 15 Apr 2019
3. UK Government: Office for Science, Distributed Ledger Technology, Beyond Block Chain (Report) (2016). https://assets.publishing.service.gov.uk/government/uploads/system/uploads/attachment_data/file/492972/gs-16-1-distributed-ledger-technology.pdf. Accessed 15 Apr 2019
4. OpenBlockchain: Researching the potential of blockchains (2017). http://blockchain.open.ac.uk/. Accessed 15 Apr 2019
5. Wilson, S.: How it works: blockchain explained in 500 words (2017). http://www.zdnet.com/article/blockchain-explained-in-500-words/. Accessed 15 Apr 2019
6. Nielson, B.: Blockchain solutions for cyber & data security (2017). https://richtopia.com/emerging-technologies/blockchain-solutions-for-cyber-data-security. Accessed 15 Apr 2019
7. Primechaintech: Blockchain security controls (2018). http://www.primechaintech.com/docs/blockchain_security_controls.pdf. Accessed 15 Apr 2019
8. Miloslavskaya, N.: Designing blockchain-based SIEM 3.0 system. Inf. Comput. Secur. 2018. **26**(4), 491–512 (2018). https://doi.org/10.1108/ics-10-2017-0075. (UK). Emerald Publishing, September
9. The rise of crypto in higher education (2018). https://blog.coinbase.com/the-rise-of-crypto-in-higher-education-81b648c2466f. Accessed 15 Apr 2019

Identifying Information Security Risks in a Social Network Using Self-Organising Maps

Rudi Serfontein(✉), Hennie Kruger(✉), and Lynette Drevin(✉)

North-West University, Potchefstroom, South Africa
{rudi.serfontein,hennie.kruger,
lynette.drevin}@nwu.ac.za

Abstract. Managing information security risks in an organisation is one of the most important tasks an organisation has. Unfortunately, due to the complexity of most organisational systems, identifying information security risks can be difficult. One way to identify possible risks in an organisation is to make use of Social Network Analysis (SNA). While they can be used to identify risks, the metrics calculated using SNA are often numerous and daunting to managers unfamiliar with SNA. Furthermore, as the data in this form tend to be uncomfortable to process, educating managers about risks in their organisation can be quite difficult. Also, as these metrics often require quantitative processing in order to be useful, SNA on its own is not always an attractive method to use to identify risks in an organisation. In this paper the use of self-organising maps to identify possible information security risks in an organisation is investigated. Risk data were obtained from an organisation that deals in risk management, which were used to build a social network. A number of metrics associated with risk were calculated from the network, and these metrics were used to cluster the various entities using a self-organising map. Certain entities that pose a possible information security risk were identified. The results suggest that it may be viable to use self-organising maps, in concord with SNA, to more easily identify risks in an organisation using visual methods.

Keywords: Self-organising maps · Social network analysis · Information security

1 Introduction

Information security risk management is one of the most crucial parts of information security and should be one of the most important actions taken by organisations [1]. Unfortunately, due to the relative complexity of most organisational systems, identifying information security risks that are inherent to people using the systems, and making managers aware of them, is often quite difficult. One of the methods proposed

Published by Springer Nature Switzerland AG 2019
L. Drevin and M. Theocharidou (Eds.): WISE 2019, IFIP AICT 557, pp. 114–126, 2019.
https://doi.org/10.1007/978-3-030-23451-5_9

in recent years to address such risks involve the use of Social Network Analysis (SNA) [2–4]. SNA is a method that can be used to evaluate an organisation, for instance a community or business, in such a way that social interactions can be studied quantitatively, rather than qualitatively [5]. It does however have a significant drawback in that large networks, when visualised, may have so many nodes and arcs that the network is visually incomprehensible. In order to address this drawback, a number of studies have employed techniques that alter significant nodes and edges of a visualised network in order to draw attention to certain aspects. Some of these techniques include differentiating the colour of nodes and edges [6], using differing sized nodes to correspond to certain metrics [7], and using labels of various sizes [3]. A somewhat more novel technique makes use of Self Organising Maps (SOMs) to directly visualise network data [8]. A SOM is an effective technique that can be used not only to visualise high-dimensional data, but to visualise it in such a way that the result can act as both a similarity graph and a clustering diagram [9]. The SOM technique can be used to identify similar nodes within a social network, even in the presence of seemingly contradicting attributes, and present this data in a way that managers are quickly informed of risks in the network. SOMs have also been used in information security research to propose improvements to intrusion detection methods [10], and as a method for analysing information security behavioural data [11, 12]. While the approach suggested by Boulet, Jouve, Rossi and Villa [8] does allow for social networks to be visualised as SOMs, it has a shortcoming in that the SOMs generated can not necessarily be used in a way that is relevant to the process of identifying possible information security risks. This is mainly as a result of the fact that, in order to identify risks within a social network, a number of metrics calculated from the network data is used rather than the raw data itself.

In this paper the feasibility of using existing SOM techniques to inform managers of possible risks in an organisation is discussed. The value of such an application is twofold; firstly, by using a visualisation method that reduces the amount of data that is visualised, the often confusing graphs produced by traditional SNA visualisation techniques can be replaced with SOMs that are easier to process graphically. Furthermore, as SOM algorithms produce maps that naturally display data of interest, analysis and evaluation of the data should no longer require the visualisation results to be adapted (node enlargement, colouration, etc.) in order to be meaningful. Secondly, as SOMs organise similar data into clusters, their application should make it easier to inform a manager of groups of similar at-risk entities. This is thanks to the clustering done by the SOM algorithms, as, due to the relationship between certain SNA metrics and the CIA triad (Confidentiality, Integrity and Availability), as will be discussed in Sect. 2, clustering the nodes according to these metrics allows an evaluator to quickly identify similar problematic nodes. Furthermore, because the SOM algorithm uses the calculated SNA metrics as attributes to determine the clusters, the clusters themselves can be used to infer similarities that may not be readily transparent from the available data. Another advantage is that managers can be informed and educated of possible risks in an organisation early on, which may aid in developing effective awareness, education, and training programs. The graphical nature of SOM may also make it a useful tool for training inexperienced risk managers, and can potentially aid in identifying standard trends and patterns.

In the remainder of the article the background, research methodology, and results, will be discussed respectively. The background discussion will focus on SNA in the context of information security, as well as SOMs. The discussion of the method will focus on both the application of the techniques, and the data collection phase. The paper will then conclude with a discussion of the results and implications.

2 Background

The primary theme of this paper is the use of Social Network Analysis (SNA) metrics as inputs for a Self-Organising Map (SOM), which should aid in evaluating risk in an organisation. In order to demonstrate how this can be done, five SNA metrics will be discussed briefly. While there are dozens of SNA metrics that can potentially be used, the five discussed here were chosen based on their established relationships with risk in the literature. The section will start with a description of SOMs, followed by the evaluation of the selected SNA metrics in relation to risk.

2.1 Self-Organising Maps (SOM)

The self-organising map (SOM) is a neural network technique that can be used to visualise and evaluate high-dimensional data [13]. The SOM technique uses given data to produce a self-organising neural network wherein the data points are clustered into topographical regions [14]. This visualisation technique has a wide range of known applications, from evaluating comparable biological adaptations [15] and improving optimisation algorithms [16, 17], to clustering data for problem-solving purposes [14, 18]. One of the greatest advantages SOM has over other high-dimension visualisation techniques is that it produces a two-dimensional topographical map that can be evaluated and interpreted without any special knowledge or skills. In addition to clustering known data points, depending on the data, the technique can also be used in vector quantisation, and as a regression modelling technique [13]. All these methods can arguably be used to obtain valuable information about data, but in the context of this paper only the clustering function of SOM will be considered. The algorithm for developing a SOM [19] is shown below.

Input: Dataset N
Output: A topographical map M containing the data from N, sorted into topographical areas

Variables:
w_{ij} – Weight vector describing topographical area ij; either randomised or defined at start
x – An input vector contained in N
α – Learning rate that is a slowly decreasing function of time

```
while Stop condition is false
  For each x in N
    For each vector j
      | Compute D(j) = \sum_i (w_{ij} - x_i)^2
    end
    Find index J such that D(J) is a minimum
    For all units j in a topographical area J, and for all i:
      | Compute w_{ij}(new) = w_{ij}(old) + \alpha[x_i - w_{ij}(old)]
    end
  end
  Update \alpha
  Reduce radius of topographical area at specified times
  Test Stop condition
end
return M
```

This algorithm produces one map with all of the entities sorted into clusters. Certain software suites, such as Viscovery SOMine [20], provide additional information by colouring the same map using values from different attributes.

As stated, SOMs can be used to cluster high-dimensional data on a two-dimensional map, producing a result that can be interpreted easily without training. This makes the technique especially valuable to those in managerial positions, as these individuals may not have the time to study large reports and data sets in detail, and may also hold true for the outcomes of SNA based studies – especially if the resulting network is particularly large or complex. By calculating the SNA metrics, as discussed in the next section, and applying SOM to the resulting data set, the risks posed by certain individuals or groups can be determined and presented visually in a way that is easy to process and interpret. Additionally, a number of at-risk individuals may be identified that would not necessarily have been evident through the use of more traditional visualisation techniques such as bar-graphs. It is possible for an individual to have all the traits of a high-risk individual and not be an obvious risk from the data itself. In these instances, a clustering technique such as SOM can be used to identify individuals that have similar, possibly hidden, attributes. This makes it significantly easier to address certain information security risks, as larger scale programmes can be developed to target groups consisting of similar individuals.

In summary, SOM is a valuable technique to use in addition to SNA, as the clustering function of SOM can be used to infer invaluable information about information security risks if the correct and relevant SNA metrics are used.

2.2 Social Network Analysis (SNA) in the Context of Information Security

One of the most well-known frameworks for information security is the CIA triad [21], which references Confidentiality, Integrity, and Availability. ***Confidentiality*** describes the access rights that users have to a piece of information. For example, a manager having confidential access to certain business data that his employees do not, or should not, have. One possible SNA metric that can be used to evaluate a risk to confidentiality is *closeness centrality*. Closeness centrality is calculated by determining all the shortest distances to all other nodes within the network [22], so a node with a high closeness centrality has a large number of close relationships to other nodes in the network. Such a node may therefore have access to information that it should not have access to. Alternatively, if the node is an object or a resource, such as a shared computer or a photocopier, it could become a significant confidentiality risk if malware or untrustworthy maintenance personnel are involved.

Integrity describes not only how accurate any piece of information is but, by extension, how trustworthy it is. One of the SNA metrics that can be used to evaluate the risk a node poses to the integrity of the information in the network is *total degree centrality*. The total degree centrality measure is concerned with an individual node's position within the network [22, 23], and is determined by using the number of nodes leading into and out of a node. A node with a high total degree centrality is well connected within the network, and may have enough influence over other nodes to impact the integrity of the information passing through them. Consider, as an example, an office worker with a high total degree centrality that has to capture data for a corporate database. If this worker were to make a mistake in capturing the data, the integrity of the data that a large number of nodes rely on may be compromised.

The *betweenness centrality* measure can be used to identify nodes that are risks to both integrity and confidentiality. This measure is a representation of the number of times that a particular node is part of the shortest path between any two nodes in the network [24]. It is reflective of the number of indirect nodes that are connected to that node. To demonstrate the rationale behind using betweenness centrality as an indicator of risk to both integrity and confidentiality, consider a department with a "go-to" individual. This individual will likely have access to greater amounts of information than is ideal, and would be in a position to alter the information flowing through the network. Furthermore, as nodes with high betweenness measures tend to act as brokers, this individual may be seen as a trustworthy shortcut to obtain information in the network, which places it in a position to obtain greater amounts of information, as well as manipulate information as it flows through the network.

The final member of the triad, ***availability***, deals with the ability to access the data in a timely manner. Availability is often at odds with both confidentiality and integrity, as systems meant to protect availability and confidentiality often impact on the availability of the data. With regards to SNA, one of the metrics that may identify a high risk node in terms of availability is the one that identifies a node as a *boundary spanner*. A boundary spanner is a node that, if removed, will cause one part of the network to become completely isolated [25], thereby negatively impacting the availability of information in certain parts of the network.

The final SNA metric to be mentioned here is *eigenvector centrality*. Eigenvector centrality measures the extent to which a particular node is connected to highly connected nodes [22]. Nodes that have a high eigenvector measure are considered to possess emergent leadership properties [26] and may be considered a potential risk to confidentiality, integrity, and availability. For example, consider the impact an informal leader can have on information in a network. Confidential information may be shared with such a node as a result of the connections with highly connected nodes, whereas the integrity of the data in the network may be impacted by the additional knowledge the node obtains. Availability may also be impacted negatively if the emergent leader convinces other nodes to delay the flow of information, or if the information is redirected through the network along suboptimal routes. A summary of the SNA metrics discussed, and how they relate to the CIA triad, is given in Table 1.

Table 1. SNA metrics in the context of information security

SNA metric	CIA Triad			Rationale
	C	I	A	
Total degree centrality		X		Nodes with a high total degree centrality have influence in the network and are connected to a significant portion of the network
Closeness centrality	X			Nodes with a high closeness centrality have access to a significant amount of information in the network
Betweenness centrality	X	X		Nodes with a high betweenness centrality may be prone to information brokering and tampering
Boundary spanner			X	If a boundary spanner node is removed, an entire section of the network becomes isolated
Eigenvector centrality	X	X	X	Nodes with a high eigenvector centrality are considered emergent leaders and, depending on their influence and attitude, may be a general risk, depending on the circumstances

It should be emphasised that, while this brief discussion focussed on each member of the CIA triad individually, confidentiality, integrity, and availability are all interconnected. It is possible, for instance, for a significant enough increase in confidentiality to result in a significant reduction in availability. This is also true for the relationship between confidentiality and integrity, and the relationship between integrity and availability. The goal is typically to find a balance between these three aspects that is appropriate to the particular situation. This interrelatedness should be kept in mind when evaluating risks using SNA, as well as when selecting controls to address these risks.

From this short discussion it is clear that SNA metrics can be used to identify and possibly evaluate risks in terms of the CIA triad. The use of SNA metrics as input data for a SOM is therefore appropriate, and its use in this manner may help to identify and visualise risks in an organisation. This should help to improve overall awareness of risks in the organisation, aid in training managers, and may even help to determine overall preventative measures. The application in the rest of the paper uses the five SNA metrics discussed in this section as input for a SOM.

3 Method

The study was conducted using data provided by a manager from a large company that deals with risk evaluation. The data are confidential, and were subsequently anonymised prior to publication. Using this data, a network was built that describes the relationship between various entities. This network is shown in Fig. 1.

The entities, or nodes, of the network include 26 real-world risks, 612 controls, 6 risk owners, 26 control owners, 13 risk coordinators and 12 governing bodies. The risks are those risks that the organisation has to manage, whilst the controls are those controls used to manage the risks. The risk- and control owners are ultimately responsible for the risks and controls respectively, whereas the risk coordinators ensure that the correct risks are managed using the appropriate controls. The governing bodies are responsible for determining which control is used with which risk. These bodies also determine what the probability of a risk occurring is, as well as the severity of such an occurrence. The network is undirected, as unidirectional relationships between entities such as risks and risk owners do not seem realistic.

The network data were processed using the software suite ORA-Lite [24], while the SOMs were generated using the Viscovery SOMine Suite [20]. The data for the SOM consists of the 5 SNA metrics for each node. In total, 695 nodes are contained in the network, and a total number of 1738 links exist between them. The focus of the network is on managing real-world risks, and it was subsequently processed in a risk centric way, i.e. the relationships between the nodes are based on similar relationships to particular risks. This means that the relationship between a risk coordinator and a control owner, for example, is described only in terms of their shared relationship to the same risk.

With networks of this size, the large number of metric values that are produced can be quite complex. In order to help evaluate such complex data in a simpler, graphical way, the SOM algorithm is used. The SOMs can be used to quickly identify problem areas, which should make it easier to evaluate the data. Additionally, as SOMs are graphical in nature, they can be applied iteratively to investigate how the risk in a network changes over time, or as certain controls are introduced that aim to manage those risks.

When applying this technique to training risk managers, one of the aims is to highlight certain trends or groups that may pose a natural risk in the network. In doing so, the risk manager should be better informed of the nuances of the network and may be able to introduce more effective risk mitigation measures than would have been possible otherwise. Consider, for example, a network, such as the one shown in Fig. 1, with risks, control coordinators, and controls. If a SOM is developed for the network, the manager should be able to readily identify groups of nodes that have similar risk profiles based on their clustering. If a certain grouping of controls and control coordinators are found in the same cluster, for instance, it may indicate that there is a problem with the way in which the controls are managed. Alternatively, if all of the

Fig. 1. Social network showing relationships between risks (blue), risk controls (purple), risk coordinators (yellow), risk owners (orange), control owners (pink) and the governing bodies (green) responsible for appointing the various role-players. (Color figure online)

control coordinators are grouped into one high risk cluster, it may be appropriate to introduce measures, such as policies, to address the risks posed by these nodes.

Another way in which the technique can be used in training is to monitor how the risk profile of certain clusters change when new controls are implemented to address the identified risks. As a SOM is graphical in nature, and the geographical structure of the map changes as the risk values for the nodes change, it should be possible to identify the changes in the network graphically. This is especially true for clusters that lose nodes, as the area of the map that the cluster occupies should be reduced. By using the SOMs as a graphical aid, the manager should be able to identify which approaches work best, and under which circumstances.

4 Results and Discussion

The SOM algorithm produced a map with three regions, or clusters, when applied to the network data. This map is shown in Figs. 2, 3, 4, 5 and 6. Each figure shows the same map, but with different colourations. The colourations are used to show how the values of the five measures differ for various nodes. The clusters are the same in each image, as one map, built using all five SNA metrics as node attributes, was obtained.

In Fig. 2, where the boundary spanner measure is used to colour the map, the red colouration that covers most of Cluster C2 indicates that the nodes in C2 pose a significant possible risk, as the nodes in this cluster have a much higher boundary spanner value than the nodes in other clusters. A cursory evaluation of the cluster's data shows that C2 exclusively contains all of the nodes that represent the risks. It should be noted that, while the risks are all found in the same cluster for this network, this will not necessarily be the case for all networks. As the boundary spanner metric indicates that a node's removal will completely isolate a part of the network, this suggests that the current structure in the network includes nodes that will be isolated if any of the risks are resolved. The network data itself shows that these nodes are primarily controls. If, for example, the risk "Corporate Brand" is completely resolved, i.e. if the company finds itself in a situation where there is no risk at all to the company brand, then the controls that exist to manage that risk, such as "Social Media strategy and protocols" and "Expert communications resources", are no longer needed. In order to ensure that these controls are not kept in place unnecessarily, additional measures need to be implemented.

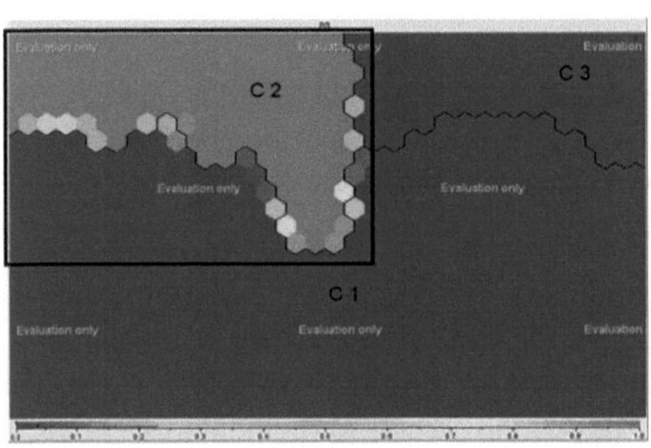

Fig. 2. SOM (boundary spanner) (Color figure online)

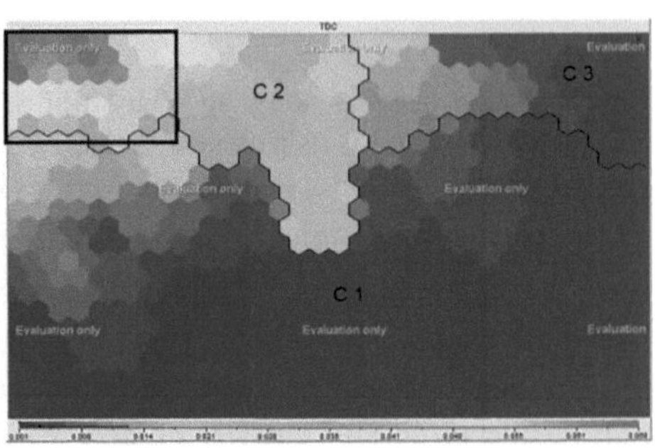

Fig. 3. SOM (total degree centrality) (Color figure online)

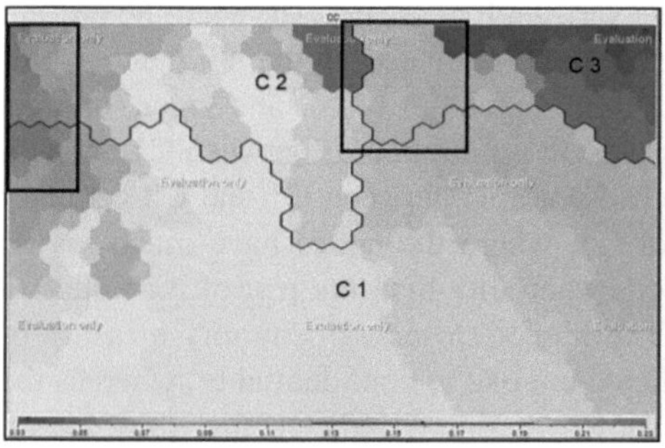

Fig. 4. SOM (closeness centrality) (Color figure online)

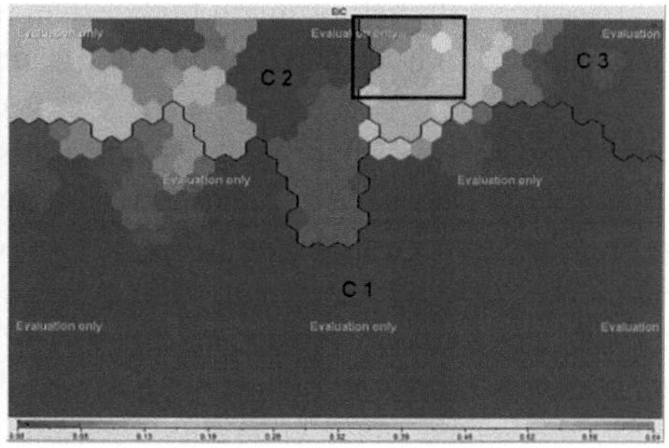

Fig. 5. SOM (eigenvector centrality) (Color figure online)

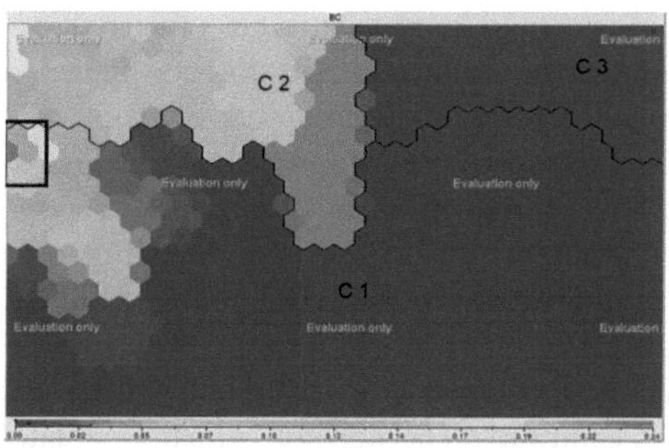

Fig. 6. SOM (betweenness centrality) (Color figure online)

The colouration, based on the total degree centrality, used on the SOM in Fig. 3 shows that there is an area in cluster C2 where the nodes have unusually high total degree centrality values, which is associated with a higher level of risk to integrity. Of the nodes in C2, there are six nodes, indicated by the red area in C2, that have a significantly higher amount of total degree centrality than the rest of the nodes. These nodes are the risks "Forest fires", "Environmental impacts", "Interruption to supply networks", "Waste Treatment Capacity", "Urban Resource Capacity", and "Rural Resource Capacity". All of these risks can have a significant impact if realised, which is why the influence they have is so substantial. This also means that any errors with regards to these risks, such as the risk of forest fires being over- or underemphasised, can have a significant impact on the information that is ultimately used in the network to manage other risks. If, for example, the integrity of the information with regards to the chances of a forest fire occurring is compromised, then there may not be enough water available to address the fire. If the fire affects any industrial assets, this may have environmental impacts, which in turn could negatively affect the company's corporate brand image. To protect the integrity of the information of these nodes, additional controls should be implemented.

An area with values much higher than the surrounding areas is shown to be present in cluster C3 in both Figs. 4 and 5. This area, which is situated on the left hand side of cluster C3 where it borders Cluster C2, is coloured green in Fig. 4 and green, orange, and red in Fig. 5. Additionally, a hotspot is present on the border between C1 and C2, as shown in Fig. 4. While the nodes in the hotspot area between C1 and C2 certainly pose a risk to confidentiality, the section of C3, where the nodes have much higher values for closeness centrality and eigenvector centrality than the rest of the nodes in the cluster, warrants further investigation. The higher closeness centrality measure of these nodes, shown in Fig. 4, suggest that they are a risk to confidentiality, whereas the very high eigenvector centrality measure shown in Fig. 5 indicate that they are an overall risk. There are two nodes in particular that fall into this region, one being a risk owner that is responsible for 11 out of the 26 risks, and the other being a risk coordinator that is responsible for 6 risks. The remainder of C3 is low risk and, as both of these nodes are in the cluster, it intimates that the risk posed by this risk owner and risk coordinator could be alleviated by reducing the number of risks that they are responsible for. Some of the risks could be transferred to other risk owners and coordinators. Alternatively, the risks can be co-owned and co-coordinated with owners and coordinators that are responsible for a smaller number of risks.

With the exception of the small area of low risk in C3, Fig. 4 shows that most of the nodes in the network have a high measure of closeness centrality. This suggests that controls should be in place to protect the confidentiality of the information in the network in general, as almost any one of the nodes could be responsible for compromising confidentiality.

Figure 6 highlights the existence of a single hotspot that exists in cluster C1 with regards to betweenness centrality. The hotspot, which is situated on the left hand side of C1 and has a red colour, contains a single risk coordinator, which poses a risk to both the integrity and the confidentiality of information in the network. In order to resolve this risk, the dependence on the specific risk coordinator should be reduced. The dependence of the risk coordinator can be reduced in one of at least two ways. The first method involves transferring some of the coordinator's responsibilities, such as risks, to another coordinator. This coordinator should preferably be located in cluster C1, as such a coordinator is likely to have a similar amount of power and influence. The second method that could be used is to employ an additional risk coordinator to take over some of the duties. This coordinator could also assume some of the duties of the risk coordinator in C3, thereby reducing the risk of two nodes simultaneously.

Based on all the SOMS shown in Figs. 2, 3, 4, 5 and 6, there are six risks, two risk coordinators, and a risk owner that pose potential risks to the overall security of information in this network. From this discussion, the advantage of using the SOM method to visualise SNA metric data is clear: by using SOMs to visualise SNA metric data, a relatively simple process can be followed in order to evaluate the risks in a network. The advantages are especially clear when compared to the process that would be needed in order to evaluate the risks in a network, such as the one shown in Fig. 1, or when using only raw data and statistical analysis. The use of SOMs in this manner gives managers the opportunity to evaluate risks graphically, as well as to compile risk discussion reports that do not require any prior knowledge of SOMs or SNA. This, in turn, could help improve the nature and quality of risk management, as a greater number of options and plans could develop as a result. Furthermore, SOMs allow for a way to systematically identify risks, and can also be used to monitor the progress and impact of risk mitigation strategies. Depending on the situation, it may be possible to identify positive or negative changes in the network almost instantaneously using this method. The central premise, i.e. that SOMs can be used to visualise SNA risk data, and in turn help educate managers of risks in their organisation in a quick and simple way, is therefore feasible.

5 Conclusion

Information security risk management is one of the most crucial parts of information security, but it is often complicated by the complexity of most organisational systems. In order to simplify the task of identifying risks in an organisation, SOM can be used to identify possible risks in an organisation by visualising SNA metric data of the organisation. A SOM, which clusters similar entities into geographically separate regions, is relatively simple to evaluate due to its graphical nature. When compared to other risk identification techniques that employ SNA metrics, which may require risk managers to process and evaluate large tables of numbers, the use of SOM may reduce the amount of work needed, as entities that pose a threat to the organisation can be identified with relative ease. Additionally, as a SOM is easier to evaluate, inexperienced risk managers may find the use of SOM less daunting than to use numerical data and statistical analysis. Finally, as a SOM provides an additional level of information that may not be readily apparent from the data, it could aid in educating risk managers of dangers in the organisation that may not be known, or obvious.

References

1. Wangen, G.: Information security risk assessment: a method comparison. Computer **50**(4), 52–61 (2017)
2. Armstrong, H., Armstrong, C., McCulloh, I.: A course applying network analysis to organizational risk in information security, In: South African Information Security Multi-conference pp. 204–214 (2010)
3. Dang-Pham, D., Pittayachawan, S., Bruno, V.: Investigation into the formation of information security influence: network analysis of an emerging organisation. Comput. Secur. **70**, 111–123 (2017)
4. Serfontein, R., Drevin, L., Kruger, H.: The feasibility of raising information security awareness in an academic environment using SNA. In: Drevin, L., Theocharidou, M. (eds.) WISE 2018. IAICT, vol. 531, pp. 69–80. Springer, Cham (2018). https://doi.org/10.1007/978-3-319-99734-6_6
5. Scott, J., Carrington, P.J.: The SAGE Handbook of Social Network Analysis. SAGE Publications, Thousand Oaks (2011)
6. Tsui, E., Liebowitz, J.: Linking social network analysis with the analytic hierarchy process for knowledge mapping in organizations. J. Knowl. Manag. **9**(1), 76–86 (2005)

7. Dang-Pham, D., Pittayachawan, S., Bruno, V.: Applying network analysis to investigate interpersonal influence of information security behaviours in the workplace. Inf. Manag. **54** (5), 625–637 (2017)
8. Boulet, R., Jouve, B., Rossi, F., Villa, N.: Batch kernel SOM and related Laplacian methods for social network analysis. Neurocomputing **71**(7), 1257–1273 (2008)
9. Kohonen, T.: The self-organizing map. Neurocomputing **21**(1–3), 1–6 (1998)
10. De la Hoz, E., De la Hoz, E., Ortiz, A., Ortega, J., Prieto, B.: PCA filtering and probabilistic SOM for network intrusion detection. Neurocomputing **164**(Suppl. C), 71–81 (2015)
11. Hunt, R., Hill, S.: Using security logs to identify and manage user behaviour to enhance information security. In: 14th European Conference on Cyber Warfare and Security, p. 111. Academic Conferences Limited (2015)
12. López, A.U., et al.: Analysis of computer user behavior, security incidents and fraud using self-organizing maps. Comput. Secur. **83**, 38–51 (2019)
13. Bäck, T., Kok, J.N., Rozenberg, G.: Handbook of Natural Computing. Springer, Heidelberg (2012). https://doi.org/10.1007/978-3-540-92910-9
14. Pal, C., Hirayama, S., Narahari, S., Jeyabharath, M., Prakash, G., Kulothungan, V.: An insight of world health organization (WHO) accident database by cluster analysis with self-organizing map (SOM). Traffic Inj. Prev. **19**(sup1), S15–S20 (2018)
15. Nakayama, H., et al.: Comparative transcriptomics with self-organizing map reveals cryptic photosynthetic differences between two accessions of north american lake cress. Sci. Rep. **8** (1), 3302 (2018)
16. Gu, F., Cheung, Y.-M.: Self-organizing map-based weight design for decomposition-based many-objective evolutionary algorithm. IEEE Trans. Evol. Comput. **22**(2), 211–225 (2018)
17. Kuo, R.J., Rizki, M., Zulvia, F.E., Khasanah, A.U.: Integration of growing self-organizing map and bee colony optimization algorithm for part clustering. Comput. & Ind. Eng. **120**, 251–265 (2018)
18. Lee, Y.: Using self-organizing map and clustering to investigate problem-solving patterns in the massive open online course: an exploratory study. J. Educ. Comput. Res. (2018). https://doi.org/10.1177/0735633117753364
19. Fausett, L.V.: Fundamentals of Neural Networks: Architectures, Algorithms, and Applications. Prentice-Hall, Englewood Cliffs (1994)
20. Viscovey SOMine. www.viscovery.net/somine. Accessed 10 Feb 2019
21. Au, C.H., Fung, W.S., Tses, A.: An investigation on the relationship between control self-assessment, cloud security, and cloud-related business performance-using partial least squares, In: Industrial Engineering and Engineering Management (IEEM), pp. 1879–1883. IEEE (2016)
22. Armstrong, H., McCulloh, I.: Organizational risk using network analysis, In: South African Information Security Multi-conference, pp. 132–141 (2010)
23. Hanneman, R.A., Riddle, M.: Introduction to Social Network Methods. University of California, Oakland (2005)
24. ORA-Lite. www.casos.cs.cmu.edu/projects/ora. Accessed 24 Apr 2018
25. Cormen, T.H., Leiserson, C.E., Rivest, R.L., Stein, C.: Introduction to Algorithms, 2nd edn. The MIT Press, Cambridge (2001)
26. Borgatti, S.P.: Centrality and network flow. Soc. Netw. **27**, 55–71 (2005)

Organisational Aspects

Lessons Learned from an Organizational Information Security Awareness Campaign

Juan-Marc Scrimgeour and Jacques Ophoff(✉)

University of Cape Town, Cape Town, South Africa
SCRJUA001@myuct.ac.za, jacques.ophoff@uct.ac.za

Abstract. Educating end-users to improve information security awareness plays an important part in securing organizational environments. While best practice standards provide a set of minimum information security awareness controls that should be implemented, little guidance is given on how to implement these controls to ensure the effectiveness of training. This research defined and evaluated a method for implementing an information security awareness campaign (ISAC) within an organization. The method is based on prior research and standards, while assisting the subject in improving their ISAC through the creation of artefacts and measurement techniques. A design science research approach was used with several research cycles to design the method. The method was implemented within an organization and evaluated based on the impact, effectiveness and results of each step, as well as the feedback from participants (two questionnaires were completed by 47 and 36 employees respectively). The research found both positive and negative results. Certain steps within the method proved time consuming and confusing to some participants. Although improvements can be made, the method was found to be adequate as it achieved the required objective within the organization and provided the organization with a risk-based method and visual representation to measure awareness on specific information security awareness topics. The results of the study not only provided value to the organization but provides a validated method for implementing an ISAC which could be applied in other contexts.

Keywords: Information security awareness campaign · Effectiveness

1 Introduction

Research has shown that educating end-users on information security awareness (ISA) plays an important part in securing your environment [1–3]. ISA can be defined as *"a learning process that sets the stage for training by changing individual and organizational attitudes to realize the importance of security and the adverse consequences of its failure"* [4]. Best practice standards provide a set of minimum controls that should be implemented, however, little guidance is given on how to implement these controls to ensure the effectiveness of the training [2, 5, 6]. The field of ISA is popular; however, most studies focus on improving training or how to implement the training in a different way. There seems to be a lack of studies that focus on how to implement a campaign that meets the stringent requirements set by best practice

Published by Springer Nature Switzerland AG 2019
L. Drevin and M. Theocharidou (Eds.): WISE 2019, IFIP AICT 557, pp. 129–142, 2019.
https://doi.org/10.1007/978-3-030-23451-5_10

standards. In addition, research on effectiveness measurement techniques is largely focused on questionnaires, and as a result, questionnaires are the primary means of measuring effectiveness. However, researchers in this field state that the questionnaire technique can be improved upon by supplementing it with hard measures.

This research defined and evaluated a method for implementing an ISAC within an organization based on existing research and standards, while assisting the subject in improving their ISAC through the creation of artefacts and measurement techniques. The method used attempts to supplement the widely used questionnaire technique with risk management practices, such as those defined by the NIST [4], *"The program and supporting processes to manage information security risk to organizational operations (including mission, functions, image, reputation), organizational assets, individuals, other organizations, and the Nation."* This will address the research problem by implementing and evaluating a method for delivering an ISAC within an organization that is measurable and relies on the use of risk management metrics to determine its effectiveness. The current paper reflects on the lessons learned during this ISAC implementation process.

The study was conducted within a financial institution in South Africa. The training provided was created and administered by employees of the target organization (TO) and focused on one specific theme (Acceptable Usage Policy).

2 Background

Recently several studies have focused on identifying the best way to improve on an ISAC. These studies have varied in approach from simulations [5, 7, 8] to the development of educational material [2, 9]. When examining factors which influence the effectiveness of ISA the following themes emerge: the end-user's knowledge and skills, the personality of the end-user, and the environment that surrounds the end-user.

There is little guidance of what knowledge should be passed on in ISA. While some standards (e.g. PCI-DSS) state key focus areas for ISA, it is not all-encompassing and is normally focused on software developers. In addition, it is suggested that the end-user's personality can influence the effectiveness of ISAC. Studies show that end-users tend to interpret, experience, and perceive the importance of ISA differently based on personality [10–12]. These studies, in how personalities can impact the effectiveness of ISA, have highlighted the importance of how one communicates the content and importance of ISA. Lastly, studies show that context is crucial in the effectiveness of ISA training [3, 13, 14]. This aligns with standards and regulations which state that ISA training should be relevant to end-users' role and environment [15, 16]. In addition, it has been shown that demographic factors, such as age and educational level, can affect employee security policy awareness and compliance [17]. Effective training in one environment does not guarantee success in another.

2.1 Measuring the Effectiveness of ISA Training

Two primary measurement techniques can be identified from prior research: technical measures, in the form of metrics (number of reported phishing mails; incidents due to change, data leakage events, audit findings); and questionnaires or surveys, that test the knowledge of end-users.

Technical measures of effectiveness are seldomly reported in academic publications, in most part because obtaining the data required from businesses has proven difficult (if not impossible) as the data owners have security concerns around sharing the data [18, 19]. Most studies that make use of such measures are case studies using simulated phishing campaigns [5, 8, 9]. In addition, it has been seen that methods also include reporting on incidents, testing employee pre and post training, and collection feedback from stakeholders [20]. While these studies show that end-users are retaining what they have learnt and have changed their behavior, it only addressed one security concern, albeit an important one. On the other hand, questionnaires are by far the most popular means of measuring the effectiveness of ISACs, with more than three-quarters of studies performed over the past years focusing on the designing and using a variation of a questionnaire to test end-user knowledge of ISA topics. While many questionnaires are self-developed they should ideally be grounded in best-practice. For example, a formal approach is taken by Poepjes [19], which bases questions and focus areas on the ISO 27001/2 standard.

2.2 ISA Capability Model

The Information Security Awareness Capability Model (ISACM) [19] requires that several metrics be obtained to determine what awareness campaigns need to be delivered in the environment. These metrics are Awareness Importance (AI), Awareness Capability (AC) and Awareness Risk (AR). AI is derived from taking an information security best practice standard, extracting the controls and rating their level of importance regarding user awareness of the control within the environment. AC is derived from surveying a random sample of end-users on their understanding of the various controls identified as important in the AI phase. AC can therefore be defined as the end-users' understanding and knowledge around specific awareness controls. AR is then calculated by applying the values obtained to an awareness risk matrix. This matrix is used to determine the AR rating. AR can therefore be defined as the risk identified when comparing the users' AC against the AI score for each awareness control. The results of the ISACM can be used to create a targeted and measurable ISAC.

3 Implementation Methodology

We created a practical method to implement an ISAC, derived from the ISACM. The method adapted the model to the environment of a target organization (TO). Several instruments were developed in conjunction with TO personnel:

- Control framework: the control framework is a list of information security best practice controls. The framework aligns with the information security framework (ISF) that the TO uses.

- Control awareness survey: the survey contains questions to determine the AC value of controls that received an AI rating of *moderate* to *extremely important*. The survey should be updated upon any change in the control framework.
- Awareness risk matrix: this matrix is used to determine the AR rating and was adapted from the TO risk framework.

Figure 1 shows how the instruments and metrics were combined in a step-wise approach.

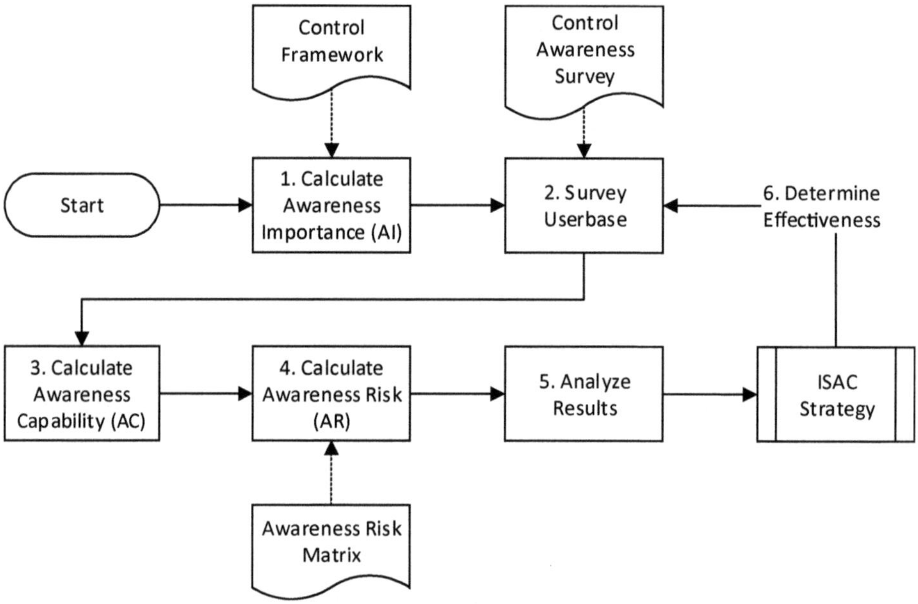

Fig. 1. ISAC methodology

3.1 Awareness Importance (AI)

The control framework is a list of information security best practice controls which will be given to Senior Staff members of the IT security department that are stakeholders in the ISAC. Each control is then rated by the IT security team to determine the AI of each control, for each end-user group. The control framework is developed by incorporating the IS/cybersecurity framework of the TO. The NIST [4] defines a cybersecurity framework as "a common language for understanding, managing, and expressing cybersecurity risk both internally and externally. Includes activities to achieve specific cybersecurity outcomes, and references examples of guidance to achieve those outcomes".

3.2 Survey Userbase

The control awareness survey is dependent on the results of the control framework. To not overburden users only the top ten controls, that are deemed *moderate* to *extremely important* for each group, are used in the survey. Additionally, the questions are tailored to the identified group's environment. The results of the survey are used to calculate the group's AC.

3.3 Calculate Awareness Capability (AC)

The results of the survey are then used to obtain an average score for each control for each group, used as the AC metric. For example, for control X, the survey results for 10 users from group Y are 2, 3, 2, 4, 5, 2, 2, 4, 5 and 2. The scores are added together, resulting in a total of 31 out of 50. This is then divided by 10 (the number of participants) to give an AC score for control X and group Y of 3.1.

3.4 Calculate Awareness Risk (AR)

The awareness risk matrix must be applied in the TO environment so that it aligns with the organization's risk framework. This results in an awareness risk matrix that will be used to plot the AI and AC scores, to determine the AR score for each control.

3.5 Analyze Results

The AR rating for each control will be used to determine what training should be implemented in the environment for each user group. The control with the highest AR will be used to compile and implement the ISAC strategy for the coming training period. The ISAC strategy is then implemented by the information security team.

3.6 Determine Effectiveness

Once the training curriculum addressing the AR has been successfully implemented and is considered complete by the information security team, the same questionnaire that was used to measure AC will be sent to a new sample set of users for each target group (i.e. it does not contain any of the users that answered in the original sample group). The answers from the second sample group will then be reflected on the awareness risk matrix. Should the userbase have learnt anything from the ISAC, their AC score will be higher, therefore reducing the AR score. As the AR score of a control reduces, a new control with a higher AR score will become the new focus for the next ISAC period.

3.7 Target Organization Overview

The TO is required by both regulation and legislation to implement ISA within their environment, with the objective to change the behavior of staff to be more security minded. The TO is aligned with international best practices and has chosen the Information Security Forums Standards of Good Practice (SoGP) [15] as their primary

ISF. The responsibility of implementing training within the TO is given to the IT security department where there are multiple security teams, including: information security, cyber security, and access control, to name a few. Senior members of the various teams within the IT security department form part of the ISAC stakeholder group.

The TO is required by their board of directors to deploy at least four topics a year, allowing topics to be deployed every three months at a minimum. Training is deployed in multiple ways depending on the level of training or awareness the information security team needs to implement. For structured e-learning style training, the information security team makes use of a learning management system, which deploys the training to the end-user and tracks their progress and completion status. E-learnings are either sourced from an external supplier who is an expert on the topic or created internally by the TO's human resource employee education department that specializes in educating staff, with the information security team playing the role of the subject matter expert.

4 ISAC Implementation and Lessons Learned

The method was implemented and evaluated in a financial institution in South Africa over a ten-month period in 2018 (January to October). Ethical clearance from the university and permission from the organization was obtained before any data was collected. Implementation and evaluation data were collected in several ways. The first collection method was in the form of artefacts created in Microsoft Excel to capture the responses of the IT security team in a structured manner. The second method was a questionnaire that was sent to a group of end-users to obtain the participants' understanding of the material given to them. The content was obtained from documents and questionnaires previously created by the TO. Lastly, feedback regarding the method's efficacy was collected through observation by the researcher as well as from the IT security team; the team members were asked two questions: *"In your opinion, what worked well?"* and *"In your opinion, what did not work well?"*. During the research process we endeavored to minimize bias by using established frameworks and questionnaires, discussing preliminary findings for alternative explanations, and being open to contrary evidence. We are confident that bias was sufficiently considered and that the research was conducted to a high ethical standard.

4.1 Awareness Importance (AI)

The control framework is a list of information security best practice controls which was given to senior staff members of the IT security department that are stakeholders in the ISAC, to measure AI. The control framework aligns to the 2016 version of the SoGP, as the 2018 version [16] was not published until later in the year. The instrument is an adaptation of the instrument used by Poepjes [19]. The stakeholder will rate the AI on a 1 to 5 ordinal scale, with 5 being the highest level of importance.

Data for the control framework was collected by the researcher, with assistance from the information security team. The target audience for the control framework were senior members of the IT security department who are stakeholders in the ISAC. By answering the control framework, these senior members will provide the information security team with their individual understanding of what training is important for each target group (senior management, branch staff, privileged users, contact center and end-users).

The data was collected by sending the control framework to each senior IT security department team member with instructions on how to complete it. Each senior IT security department team member was given two weeks to complete the task. After three months of project prioritization sessions, the control framework was completed by all senior IT security department team members. As an example, Table 1 highlights the top six topics for the end-user group.

Table 1. AI for end-users

SoGP 2016 controls	Average score
PA2.5 Portable Storage Devices	4.3
SM1.2 Acceptable Use Policies	4.2
BA2.2 Protection of Spreadsheets	4.2
PA2.4 Employee-owned Devices	4.0
PM2.2 Security Awareness Messages	3.8
IM1.1 Information Classification and Handling	3.8

Lessons Learned. Using TO's ISF proved to be very effective, as IT security staff were already familiar with the topics and controls within the framework. As the TO strives to comply with this framework, it meant that most controls within the framework were implemented already. While the translation of this standard into a questionnaire was detailed and comprehensive, determining AI proved to be very difficult, as interpreting the importance and impact of a control can be subjective. Additionally, the length of the control framework proved to be a challenge, as the time taken to complete the AI rating resulted in a slow response rate from participants.

Additionally, participants had various degrees of understanding about the SoGP controls. While the information security team believed that all IT security department team members were familiar with the standard, this was not the case, with some participants struggling to understand the control on its own, how one control differentiates from another, or how the control changes and applies depending on the stakeholder group.

Their seemed to be a difference of opinion about the grouping of stakeholder groups with one participant stating that *"The one thing that really worked well was using the ISF framework to map out areas that needs to be addressed in the different classes of users. Identifying the user classes and applying what is relatable for them from the ISF framework, ensures that all the areas are covered for the correct audience."* While another participant stated that the groupings were inaccurate *"There should only be a grouping of three user categories – Senior Management, Privileged users and End-Users. I think although only certain controls might be applicable to certain environments or grouping of users in a certain org [organization] structure it is imperative that the business users as a whole should be made aware of all kinds of risks and attacks a business might face."*

A suggestion for improving this step would be to create ISA control groups that are mapped to the ISF. For example, many of the controls, such as data protection controls, were grouped together by the respondents and received similar, if not the same, AI score. A grouping under a control named Data Protection can represent all data protection controls, allowing for one control to supplement many of the smaller controls. This will not only shorten the length of the control framework but allow for more control variety within the various ISACs throughout the year. Additionally, this will provide a single ISAC with multiple topics (each information security control broken up into its smaller ISF controls) as well as make it easier to incorporate other ISFs to the proposed method. The grouped controls would also allow for a more generic definition of a control making it easier for participants not familiar with the ISF of the organization to answer the control framework.

4.2 Survey Userbase

While the information security team was awaiting responses on their AI control framework, the information security team started working on creating questions for the AC questionnaire based on each topic within the SoGP. The information security team were provided several artefacts to assist in crafting these questions that included: the HAIS-Q [21], questionnaire guidelines; and the AI control framework for formatting. The information security team first attempted to create Likert style questions for each topic within SoGP, which proved to be far more challenging than they expected. While theme-specific questions are easily incorporated into Likert style questions, the topics presented in SoGP were far more complex in nature and did not allow for a strongly agree to strongly disagree Likert scale format.

The information security team therefore decided to create questions that were aimed at current processes and procedures in the environment that relate to the SoGP controls. Due to several security incidents and projects throughout the environment, several ISA topics were required to be implemented as a matter of urgency, but conflicted with the topics that were identified in the AI results. It was decided by the TO that they would therefore use the AI results to define the topic for one specific target group, the end-user group. The remaining target groups will receive training based on the current need from the business. While this was not ideal, the risk of not performing the required training for the other target groups was too great to ignore.

The information security team creating the AC questionnaire was informed of the decision and immediately started focusing on delivering the questions that were required for measuring the AC of the top ten topics (out of 132) [15] for the end-user target group. The team created five questions for each topic, which was set up on Survey Monkey. An invitation with a link to the survey was emailed to a random sample of users. Users were given two weeks and a total of 47 users successfully completed the questionnaire. The information security team felt that this was enough to proceed to the next step. The challenge of competing for employee attention has also been noted in other ISA training contexts [20].

Lessons Learned. Using the results from the AI questionnaire to build a questionnaire targeting the end-users proved to have many challenges. The mapping of the ISF controls to general ISA questions or previously used questions from academic papers was near impossible. This resulted in the information security team having to create the questions themselves, as opposed to relying on past research. While the time taken to build this questionnaire took far longer than expected, the resulting questions can be easily used again in the future with little to no rework.

4.3 Calculate Awareness Capability (AC)

Table 2 shows the average score received from the questionnaire. Score ranges from 0 to 5. With a score of 5 meaning the users answered all questions correctly and 0 meaning the user did not answer any of the questions correctly, for that topic. The results show that the end-user target group is unfamiliar with several security controls within their day to day working environment, particularly information classification and handling and the processes and procedures defined in the Acceptable Use Policies (AUP). The sores in Tables 1 and 2 is then used to map to the awareness risk matrix to determine the AR score for each control.

Table 2. AC for end-users

SoGP 2016 controls	Average score
IM1.1 Information Classification and Handling	1.7
SM1.2 Acceptable Use Policies	1.9
BA2.2 Protection of Spreadsheets	2.4
PA1.2 Office Equipment	2.4
PA2.4 Employee-owned Devices	2.7
PA2.3 Mobile Device Connectivity	3.1
IM2.2 Sensitive Physical Information	3.2
PM2.2 Security Awareness Messages	3.2
IM1.2 Information Privacy	3.4
PA2.5 Portable Storage Devices	3.5

Lessons Learned. The information security team felt the results were a true reflection of the environment with one member of the information security team stating *"The one thing that really worked well was using the ISF framework to map out areas that needs to be addressed in the different classes of users. Identifying the user classes and applying what is relatable for them from the ISF framework, ensures that all the areas are covered for the correct audience."*

4.4 Calculate Awareness Risk (AR)

The TO makes use of an organization-wide risk framework that is developed by the risk management business unit and approved by the board of directors. It examines two main dimensions, impact and likelihood. For the organization impact holds greater value than likelihood, as the TO sees any impact within the short term (three years) as being significant enough to warrant attention.

The strategy applied by Poepjes [19] is then applied to this matrix, supplementing likelihood with AC and impact with AI. The result of mapping aggregated scores for AI and AC for each grouping will be an AR rating for each control. The AI and AC scores for the end-user target group were then mapped on the awareness risk matrix. Figure 2 demonstrates the AI and AC mapping.

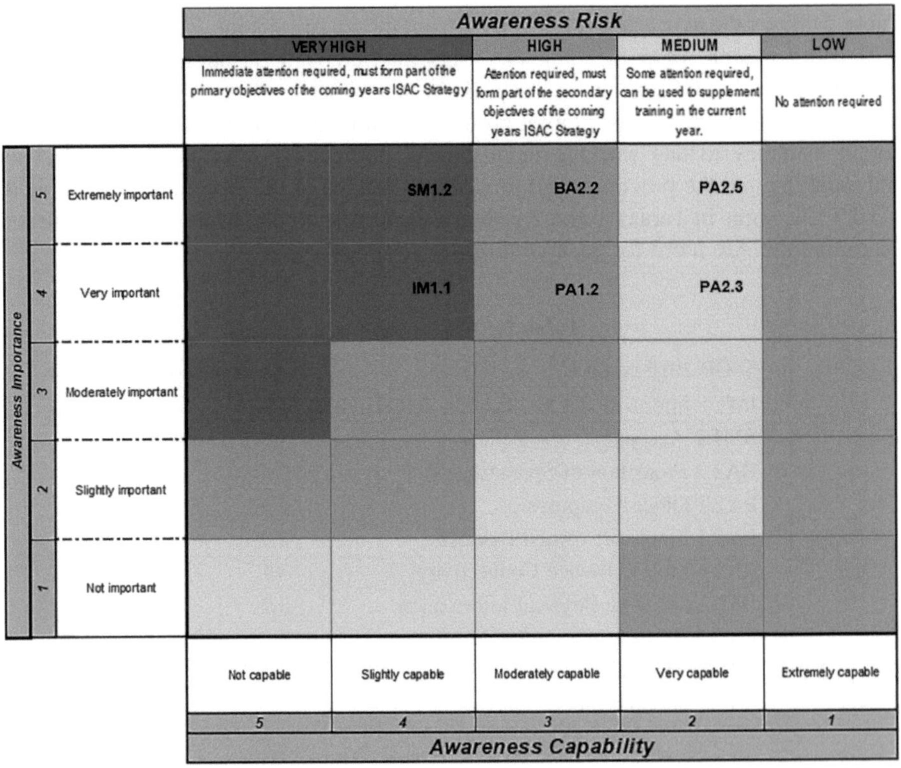

Fig. 2. End-user awareness risk matrix

The AC score is inverted to map to the risk matrix. This is done by taking the highest rating and subtracting the current score. For example, "IM1.1 Information Classification and Handling" received an AC score of 1.7 in Table 2, which is subtracted from the highest risk rating of 5, to give the risk matrix AC mapping of 3.3. On the risk matrix the area towards the top left indicates very high risk. Controls in this area require immediate attention and should form part of the primary objectives of the next ISAC strategy. As can be seen "SM1.2 Acceptable Use Policies" and "IM1.1 Information Classification and Handling" are identified as very high risk for the organization.

Lessons Learned. The plotting of the results of the AI and AC questionnaire provided a very effective means of illustrating the AR within the environment. Unfortunately, the 5×5 risk matrix results in groups of ARs, requiring the information security team to revert to the raw data to determine the highest AR. Additionally, the awareness risk matrix required the original AC score to be inverted to map to the awareness risk matrix. While this did not affect the results of the AR score, it was an unnecessary complication in an otherwise well-developed step.

4.5 Analyze Results

The results from mapping the AI and AC score showed that the largest AR score comes from the topic *"SM1.2 Acceptable Use Policies"*. The information security team agreed that this reflects what they had suspected and used this topic for the ISAC. The information security team then started building an ISAC strategy to increase end-users' awareness of AUP controls within the environment.

ISAC Strategy. The team had multiple discussions with various vendors and departments to determine the best way to deliver training for this topic. Due to the topic being organization-specific, generic e-learnings from vendors proved to be inadequate. Recommendations from the human resources employee education department within the organization required creating a very lengthy and complex, custom built, e-learning. This too was deemed inadequate, as the team knew from prior training efforts that lengthy e-learnings do not have a high completion rate.

The information security team decided to focus on an awareness campaign with the overall theme of *"Protecting the family"*. The theme was chosen because it aligned with a family-focused product which the organization was rolling out, as well as the organizational culture (communications often referred to 'our family' and 'being part of a great family'). The goal was to instill a security mind-set and a sense of responsibility in employees.

To implement the campaign posters and desktop backgrounds (wallpapers) were designed. Large (A3) posters were displayed in social areas in every building. These posters were intended to be eye-catching, with minimal text but reference to where employees could go to find out more. Smaller (A4) posters were placed behind every bathroom stall door and contained more detailed information. The desktop backgrounds also had minimal text but provided the user with the central call-to-action and link to more information.

The information security team then created a series of emails in line with the style of the posters, with the content being only a few short paragraphs. An email was sent out every two weeks, each tackling a different section of the AUP. The topics were: sharing data, laptop security, policy document awareness and importance, communicating security risks, removable media, backups and shared drives, and disposing of information. Content was in plain English and could be read in under three minutes.

Lessons Learned. The visual representation of the AR within the environment made identifying the required training very easy. The information security team felt that it was a true reflection of the current environment, with one member of the information security team stating: *"One could gain a true direction for awareness training within an organization"*.

Building the ISAC strategy proved to be quite challenging, due to the nature of the topic chosen. As the topic focused on AUP, the training needed to be customized to the environment, making it impossible to use generic training from a third party proficient in the topic. While the content was easy for the team to come by, as it came from a company policy, deciding on the method to deploy the training was not. The chosen method was a series of emails supported by a marketing campaign. The information security team could benefit from previous research, such as that done by Pattinson et al. [12], to determine what method of training is best suited for different end-users.

4.6 Determine Effectiveness

Once the information security team had deployed the training to their satisfaction, the questionnaire and email was sent to a further 255 respondents. Respondents were given three weeks to complete the survey with a reminder e-mail sent a week before final closure date. A total of 36 users successfully completed the questionnaire.

The average score received from the second questionnaire show that there was a slight increase (from an average score of 1.9 before training to 2.5 after training) in the user's knowledge of the security controls within their day to day working environment. The original AI and post training AC score for the end-user target group was then mapped on the awareness risk matrix. There was a clear move of AC to the right (more capable), making the AR decrease from a very high risk to a high risk.

Lessons Learned. Re-performing the survey, as well as calculating the new AC and AR scores was done significantly faster than many of the other steps. The artefacts created at the start of this method made this step very efficient.

The move of the AC of the target group from very high to high proved to be a very effective illustration of the effectiveness of the training implemented. The information security team believed that the method used to train the staff was not the most effective but believed that the slight move was an accurate view of the effectiveness of the ISAC and were therefore pleased with the results.

5 Conclusions

While we acknowledge the limitations of statistical generalization within a single case study we propose that analytic generalization is possible. Such lessons learned may potentially apply to a variety of contexts. Our study reflects on the practical steps required in an ISAC and the hurdles staff who implement it will have to overcome. These include identifying and prioritizing training topics, creating training material, and effectively measuring learning.

Several limitations should be considered in this study. The TO comes from a highly regulated industry, which requires compliance with many controls. This requirement drives some of the decision-making in this case. Due to compliance requirements and risks prevalent in the environment, the method was only used on a single target group that was considered less risky by the TO. The implementation of this method over a longer period would provide the opportunity to not only collect more data but help improve and evolve the method. Additionally, the content and mechanisms used to deliver training was decided on by TO staff. While TO staff were sure of its effectiveness as a training delivery method, there is no evidence to validate their assumption, other than their experience in the field and knowledge of the environment.

While our study contributes to the validation of the model proposed by Poepjes [19] it also indicates the need for further research. Within the field of ISA training ways to efficiently measure the effectiveness of a campaign are needed. Further research could also investigate the methodology used to conduct the training, and how this impacts the effectiveness of the ISAC. Additionally, the incorporation of hard measures, such as phishing simulation results and other user behavior metrics, could prove effective but more research is required on what those hard measures should be.

Acknowledgements. This work is based on the research supported wholly/in part by the National Research Foundation of South Africa (Grant Numbers 114838).

References

1. Daniel Ani, U.P., He, H.M., Tiwari, A.: Human capability evaluation approach for cyber security in critical industrial infrastructure. In: Nicholson, D. (ed.) Advances in Human Factors in Cybersecurity, pp. 169–182. Springer, Heidelberg (2016). https://doi.org/10.1007/978-3-319-41932-9_14
2. Denning, T., Lerner, A., Shostack, A., Kohno, T.: Control-alt-hack: the design and evaluation of a card game for computer security awareness and education. Presented at the Proceedings of the 2013 ACM SIGSAC Conference on Computer & Communications Security (2013). https://doi.org/10.1145/2508859.2516753
3. Yildirim, E.: The importance of information security awareness for the success of business enterprises. In: Nicholson, D. (ed.) Advances in Human Factors in Cybersecurity, pp. 211–222. Springer, Heidelberg (2016). https://doi.org/10.1007/978-3-319-41932-9_17
4. National Institute of Standards and Technology: Glossary—Computer Security Resource Center. https://csrc.nist.gov/glossary/
5. Aloul, F.A.: The need for effective information security awareness. JAIT **3**, 176–183 (2012). https://doi.org/10.4304/jait.3.3.176-183
6. Stewart, G., Lacey, D.: Death by a thousand facts: criticising the technocratic approach to information security awareness. Inf. Manag. Comput. Secur. **20**, 29–38 (2012). https://doi.org/10.1108/09685221211219182
7. Arachchilage, N.A.G., Love, S.: Security awareness of computer users: a phishing threat avoidance perspective. Comput. Hum. Behav. **38**, 304–312 (2014). https://doi.org/10.1016/j.chb.2014.05.046
8. Young-McLear, K., Wyman, G., Benin, J., Young-McLear, Y.: A white hat approach to identifying gaps between cybersecurity education and training: a social engineering case study. In: Nicholson, D. (ed.) Advances in Human Factors in Cybersecurity, pp. 229–237. Springer, Heidelberg (2016). https://doi.org/10.1007/978-3-319-41932-9_19
9. Pattinson, M., Butavicius, M., Parsons, K., McCormac, A., Calic, D.: Managing information security awareness at an Australian bank: a comparative study. Inf. Comput. Secur. **25**, 181–189 (2017). https://doi.org/10.1108/ICS-03-2017-0017

10. Kajzer, M., D'Arcy, J., Crowell, C.R., Striegel, A., Van Bruggen, D.: An exploratory investigation of message-person congruence in information security awareness campaigns. Comput. Secur. **43**, 64–76 (2014). https://doi.org/10.1016/j.cose.2014.03.003
11. McCormac, A., Zwaans, T., Parsons, K., Calic, D., Butavicius, M., Pattinson, M.: Individual differences and information security awareness. Comput. Hum. Behav. **69**, 151–156 (2017). https://doi.org/10.1016/j.chb.2016.11.065
12. Pattinson, M., et al.: Adapting cyber-security training to your employees. In: Clarke, N.L., Furnell, S.M. (ed.) Proceedings of the Twelfth International Symposium on Human Aspects of Information Security & Assurance, pp. 67–79. University of Plymouth (2018)
13. Tsohou, A., Kiountouzis, E., Karyda, M., Kokolakis, S.: Analyzing trajectories of information security awareness. Info Technol. People **25**, 327–352 (2012). https://doi.org/10.1108/09593841211254358
14. Waly, N., Tassabehji, R., Kamala, M.: improving organisational information security management: the impact of training and awareness. In: 2012 IEEE 14th International Conference on High Performance Computing and Communication & 2012 IEEE 9th International Conference on Embedded Software and Systems, pp. 1270–1275 (2012). https://doi.org/10.1109/HPCC.2012.187
15. Chaplin, M., Creasey, J., Thathupara, S.: The standard of good practice for information security 2016. Information Security Forum Limited (2016)
16. Jordan, A., Haken, G., Creasey, J.: The Standard of Good Practice for Information Security 2018. Information Security Forum, United Kingdom (2018)
17. Chua, H.N., Wong, S.F., Low, Y.C., Chang, Y.: Impact of employees' demographic characteristics on the awareness and compliance of information security policy in organizations. Telemat. Inform. **35**, 1770–1780 (2018). https://doi.org/10.1016/j.tele.2018.05.005
18. Lebek, B., Uffen, J., Breitner, M.H., Neumann, M., Hohler, B.: Employees' information security awareness and behavior: a literature review. In: 2013 46th Hawaii International Conference on System Sciences, pp. 2978–2987. IEEE, Wailea (2013). https://doi.org/10.1109/HICSS.2013.192
19. Poepjes, R.: The development and evaluation of an information security awareness capability model: linking ISO/IEC 27002 controls with awareness importance, capability and risk (2015). https://eprints.usq.edu.au/28067/
20. Alshaikh, M., Maynard, S.B., Ahmad, A., Chang, S.: An exploratory study of current information security training and awareness practices in organizations. In: 51st Hawaii International Conference on System Sciences, HICSS 2018, Hilton Waikoloa Village, Hawaii, USA, 3–6 January 2018, pp. 1–10 (2018). https://doi.org/10.24251/HICSS.2018.635
21. Parsons, K., McCormac, A., Butavicius, M., Pattinson, M., Jerram, C.: Determining employee awareness using the human aspects of information security questionnaire (HAIS-Q). Comput. Secur. **42**, 165–176 (2014). https://doi.org/10.1016/j.cose.2013.12.003

A Comprehensive Framework for Understanding Security Culture in Organizations

Alaa Tolah[1,2](✉), Steven M. Furnell[1,3,4], and Maria Papadaki[1]

[1] University of Plymouth, Plymouth, UK
{alaa.tolah, steven.furnell, maria.papadaki}@plymouth.ac.uk
[2] Saudi Electronic University, Riyadh, Saudi Arabia
[3] Nelson Mandela University, Port Elizabeth, South Africa
[4] Edith Cowan University, Joondalup, Australia

Abstract. Organizational security is exposed to internal and external threats, with a greater level of vulnerabilities coming from the former. Drawing upon findings from prior works as a foundation, this study aims to highlight the significant factors that influence the security culture within organizations. Phase one of the study reports upon an interview-based investigation undertaken with thirteen experienced, knowledgeable security specialists from seven organizations. The main findings confirmed the importance of the identified factors from the previous work. The focus to emerge from the interviews concludes that continuously subjecting employees to targeted training and awareness development improves security culture. Indeed, there was a clear lack of awareness and compliance regarding the implementation and clarity of security policies in organizations. Also, the inefficient training program and limit to specific employees in organizations leads to a lack of awareness and compliance.

Keywords: Security culture · Human factors · Qualitative study

1 Introduction

Nowadays, a knowledge-based economy has become more dynamic than at any time in history, which continues to progress. Technology enables all business operations and information technology to develop into a central concept for most aspects of life. However, information technology developments continually initiate new risks to the security of information assets. The use of ICT can make the violation of information security easier, while many technical approaches to security and counter-measures have augmented in organizations; although this development needs to increase, as many researchers perceive security to be both a "people" and "technical" issue [2, 4]. Nonetheless, technology is less likely to cause problems than human error, which is a cause of the majority security breaches (75% of organizations suffer security breaches by insiders) [13]. Therefore, organizations need to focus on employees' behavior to achieve information security, as many studies examined the human factors and their relation to information security with social psychology issues that determine reasons

Published by Springer Nature Switzerland AG 2019
L. Drevin and M. Theocharidou (Eds.): WISE 2019, IFIP AICT 557, pp. 143–156, 2019.
https://doi.org/10.1007/978-3-030-23451-5_11

for unacceptable behavior that leads to security breaches [12]. One approach the organization can take to manage the security would be developing strategies that enhance security culture [1, 7].

A positive security culture contributes to support organizations in guiding employees to follow security policies, which lowers the potential risk of harmful information interaction by employees, as they develop knowledge and advance their skills correctly, and behave securely in their working environments [2, 17]. The culture that promotes secure human behavior through knowledge, values, and assumptions is better than regulations that merely mandate employees' behavior [1]. Various studies suggest that organizational security culture could lead an employee to act as a "human firewall" [1]; where acting correctly is commonplace [15]. Consequently, organizations are required to use understandable guidelines to develop a culture of security awareness, which utilizes various approaches to improve comprehension [2, 17].

The proposed paper extends the proposed framework by [16], which facilitates an understanding of security culture and its elements. It initially assists in comprehending whether the level of security culture enhances the security of information assets, and also assesses the relationship between influential factors and factors that constitute security culture.

The development of an initial framework is based on Alnatheer's model and a review of academic literature in the security culture. In the proposed framework, the security culture comprises several factors, as the components are structured into: factors that influence security culture (top management, security policy, security education and training, security risk assessment and analysis, and ethical conduct); factors that constitute security culture (security awareness, security ownership and security compliance); and factors of organizational behavior that contribute to workplace behaviors and could influence the security culture (personality traits and job satisfaction) (see Fig. 1). These factors appear to be the most influential factors and are considered as part of the security culture's conceptualization. By understanding the influential factors or reflection factors, it is possible to aid in directing the interaction of humans with information security. These factors provide management with a means to implement adequate security management approaches that include the guidance provision and control implementation in the assessment of security culture.

As this study relied on prior literature to develop an initial security culture framework and to explore a detailed perception and understanding of human behavior, it was considered that using an interview method would enable in-depth information from employees involved in an organization's information security, and understand factors affecting security culture with which are more critical from the perspective of participants. The main aims of the interview were to explore whether all the ten factors within the proposed framework are necessary; which factors are the most important, whether new factors should be incorporated, and to identify new issues that had not previously been considered to alter security culture potentially.

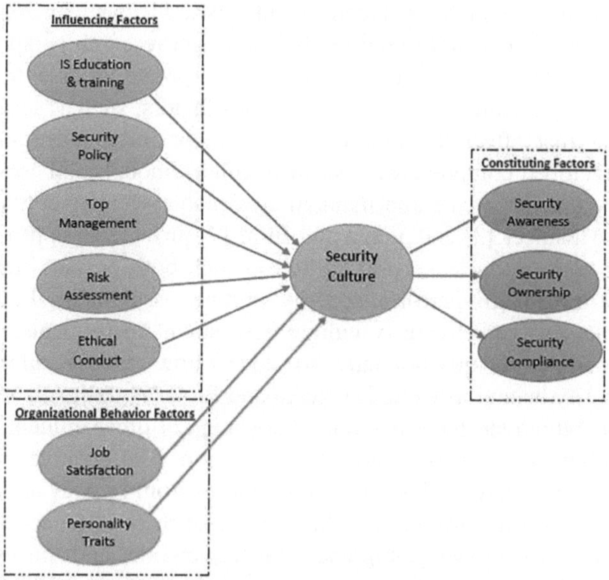

Fig. 1. The comprehensive security culture framework [16]

Therefore, this paper presents the findings from exploratory interviews with IT/security professionals and combines these with the literature review to investigate whether the identified factors are vital for organizations and to determine a base for more comprehensive research through quantitative techniques. The paper initially provides a review of related work for security culture frameworks. Subsequently, the current research method is described with the analytical approaches used to interpret the results. The paper concludes by outlining the research implications and future research.

2 Literature Review of Existing Security Culture Approaches

Instilling an effective culture is vital to create adequate levels of information security. Various studies have focused on security culture, while literature reviews offer an overview that focuses on security culture (Alhogail [2]; Glaspie and Karwowski [8]). Their literature analyzes concluded that most investigated issues in security culture relate to: the conceptualization of culture to identify concepts and factors that affect security culture, the creation of security culture, or an assessment of security culture to measure whether it is an adequate level. Many studies provide various approaches and models that highlight security culture's importance, promote its benefits and provide guidelines to create and assess security culture. The literature analysis showed that most studies demonstrated various essential factors that may shape or change security culture [2]. A comprehensive review of security culture was conducted to gain an overview of the current security culture frameworks, which focused on studies that assess security culture, which presented essential knowledge with regards to factors that assist in developing security culture [16]. Thirteen research perspectives relate to the creation of security culture and five studies incorporate an assessment of security culture. The security culture is a product of various factors, such as security policy and security training that affect the individual's behavior in organizations [16]. These studies have developed comprehensive security culture models and contributed to how organizations potentially create and maintain acceptable security culture levels.

Studies by Alnatheer [3] and Veiga and Eloff [7] provide an approach that utilizes the same framework to assess security culture, which both provide statistically sound assessment instruments to perform security culture assessment. Few studies have provided reliable and valid security culture assessment instruments; Schlienger and Teufel [15] designed a questionnaire to detail how proper rules impact upon employees' security behavior, while Da Veiga and Eloff [7] designed a security culture assessment tool. Moreover, there is minimal coverage of other influential factors, such as individual difference variables and job satisfaction. The positive impacts of these factors on workplace behaviors had proven by studies from D'Arcy and Greene [5] and McCormac [11]. The literature review illustrated that there is a need for more investigation in the area to provide comprehensive frameworks and the best practices of security culture cultivation and assessment. Hence, this study proposed an initial framework that integrates the most important factors that influence security culture. The interview method was adopted to explore and examine the identified factors.

3 Methodology

This study used the pragmatic philosophical approach with mixed methods of data collection. The initial phase was a qualitative design to acquire sufficient information regarding security culture from IT/security specialists in organizations and to explore influential factors. The second phase will be quantitative data for a survey with a minimum sample size of 250 employees from several organizations to develop an understanding of the relationship between factors and to test the framework's validity. The findings from the qualitative phase will be incorporated with the literature review to identify constructs that influence security culture and related survey items. To enhance theoretical propositions, an exploratory interview was adopted to investigate whether all identified factors are necessary for organizations, which also assist in the survey design.

3.1 Sample

It is essential to select organizations from a broad range of sectors and industries, which may require various levels of security. It will help organizations to make individual decisions regarding security culture programs and guide investments in security awareness and training sessions [14]. Access to appropriate organizations was difficult, as certain organizations are restricted against discussing security management. The initial choice of organizations' location was in the UK, due to the study's location. However, the low number of respondents in the UK resulted in an invitation e-mail being sent to international organizations' members that had cooperated on past occasions in Saudi Arabia and the USA. The study managed to interview seven individual organizations: two in the UK, one in the USA, and four in Saudi Arabia, which covered private, public and semi-public sectors, and included various industries: four in education, and one insurance, law, and mining, respectively. These organizations have the security infrastructure in place; have technology adoption, and used security management practices. However, the diversity of organizations' geographical locations would assist in advancing the understanding of security culture from varied backgrounds.

A semi-structured was utilized in an exploratory manner, and there was no restriction in sample size. This study does not aim to demonstrate the representation of security culture; it aims to identify factors of more critical importance within organizations. This exploratory study could provide indications of the validity of factors intended in the framework. The results cannot be generalized, although it is possible that the findings from the quantitative survey in the next phase could be generalizable. Access to people with relevant knowledge and experience of organizations' security was sufficient. Nevertheless, only thirteen participants from the IT/Information security department agreed to participate in the interview; experience and knowledge of respondents yield rich data. Table 1 below lists the demographic features for participant organizations.

Table 1. Organizations demographic profile

Org	Type	Size	Location	Sector	No. of interviewees	Interviewees position
A	Public	4000	SA	Education	3	IT assistance director and IT specialists
B	Public	5000	SA	Education	2	IT specialists
C	Private	6000	USA	Education	2	IT specialists
D	Public	5000	UK	Education	1	Enterprise security architect
E	Private	400	SA	Insurance	3	IT supervisor and IT specialists
F	Semi-Public	4000	SA	Mining	1	Security manager
G	Private	1500	UK	Law	1	Security manager
Total					13	

3.2 Data Collection

The primary method for collecting data for discourse analysis was individual interviews from October 2017–January 2018, conducted face to face or through Skype. An interview guide was designed and utilized during the interview to ensure data consistency and minimize bias. The interview questions consisted of four parts, with the first part on demographics and a general overview of participants. The second part included questions with open-ended answers related to organizations' security practices, how employees are educated and acquire security regulations' awareness. The third part includes questions with open-ended answers that determine security culture behaviors, knowledge, and practices of employees; and part four enabled interviewees to construct individual interpretations.

A pilot study with three respondents was conducted to ensure that the interview guide was appropriate, and participants understood the questions. Subsequently, the language was either in English or Arabic, depending on the preference of each interviewee, although the transcripts were transcribed in English. The average interview time was twenty-five minutes, while certain interviewees refused to have their interviews recorded, due to the perceived sensitive nature of their information, even though the identity of the interviewees and the data were kept confidential.

3.3 Data Analysis

A within-case analysis was used for data analysis, which includes detailed interviews. Each interview assists in providing insight into the identified factors and how different constructs are perceived within real life situations. The interviews provided data regarding security culture in the form of a narrative discussion, instead of analyzed interpretation. The understanding was obtained by reviewing the significant findings and reflecting upon personal views following a review of past literature. The data analysis process in the study includes developing a coding scheme to capture the data's critical content; applying the coding scheme to each identified comment made by the interviewee; and exploring the results' frequencies and patterns, where pieces are taken individually from the analysis and compared with other forms of data to determine which parts are similar or different to establish data correlations.

During the analysis, both explicit and implicit results derived from the interviews. By coding the data, the interviews were sufficiently analyzed, as this was a repetitive process that involved determining consistency and providing data links to the framework's constructs. The data from this repetitive process were correlated and coded into constructs during the analysis stage and resulted in data points for further analysis. Furthermore, data categories were identified, which are: top management, policy, education and training, ethical conduct, risk assessment and analysis, awareness, compliance, ownership and job satisfaction. The selected comments focused on various levels of analysis, such as the comments' structure, the overall content of what was said, and the vocabulary.

4 Results

The interview analysis depicted the perception of employees towards security culture. The findings of the interviews illustrated the relevant signify factors and correlation regarding security culture. The participants responded to the interview questions concerning their organization's practices: the security culture practices, the employee security behavior patterns, and the perceptions for improving security culture.

Quotations are used to highlight explanations of the findings, followed by a symbol that denotes the organization's name and the participant's number [A1].

4.1 Security Culture Practices

This section determines information regarding security practices; how employees educate; and acquire the awareness of related security regulations and risks.

- **The Main Information Security Practices and Rules used in the Organization.** Interviewees provided the main security practices used in organizations, which indicated that all seven participating organizations use general security practices, such as security policies, security training, physical and technical measures.
- **Security Education and Training Courses in the Organization.** Interviewees reported whether their organizations provide security training sessions. Eight participants from organizations located in Saudi Arabia and the USA reported an absence of security training programs. Five participants reported security training courses in their organizations: two organizations located in the UK and one in Saudi Arabia. Each organization informed its members regarding information security matters through induction training.
- **Different Methods of Security Awareness and Training Sessions.** The participating organizations use various channels to distribute related security awareness to employees, such as sending e-mails' notification, conducting seminar and training courses, sending text message notification, using posters or displaying information security in the organization website. Organization A usually uses e-mails, text message and training sessions to make the members aware of any security issues. While participants from organizations B and C reported that e-mails and posters are the main security awareness activities utilized in their organizations. In organization D, the main security awareness methods are e-mails, training courses and displaying information security on the organization website. Organizations E and F adopted the same security awareness activity of e-mails. Finally, organization G uses e-mails, text messages, training courses, and displays information security on the organization website as the main awareness methods.
- **Alerting Regularly about Risks and Dangers in the Organization.** Three interviewees reported that their organization's employees are not alert to any security risks, such as B and G. Ten interviewees reported that all employees in the organization are alert to security risks and dangers inherited in the work environment.
- **Information Security Level in the Organization.** To attain quantifies data, interviewees rated the level of information security in their organizations. Six participants believed that their organizations have a moderately acceptable level of information security; four participants believed a slightly acceptable level of information security; two participants claimed a very acceptable level; and one believed that it is completely acceptable.

4.2 Employee Security Behavior Patterns

This section attempts to uncover information regarding the employee's security culture behavior, knowledge, and practices in organizations.

- **Employee's General Security Behaviors.** Participants rated the employee's security behavior to obtain a broad picture. Eight participants believed that the security behavior in their organizations is "OK"; whereas four participants thought it to be "poor or very poor"; one believed it to be "good".
- **Identification of the Most Effective Security Practices on Employee's Security Behavior.** Interviewees were given several security practices to rank the level of effectiveness, including: top management, IT department initiatives, technical security countermeasure and personal values and beliefs regarding information security. Eight respondents stated top management involvement as a high priority. Following the IT department's initiatives, there was a priority for technical security countermeasures, and less priority for personal values and beliefs.
- **Perceptions of an Effective Security Culture.** Participants made a range of statements that aimed to form an effective security culture. All thirteen participants stated that conducting security training programs would be effective upon acceptable levels of security culture in organizations. Nine participants affirmed this statement: "Educating employees about the information security to increase their knowledge and make the right decision is important to have an adequate level of security culture." [B1]. The comparative analysis demonstrated that participants from the USA and Saudi Arabia organizations agreed and indicated that developing security policies and support from all levels of leadership are essential to develop an effective security culture. Participant C7 highlighted this: "To create or expect an efficient security culture, there should be an active, continuous engagement and endorsement of the information security by all levels of leadership and managers in the company". The participants from the UK and Saudi Arabia organizations stated that increasing security awareness is necessary for security protection that supports security culture. Four participants from Saudi Arabia organizations suggested that enhancing security ownership in employees would help to promote an acceptable level of security culture.
- **The Main Contributory Factors Establishing Security Culture**. There has been an agreement among participants from the UK and Saudi Arabia organizations that a security training program is one of the most important factors in security culture. Nine participants revealed that developing security training sessions for employees in the organization is one of the highest contributory factors in establishing security culture. Participant A2 assured this: "the security training program is one of the key factors for educating employees to adopt security and influence the employee behavior which will lead to establishing the security culture". Seven participants indicated that developing clear security policies as a second top contributing factor; they affirmed the effectiveness impact of security policy in security culture. Participant E3 commented that: "implementing security policies in the company will be efficient because it helps employees to clarify and get a detailed understanding about the security requirements, and the way to comply with the security rules".

Five participants mentioned that increasing security awareness is a third factor that supports security culture; while three participants signified that a periodical risk analysis is another factor that has to be considered. Two participants revealed that security culture could be effective if there is support from top management, as well as employee's compliance with security policy. One participant stated that understanding the ethical obligations of the organization and employees' job satisfaction are also vital in improving security culture.
A comparative analysis illustrated that four participants from the US and Saudi Arabia organizations believed that top management support and employees' security compliance are contributory factors in developing security culture; participant E3 stated that: "the security culture can be established effectively if all members of the company comply with security policy and regulations". Five participants from the Saudi Arabia organizations considered additional factors, such as security risk analysis, ethical conduct and job satisfaction, to contribute to the security culture. As participant A3 stated that: "Understanding the risk involved with information security and more importantly conducting a periodical risk assessment is a vital key for establishing the security culture environment". Participant B4 affirmed the effectiveness of ethical conduct policies in advancing an organization's security culture: "understanding the ethical codes and obligations is essential to improving security culture". Participant E10 suggested that job satisfaction can motivate employees to comply with organizations' security requirements: "one of the issues that should be considered in a company is the employee's job satisfaction; when the employee has a positive feeling, he/she will be more likely to comply with company security policies".

- **The Main Barriers to Achieving Improved Security Compliance.** The findings indicated that nine participants considered that the lack of awareness and training programs to be the first obstacle; the lack of clear direction in security policies was second; followed by a lack of leadership support and ownership. Two participants signified certain obstacles related to faulty human behavior by misunderstanding the ethical obligations and having no consequences to employees who fail to comply with security procedures. There has been some agreement among seven participants' perceptions of organizations in the UK and Saudi Arabia regarding the main obstacles. Seven interviewees believed that the security training sessions tend to achieve security compliance with the security policy of organizations; participant F1 stated that: "we have simple security policies, but most of the employees lack relevant training and hardly follow any security policies; the training program is vital in educating all employees to comply with security rules and guidelines". The comparative analysis illustrated that four participants from the USA and Saudi Arabia organizations expressed that the absences of clear security policies contribute significantly to the lack of compliance with information security. Three participants revealed that some of the organizations' top management lack the appropriate commitment to promote security policies; participant C2 stated that: "in my company, I have not observed any serious commitment from the top management to enforce enhancing security". One participant from Saudi Arabia considered ethical conduct as an additional factor, while one in the USA focused on the lack of security compliance.

4.3 Perceptions for Improving the Security Culture

The Participants had different recommendations that aimed to develop a security culture. There was some agreement among participants' perceptions of organizations in the UK, the USA and Saudi Arabia. Four participants agreed that the top management support in enhancing information security in organizations would improve security culture. Eight participants from the UK and Saudi Arabia organizations considered implementing security awareness as useful in developing security culture. Nine participants in the USA and Saudi Arabia organizations signified that conducting security training sessions and developing clear security policies are the most positive factors that help in improving security culture. Four participants from Saudi Arabia suggested additional factors, such as enhancing the sense of security ownership, developing ethical conduct, conducting a periodical risk assessment, and enhancing the employees' job satisfaction. Meanwhile, one USA participant suggested the importance of improving security compliance. Moreover, three participants from the UK and Saudi Arabia organizations stated the need for a tool or a model that could be used as guidance in implementing the required security culture factors that are targeted at the appropriate tiers of employee behavior, and to inculcate acceptable levels of security culture.

5 Discussion

Internal threats continue to exist within organizations. It was evident that factors identified in previous research continue to be significant. Phase one in this study provides rich data from thirteen experienced and knowledgeable respondents in seven organizations in the UK, the USA, and Saudi Arabia. The interview also revealed an apparent gap in the efficiency of providing training programs and security policies. Participants stated the requirement for periodic security training, as information security is mentioned once on induction day when the employee starts working for an organization. Participant A1 disclosed that: "education and training are not memorized for long; once the new employee finishes the first week of training, information security is forgotten." There was also concern regarding the limitations of training programs to key managers and IT members. They concluded the need for a structured training program aimed at all the organization's members.

Moreover, respondents suggested that they were unclear how their policies were implemented and updated, which is important due to the changing nature of threats. There was concern about the possible clarity of organizational policies to follow. Participant C1 suggested that: "the threats are always changing, the environment is always changing, and information security is always changing. Hence, it is vital for a company to have clear policies that are clearly described; improve the security policies by reviewing it continuously and maintain it up to date". Thus, phase two takes these points into consideration when constructing the questionnaire.

However, a comparative analysis suggested some differences in the data sets, including data collected in the UK, the USA and Saudi Arabia. In particular, there are both similarities and differences among the participants' perceptions based on their country regarding the main factors in terms of cultivating an effective security culture. There has been an agreement among the participants' perceptions regarding the important factors in establishing organizations' security culture. Based on the findings, it appears that security education and training programs, as well as security awareness and the security policy are the most significant factors that contribute toward security culture. Security education and training are considered as the most important factors to influence security culture's effectiveness. It is essential to implement and conduct periodic security training sessions in organizations to develop security culture and to improve employee's awareness, which tends to encourage security compliant behavior [7]. Additionally, it was indicated that in three organizations the security lessons had been learned following specific incidents.

The interviews indicated the importance of security awareness in promoting security culture. Both security education programs and security policy encourage compliant behavior by increasing employees' security awareness. The findings show that some organizations viewed security awareness as important in establishing a common understanding of security culture. It helps structure how employees think about information security and provides the common language and base of useful knowledge when discussing various security-related topics. Participant G1 indicated that: "it is important to create a mindset within employees; you have to develop active awareness programs, and that will give the employee a high level of awareness". Three participants stressed that sometimes security awareness might be inadequate if members are not aware of possible consequences of security breaches and cannot see the value of their security role in the organization's holistic security work. Demonstrating a high level of security awareness would lead to security-cautious behavior, which tends to encourage security compliance, while also improving security culture [6]. The findings also demonstrate that clear and sufficient security policy could promote security-cautious behavior through security awareness and establish an acceptable level of security culture. Four participants stated that security policy is an important measure, although it might be insufficient if members are not well-informed about the existing security policies.

The interviews revealed other factors that should be considered in establishing organizations' security culture: top management support and security ownership. Respondents from the UK, the USA and Saudi Arabia agreed that gaining top management commitment and support is significant in increasing organizations' security effectiveness. The support and commitment from top management help to form organizational security and predict security culture quality [9]. There were concerns regarding the failure of top management in enhancing security culture through developing appropriate training sessions, as an organization can subsequently face major issues in daily operations. Participant E2 indicated that: "employees in the company understand the importance of security; although we do not yet have a robust security policy because of that the top management is still in the process of establishing the company security activities and structures". Also, respondents from the UK and Saudi Arabia revealed that when employees understand security responsibilities and personal ownership, they comprehend security risks and behave more securely, which tends to increase security awareness and compliance; thus, better security culture [3]. Participant B1 asserted: "we do not expect to establish the security culture if our employees do not understand the importance of protecting information and it is their responsibility."

The participants from Saudi Arabia and the USA suggested three factors: security risk analysis and assessment; ethical conduct; and security compliance. The findings demonstrated that security risk assessment and analysis tend to assist organizations and employees to become capable of understanding potential damage to security, which helps to increase awareness and knowledge of security culture [3, 10]. The interview also suggested that ethical conduct is a vital factor that influences security culture, as it supports employees to integrate ethical behavior, ensuring the security of information and what is accepted by the organization [3, 10]. The findings illustrated the importance of improving security compliance in security culture creation to increase an organization's security and ensure that employee behavior complies with security policy. Participant C1 stated that: "employees are often unaware of the consequences of security breaches caused by their actions; the company should have a method that ensures employees' behavior continues to be monitored to the compliance program's effectiveness". Furthermore, another vital factor that was suggested by one respondent from Saudi Arabia is employee job satisfaction tends to promote security-cautious behavior, which develops security culture [5].

Interview analysis supports other studies and highlights the significance of factors that have an impact upon employees' security behavior and is important to be considered as part of security culture conceptualization. These factors have a positive influence on each other, and thus, have a positive influence on the security culture. The possible relationships between factors will be tested statistically in order to determine whether the proposed framework is valid. However, personality traits have received little attention from researchers, despite indications that personality traits directly affect individual behavior [11]. This is important for future research and will be an essential factor in the construction of the survey items. This paper provides some insights, although cannot be generalizable, as additional investigations are required. The study will be expanded to develop a statistical framework that would identify the correlations between factors. Knowledge management would be integrated to develop a framework that would help organizations to create the culture efficiently and predict how the security culture could be improved. Consequently, the study adopts a quantitative survey on a range of different sizes of organizations with sample size range from 250 to 300 employees.

6 Conclusion and Future Work

This study has aimed to build further comprehension of various factors that positively assist with organizations' security culture from employees' perspectives. Existing literature states factors regarding security culture adoption, while all top factors should be considered to create an environment that promotes better security culture. The study conducted an exploratory interview to present important factors that potentially affect organizational security culture and to identify existing gaps in what employees are aware of. The interviews comprised of thirteen experienced and knowledgeable security specialists from different organizations located in the USA, the UK and Saudi

Arabia. These interviews were analyzed to highlight the significant factors in security culture stemming from participants' experiences.

The findings from this study contribute to the existing knowledge by providing factors that are significant in affecting human behavior and vital in security culture. The information gained from interviews provided further knowledge of how different factors were viewed regarding reality settings. The findings also revealed an apparent gap in the organizational policies' implementation and ineffective training programs that lead to a lack of awareness and compliance. The result of this study cannot be generalizable but can be viewed to be indicative. In addition, the findings from this study demonstrate certain limitations, such as the how it cannot test the security culture framework's non-logical validity; the initial influence of factors on security culture; or factors that define security culture. However, the findings from the qualitative phase produced variables that are utilized in the quantitative phase to test the development framework's validity. In order to design the survey, the specific operational elements involved were measurable to the literature review, which were incorporated with the findings from the qualitative phase to identify constructs and related survey items that influence security culture.

References

1. Alhogail, A., Mirza, A., Bakry, S.: A comprehensive human factor framework for information security in organisations. J. Theor. Appl. Inf. Technol. **78**(2), 201–211 (2015)
2. Alhogail, A.: A Framework for the Analysis and Implementation of an Effective Information Security Culture Based on Key Human Factor Elements and Change Management Principles. King Saud University (2016)
3. Alnatheer, M., Chan, T., Nelson, K.: Understanding and measuring information security culture. In: Proceedings of the 16th Pacific Asia Conference on Information Systems, PACIS 2012 (2012)
4. Connolly, L.Y., Lang, M., Gathegi, J., Tygar, D.J.: Organisational culture, procedural countermeasures, and employee security behaviour: a qualitative study. Inf. Comput. Secur. **25**(2), 118–136 (2017)
5. D'Arcy, J., Greene, G.: The multifaceted nature of security culture and its influence on end user behaviour. In: Proceedings of IFIP TC 8 International Workshop on Information Systems Security Research, pp. 145–157 (2009)
6. Da Veiga, A.: The influence of information security policies on information security culture: illustrated through a case study. In: Proceedings of the Ninth International Symposium on Human Aspects of Information Security and Assurance, pp. 22–33 (2015)
7. Da Veiga, A., Eloff, J.: A framework and assessment instrument for information security culture. Comput. Secur. **29**(2), 196–207 (2010)
8. Glaspie, H.W., Karwowski, W.: Human factors in information security culture: a literature review. In: Nicholson, D. (ed.) AHFE 2017. AISC, vol. 593, pp. 269–280. Springer, Cham (2018). https://doi.org/10.1007/978-3-319-60585-2_25
9. Martins, N., Da Veiga, A.: An information security culture model validated with structural equation modelling. In: Proceedings of the Ninth International Symposium on Human Aspects of Information Security and Assurance, pp. 11–21 (2015)
10. Martins, A., Eloff, J.: Assessing Information Security Culture. In: 2nd Annual Conference on Information for Security for South-Africa, pp. 1–14 (2002)

11. McCormac, A., Zwaans, T., Parsons, K., Calic, D., Butavicius, M.: Individual differences and information security awareness. Comput. Hum. Behav. **69**, 151–156 (2017)
12. Parsons, K., Calic, D., Pattinson, M., Butavicius, M., McCormac, A., Zwaans, T.: The human aspects of information security questionnaire (HAIS-Q): two further validation studies. Comput. Secur. **66**, 40–51 (2017)
13. Pwc.co.uk. (2015). https://www.pwc.co.uk/assets/pdf/2015-isbs-executive-summary-02.pdf. Accessed 25 Feb 2017
14. Roer, K., Petric, G.: Indepth insight into the Human factor: The Security Culture Report 2017. 1edn. CLTRe North America, Inc (2017)
15. Schlienger, T., Teufel, S.: Information security culture-from analysis to change. S. Afr. Comput. J. **2003**(31), 46–52 (2003)
16. Tolah, A., Furnell, S., Papadaki, M.: A comprehensive framework for cultivating and assessing information security culture. In: Proceedings of the Eleventh International Symposium on Human Aspects of Information Security and Assurance, pp. 52–64 (2017)
17. Emma, W.: Growing positive security cultures – National Cyber Security Centre. Ncsc.gov.uk (2017). https://www.ncsc.gov.uk/blog-post/growing-positive-security-cultures. Accessed 22 Feb 2019

Using Gamification to Improve Information Security Behavior: A Password Strength Experiment

Jacques Ophoff(✉) and Frauke Dietz

University of Cape Town, Cape Town, South Africa
jacques.ophoff@uct.ac.za, DTZFRA001@myuct.ac.za

Abstract. Information security emphasizes the importance of motivating end users to improve their security behavior towards protecting their private and organizational information assets. Password authentication is widely used as a user authentication method to safeguard information resources from unauthorized access. Despite its prevalence password best practice is not often followed and the use of weak passwords persist. Although password strength feedback mechanisms commonly aim to extrinsically motivate users to improve their password creating behavior, it is not yet clear how other methods, specifically gamification, influences security behavior regarding password creation behavior. The purpose of this study is to examine the effect gamification on user information security behavior, specifically regarding password creation. This study presents results from an online experiment of 232 respondents, who interacted with two different password strength feedback methods, namely a meter feedback method and a gamified feedback method using gamification points. A significant difference between the methods was found when measuring password strength using the number of guesses needed to crack the password, with the points method resulting in stronger passwords. The results of the study reveal that gamified feedback can lead to increased engagement and stronger password creation.

Keywords: Information security behavior · Gamification · Authentication · Password strength feedback

1 Introduction

A common approach used to protect user's information assets from unauthorized access, is using user authentication methods [1]. A popular form of authentication that is used in information security is password verification and hence, it is especially important to motivate users to improve their security behavior regarding password creation [2–4]. To motivate users to improve their security behavior regarding password creation, users are often exposed to password strength feedback mechanisms, such as password meters, that commonly extrinsically motivate users to create stronger passwords through fear [4–7]. Considering human motivation, intrinsic motivation is increasingly found to be more effective than extrinsic motivation [8, 9], hence

Published by Springer Nature Switzerland AG 2019
L. Drevin and M. Theocharidou (Eds.): WISE 2019, IFIP AICT 557, pp. 157–169, 2019.
https://doi.org/10.1007/978-3-030-23451-5_12

increasing the interest in investigating the effects of intrinsic motivation on user information security behavior.

Within the context of information security behavior, the effects of gamification on user information security behavior, specifically regarding password creation behavior, are still undiscovered. This study contributes to information security behavior research by investigating this phenomenon. The main objective of this study is to examine the effect of gamified feedback on user information security behavior, specifically regarding password creation. Thus, the primary research question to be addressed in this study is: *How does gamified feedback affect user information security behavior regarding password creation?* This study further aims to investigate an alternative password strength feedback method to existing fear-driven methods (password meter), to potentially motivate users more effectively to create strong passwords. The research question is evaluated using empirical data, which is collected using an online experiment.

The remainder of this paper will proceed as follows. First, the conceptual background relating to information security behavior around password creation and the adopted research model will be presented, along with research propositions for this study. In Sect. 3, the research design will be discussed in detail. This is followed by the data analysis and discussion of the project findings. Finally, this paper concludes by discussing the limitations of this study, along with opportunities for future research.

2 Literature Review

Password verification is the most commonly used form of authentication in information security [2–4]. Password authentication is a user authentication method that protects valuable information assets and resources within computer-based systems from unauthorized access and violation [10] by "matching the combination of username and password against credentials stored on the server" [3]. Although passwords form an important barrier limiting unauthorized access to information assets, users still engage in poor password practices, such as creating insecure passwords and reusing passwords [2]. Mwagwabi et al. [2] argued that poor password practices amongst users occur because users find it difficult to remember passwords and consider it annoying to have to comply with inconsistent password guidelines. Using weak passwords increases the user's vulnerability to threat, as weak passwords can be cracked without difficulty by easily accessible password cracking software [3, 4]. Given the threats to password security, it is especially important to find ways to improve the security behavior of users by motivating end users to create strong and effective passwords [2–4].

2.1 Extrinsic and Intrinsic Motivation

Fear appeals, and theories related to fear, including the protection motivation theory and deterrence theory, are extensively used in the field of information security to assist in motivating end users to change their security behavior [11–13]. Fear appeals present end users with persuasive messages that warn the end user of potential threats and recommend security behavior to counteract the threat [11]. Fear appeals refer to persuasive messages designed to highlight "the seriousness of a threat and a user's ability to cope with it" [4]. Johnston and Warkentin [13] defined fear appeals as messages that aim to encourage individuals to act in a recommended way through the initiation of fear related to a threat.

Fear appeals act as an extrinsic motivator for human behavior, as these propel users externally into choosing stronger passwords. Extrinsic motivation refers to human behavior that is driven by external rewards [14, 15]. Ryan and Deci [15] further pointed out that, if individuals are externally pushed into performing an action, the motivation behind performing that action is extrinsic. When taking human motivation into consideration, intrinsic motivation has sometimes been found to be more effective regarding human motivation than extrinsic incentives [8, 9]. Intrinsic motivation refers to behavior that is driven by personal interest and enjoyment in doing something [14, 15]. The idea of intrinsic motivation is also reflected in the self-determination theory (SDT), which focuses on the degree to which an individual's behavior is self-motivated without external rewards [16].

2.2 Password Meters as Password Strength Feedback Mechanisms

A common existing measure for motivating users to create stronger passwords is the use of password meters as a real-time password strength feedback mechanism to communicate a password's strength visually as the password is typed [4–7]. Feedback mechanisms, also referred to as feedback loops, "provide people with timely information about their actions and opportunities to improve them", hence pushing people towards improved behaviors [6]. Password meters generally appear as a colored bar that changes its color and its length based on the strength of the password entered, and it is often accompanied by a word explicitly representing the strength (e.g., weak, medium or strong) of the password [5]. An example of a password meter, which is displayed during account registration, is depicted in Fig. 1.

The strength and quality of a given password is commonly measured by either enforcing strong password requirements around password length and character set complexity, or by detecting "weak patterns such as common words, repetitions and easy keyboard sequences" [5]. Past studies conducted around the use of password meters concluded that password meters as a password strength feedback mechanism, in general, effectively influence users' security behavior towards choosing stronger passwords [5, 7, 17]. However, Ur et al. [7] observed that password meters with too-strict evaluations had a negative impact on users, resulting in users getting irritated and therefore losing the motivation to satisfy the meter.

Password meters persuade users to create stronger passwords through fear by warning the users that the chosen password is weak or not strong enough. However, it has been found that methods using fear appeal are not necessarily the most effective in achieving security behavior by users [12]. D'Arcy and Herath [12] argued that the increased deterrence through fear appeals does not work for all users. It is, therefore, of increasing interest to research and investigate alternative password feedback mechanisms that will motivate users more effectively to create stronger passwords.

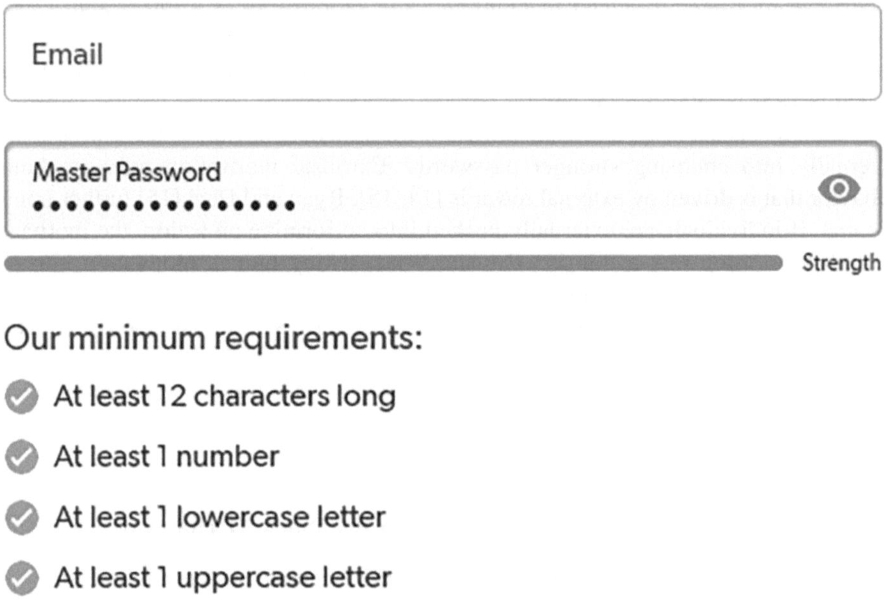

Fig. 1. Password meter example (https://lastpass.com/)

2.3 Gamification as an Opportunity to Improve Password Security Behavior

Deterding [18] argued that the SDT framework models and explains an individual's gaming motivation and enjoyment very accurately. Over the last five years, gamification has become an emerging trend and has gained increasing popularity within the academic context regarding intrinsically motivating an individual's behavior [19]. Making use of gamification in the security context, specifically regarding authentication, could increase the motivation of users to act more securely [20, 21].

Gamification can be briefly defined as "the use of game design elements in non-game contexts to motivate and increase user activity" [22]. To emphasize the behavioral effects of gamification, an alternative definition of gamification presented by Hamari et al. [19] is acknowledged as "a process of enhancing services with (motivational) affordances to invoke gameful experiences and further behavioral outcomes." Recently, human-computer interaction research has become increasingly interested in the idea of utilizing game design for designing interactive systems for motivation and enjoyment [e.g. 18, 23, 24].

Blohm and Leimeister [25] argued that game design elements can be utilized within processes and services to influence users' motivation, productivity and behavior positively. Game design elements refer to motivational affordances that drive psychological and behavioral outcomes of users [19].

Game design elements consist of game mechanics and game dynamics. Game mechanics are functional components used to gamify processes or applications. Game dynamics, on the other hand, determine the effects of game mechanics on a user's long-term user experience of the implemented mechanics. These game dynamics correspond to specific user motives that drive specific user behavior [25, 26]. For example, game mechanics such as scoring systems (i.e. gamification points) induce collective dynamics that relate user activities to measurable improvements and thus satisfy the aspiration for achievement. Blohm and Leimeister [25] further argued that, depending on the specific design of a mechanic, a specific mechanic may induce various dynamics and hence may lead to different motives.

Past studies conducted around improving the impact of password meters as a feedback mechanism for password strength, focused solely on variation in scoring algorithms and visual representations of password meters [5, 7, 17]. Shay et al. [27] pointed out that "past research has not looked at the impact of presentation and instructions (beyond password meters), or at ways to help users cope with strict [password] requirements." After conducting literature searches relating to this literature review, it has been found that no research has focused on the use of gamification within the context of password feedback mechanisms. This gap in the literature, therefore, offers an opportunity to research whether password feedback mechanisms that make use of gamification could potentially enhance motivation towards better password choice. Specifically making use of gamification points for password strength feedback is of great interest, as a point system is the game mechanic that can be considered most like the percentage calculation used by the password meter approach. The theoretical proposition in this study therefore is that *the use of gamification points, as opposed to conventional password meters, as a password feedback mechanism will result in users creating stronger passwords.*

3 Methodology

This study used a true experiment, as participants were randomly assigned to treatment groups, namely the experimental group and the control group [28]. More specifically, a Posttest-Only Control-Group Experimental Design was utilized, as the treatment groups were measured only on the posttest provided after the experiment.

The experimental group (Group A) were given a treatment or planned intervention, while the control group (Group B) were not given a treatment. For this study, the experimental group were given a point feedback method as treatment, while the control group were presented with the standard password meter. Both treatment groups were measured on the posttest only, as the study aimed to investigate whether user security behavior differs based on different feedback methods. Treatment groups were not administered a pretest, as the study was not focusing on the change in security behavior before and after a specific treatment.

To add realism to the experiment, the experiment was designed to look like a standard sign-up form to create a new online account. Participants were also presented with pre-experiment instructions that emphasized that participants should fill in the sign-up form as they would in a normal sign-up process for an account that holds sensitive personal information. However, it is acknowledged that participants cannot be forced to treat the sign-up process in the experiment the same way they would treat a sign-up process in a real-world situation.

3.1 Sampling

For this study a non-probability convenience sample was selected, consisting of students and staff at a large South African university, as these individuals were readily available and could be reached via email. The sample is believed to be a fair representation of the target population (general users of information systems) – the sample uses several information systems and includes individuals of different ages and genders, who have different levels of technical skills and password creating experience. All individuals in the sample operate within a tertiary institution, which requires them to create passwords for numerous electronic applications, often containing sensitive personal information.

3.2 Data Collection Method

An online experiment, followed by an online questionnaire, was conducted to gather primary data for this research. An email, briefly explaining the purpose of the study and providing a link to the online experiment, was sent out to the individuals in the identified sample. Potential participants were provided only with a brief description of the study (investigation into information security behavior), as informing participants that the study was investigating information security behavior specifically around password strength might have influenced their password-creating behavior. Telling participants about the purpose of the study may lead to demand characteristics, which results in participants interpreting the purpose of the experiment and subconsciously behaving differently to meet their interpretation [29].

The experiment consisted of two different simple account registration interfaces, each representing a different password strength feedback mechanism. One registration interface represented the conventional password meter feedback method (see Fig. 2), while the other registration interface represented a feedback method that used gamification points (see Fig. 3).

Fig. 2. Registration form with a conventional password strength meter

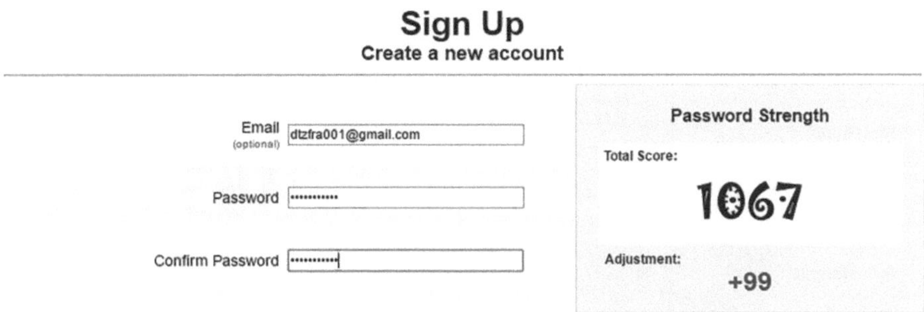

Fig. 3. Registration form with gamification points

Each participant was randomly presented with one of the interfaces and was asked to complete the registration process, which required the user to create a password. Only the password and the confirmation of password were compulsory. These two fields did not have to match to proceed to the questionnaire, however it was recorded whether they matched or not (94% of participants entered matching passwords). The password strength feedback mechanism was updated in real time as a participant entered a password. The real-time calculated password strength score was stored as primary data, avoiding the permanent storage of the actual password created. The password strength was calculated using the zxcvbn library developed by Dropbox. Zxcvbn is a password strength estimator, which recognizes and weighs "several dictionaries (English words, names and surnames, Burnett's 10,000 common passwords), spatial keyboard patterns (QWERTY, Dvorak, and keypad patterns), repeats (aaa), sequences (123, gfedcba), years from 1900 to 2019, and dates (3-13-1997, 13.3.1997, 1331997)" through pattern matching and conservative estimation [30].

The zxcvbn library awards the password strength with a score of 0 (too guessable/very weak), 1 (very guessable/weak), 2 (somewhat guessable/moderate), 3 (safely not guessable/strong) or 4 (strongly not guessable/very strong) [30]. The zxcvbn library was also utilized to calculate additional properties (other than the password score) of a participant's password, including the estimated number of guesses needed to crack the password, the estimated time (in seconds) to crack the password, and the number of milliseconds it took zxcvbn to calculate the password score. These properties were all calculated in real time during password creation and were stored after questionnaire completion. The conventional strength meter (the color and the length of the bar) was populated based on the calculated password score.

For the feedback method that used gamification points, the guesses_log10 password property was used to calculate and update the total point score. The guesses_log10 is the estimated guesses needed to crack a password, expressed as base-10 logarithm [30], thus yielding a user-friendly indication of password strength. For each character that was added or removed from the password during password creation, the difference between the old and new guesses_log10 value was calculated, multiplied by one hundred and displayed as the adjustment, while the total score was adjusted accordingly (see Fig. 4).

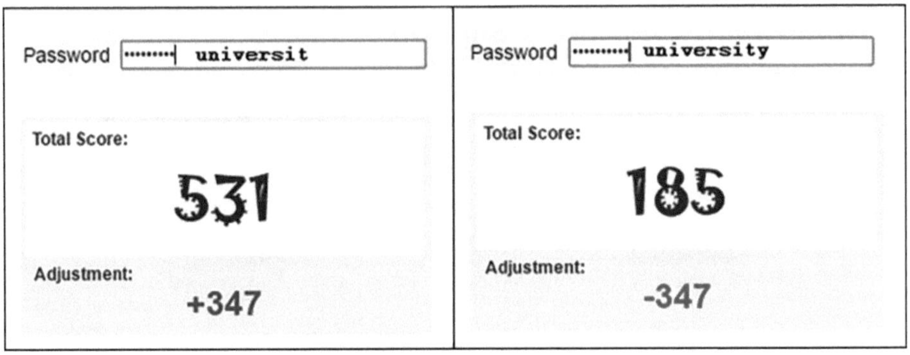

Fig. 4. Password strength points feedback concept

The example in Fig. 4 shows how the password score could be negatively affected by using a dictionary word: going from 'universit' to 'university' decreases the password score by 347 points. Unlike the strength meter, the points feedback method does not have a maximum password strength limit, as the guesses_log10 password property can still increase further even if a password has a strength score of 4 (100%) already. This enabled users to score an infinite amount of points.

Qualtrics, a web-based survey service, was used to host the online experiment, create the online questionnaire, and collect and record the response data in the cloud. Response data refers to data that the respondents provide by participating in the experiment and answering the questionnaire.

4 Data Analysis and Findings

A total of 445 responses were recorded. Of this 232 (52%) were considered valid for analysis due to fully completing the entire experiment. Out of the valid responses, 112 (48%) respondents were presented with the meter feedback method and 120 respondents were presented with the points feedback method.

Most respondents were female (56%). Age groups were divided into seven categories. Most respondents (45%) were 18–24 years old, containing mostly students at UCT. Twenty-one per cent of respondents fell within the 35–44 age group, closely followed by 19% in the age group 25–34 years and 12% in the age group 45–54 years. Only 4% of respondents fell within the age group 55–64 years. Respondents were asked whether they play any form of digital, computer or video games. A large number (59%) of respondents play games, while 41% do not play any form of digital, computer or video games.

4.1 Assessment of the Average Password Strength

Both password strength feedback methods assigned the password strength with a score of 0, 1, 2, 3 or 4 (0 representing very weak and 4 representing very strong). A t-Test for independent means was performed to test whether there was a significant difference in the average password strength between the two treatment groups, which were independent of one another. The two treatment groups are referred to as being independent, as these groups were unrelated, and each participant was tested only once. IBM SPSS Statistics 25 was used to perform an independent-samples t-Test. The summary results of the t-Test are shown in Table 1.

Table 1. Password strength t-Test data summary

Strength calculation	Score (0–4)		guesses_log10	
Feedback method	Meter	Points	Meter	Points
Mean	2.85	2.87	9.19	10.51
Std. deviation	1.21	1.23	3.69	6.29
Observations	112	120	112	120
Degrees of freedom	230		230	
t statistic	−.115		−1.929	
p value	.461		.010	

The results of the analysis show that, although Group A (points feedback method) did have a slightly higher average password score than Group B (meter feedback method), that score was not significantly different. However, when examining password strength in terms of estimated guesses needed to crack the password (guesses_log10) a significant difference was observed, with Group A having more secure passwords.

In addition to the password score, other properties relating to each feedback method were recorded or calculated. One such property is the time spent on the sign-up form, while another is the time taken to calculate the password score (a higher time indicates a more complex password). Averages scores for these metrics, across all participants, are shown in Table 2.

Table 2. Additional analysis of experiment and passwords

	Meter	Points
Average time spent on sign-up form (in seconds)	54.19	72.62
Average time to calculate password score (in milliseconds)	4.84	8.25

Respondents who were presented with the points feedback method, on average, spent more time on the simulated sign-up process than did respondents who were presented with the meter feedback method. This time, also referred to as dwell time, can be seen as a possible proxy measure for engagement [31]. The average time it took zxcvbn to calculate the password score (like the average time to crack a password) was higher for passwords created by respondents who received the points feedback method. This corresponds with the slightly higher average password score attained by respondents who were presented with the points feedback method on the sign-up page.

The findings therefore partially (except for the use of score for calculation of password strength) support the proposition that *the use of gamification points, as opposed to conventional password meters, as password feedback mechanism will result in users creating stronger passwords.*

4.2 Discussion

Although the difference in password score was not statistically significant, the average password score and averages of other password properties were found to be higher for passwords created with the points feedback method and therefore revealed a slight increase in password strength for passwords created with the gamification feedback method. Interestingly, the findings of this study revealed that, on average, respondents who were presented with the points feedback method spent more time completing the sign-up page than respondents who were presented with the meter feedback method. This could be explained by arguing that the respondents who interacted with the points feedback method might have been more engaged in creating a password, when compared with the respondents, who, on average, spent less time interacting with the meter feedback method.

The findings of this study further revealed that the average time to crack a password was significantly higher for passwords created by respondents who received the points feedback method. This could be explained by the fact that the crack time property of a password can still increase further even if a password has a strength score of 4 already. Since the points feedback method did not visually indicate an upper strength limit (i.e. password score of 4 represented as "very strong"), when compared with the conventional meter feedback method, users may have been encouraged to continue to improve the strength of their password (in terms of crack time) even if their password achieved the highest attainable password score of 4 already.

The implications of the above are twofold. First it shows potential for gamification to enhance user engagement in password creation, possibly resulting in stronger passwords. Second it points to a deficiency in password strength meters in that once a maximum (or good enough) score is reached users likely stop. Switching to a strength indication with no upper bound (e.g. estimated guesses needed to crack a password) would likely result in stronger passwords.

5 Conclusion

Information security is becoming increasingly important owing to increasing globalization and computing complexity and hence, it is becoming more and more important to motivate end users to improve their security behavior towards safeguarding their information assets and resources. This study contributed an alternative password strength feedback method to existing fear-driven methods (password meters), which used gamification points, and further investigated this password strength feedback method using empirical data.

The results of this study revealed that gamification points as a password strength feedback method did not significantly influence users' security behavior more positively than the meter feedback method, as no statistically significant difference regarding password strength and intrinsic motivation towards better password choice was found between the two password strength feedback methods. However, considering the average password score and averages of other password properties (e.g. the time to crack a password), the findings still revealed a slight increase in password strength for passwords created by respondents who were presented with the points feedback method.

This study is limited by the sample and context. The data, therefore, should be interpreted in this context and cannot be generalized to all internet users. Furthermore, this study is limited by the experimental environment, which cannot force respondents to treat the sign-up process as seriously as they would in a real-world situation. This study is also not able to reveal whether password strength was influenced by the password strength feedback method or by other factors (e.g. user's personality, curiosity or password perception). It is acknowledged that potential participants were provided with a brief description of the study ('investigation into information security behavior') which may lead to demand characteristics, resulting in participants interpreting the purpose of the experiment and subconsciously behaving differently to meet their interpretation. We tried to minimize this possibility by not disclosing our focus on password strength and password-creating behavior.

Future research could expand the experiment with questions that investigate whether respondents acknowledged and interacted with the feedback method or not. Password strength should also be investigated further through the consideration and testing of passwords' estimated crack times to determine password strength. The estimated crack time of a password has no upper limit, unlike the strength score of a password, and could serve as a more accurate measure of password strength.

Acknowledgements. This work is based on the research supported wholly/in part by the National Research Foundation of South Africa (Grant Numbers 114838).

References

1. O'Gorman, L.: Comparing passwords, tokens, and biometrics for user authentication. Proc. IEEE **91**, 2021–2040 (2003). https://doi.org/10.1109/JPROC.2003.819611
2. Mwagwabi, F., McGill, T., Dixon, M.: Improving compliance with password guidelines: how user perceptions of passwords and security threats affect compliance with guidelines. In: 2014 47th Hawaii International Conference on System Sciences, pp. 3188–3197 (2014). https://doi.org/10.1109/HICSS.2014.396
3. Van Acker, S., Hausknecht, D., Joosen, W., Sabelfeld, A.: Password meters and generators on the web: from large-scale empirical study to getting it right. In: Proceedings of the 5th ACM Conference on Data and Application Security and Privacy. pp. 253–262. ACM, New York (2015). https://doi.org/10.1145/2699026.2699118
4. Vance, A., Eargle, D., Ouimet, K., Straub, D.: Enhancing password security through interactive fear appeals: a web-based field experiment. In: 2013 46th Hawaii International Conference on System Sciences, pp. 2988–2997 (2013). https://doi.org/10.1109/HICSS.2013.196

5. De Carnavalet, X.D.C., Mannan, M.: From very weak to very strong: analyzing password-strength meters. In: NDSS (2014). https://doi.org/10.14722/ndss.2014.23268
6. Kim, T.H.-J., et al.: YourPassword: applying feedback loops to improve security behavior of managing multiple passwords. In: Proceedings of the 9th ACM Symposium on Information, Computer and Communications Security, pp. 513–518. ACM, New York, (2014). https://doi.org/10.1145/2590296.2590345
7. Ur, B., et al.: How does your password measure up? The effect of strength meters on password creation. In: Proceedings of the 21st USENIX Conference on Security Symposium, pp. 65–80. USENIX Association, Berkeley (2012)
8. Bénabou, R., Tirole, J.: Intrinsic and extrinsic motivation. Rev. Econ. Stud. **70**, 489–520 (2003). https://doi.org/10.1111/1467-937X.00253
9. Lowry, P., Gaskin, J., Twyman, N., Hammer, B., Roberts, T.: Taking fun and games seriously: proposing the hedonic-motivation system adoption model (HMSAM). J. Assoc. Inf. Syst. **14**, 617–671 (2013)
10. Furnell, S., Bär, N.: Essential lessons still not learned? Examining the password practices of end-users and service providers. In: Marinos, L., Askoxylakis, I. (eds.) HAS 2013. LNCS, vol. 8030, pp. 217–225. Springer, Heidelberg (2013). https://doi.org/10.1007/978-3-642-39345-7_23
11. Boss, S.R., Galletta, D.F., Benjamin Lowry, P., Moody, G.D., Polak, P.: What do systems users have to fear? using fear appeals to engender threats and fear that motivate protective security behaviors. MIS Q. **39**, 837–864 (2015)
12. D'Arcy, J., Herath, T.: A review and analysis of deterrence theory in the IS security literature: making sense of the disparate findings. Eur. J. Inf. Syst. **20**, 643–658 (2011). https://doi.org/10.1057/ejis.2011.23
13. Johnston, A.C., Warkentin, M.: Fear appeals and information security behaviors: an empirical study. MIS Q. **34**, 549-A4 (2010)
14. Gagné, M., Deci, E.L.: Self-determination theory and work motivation. J. Organ. Behav. **26**, 331–362 (2005). https://doi.org/10.1002/job.322
15. Ryan, R.M., Deci, E.L.: Intrinsic and extrinsic motivations: classic definitions and new directions. Contemp. Educ. Psychol. **25**, 54–67 (2000). https://doi.org/10.1006/ceps.1999.1020
16. Deci, E.L., Ryan, R.M.: Handbook of Self-Determination Research. University of Rochester Press, Rochester (2002)
17. Egelman, S., Sotirakopoulos, A., Muslukhov, I., Beznosov, K., Herley, C.: Does my password go up to eleven?: The impact of password meters on password selection. In: Proceedings of the SIGCHI Conference on Human Factors in Computing Systems, pp. 2379–2388. ACM, New York (2013) https://doi.org/10.1145/2470654.2481329
18. Deterding, S.: The lens of intrinsic skill atoms: a method for gameful design. Hum.-Comput. Interact. **30**, 294–335 (2015). https://doi.org/10.1080/07370024.2014.993471
19. Hamari, J., Koivisto, J., Sarsa, H.: Does gamification work? – A literature review of empirical studies on gamification. In: 2014 47th Hawaii International Conference on System Sciences, pp. 3025–3034 (2014). https://doi.org/10.1109/HICSS.2014.377
20. Kroeze, C., Olivier, M.S.: Gamifying authentication. In: 2012 Information Security for South Africa, pp. 1–8 (2012). https://doi.org/10.1109/ISSA.2012.6320439
21. Ophoff, J., Janowski, M.: Examining gamification as a driver of individual information security behavior. In: Conference Proceedings of the 2015 Dewald Roode Workshop on Information Systems Security Research, IFIP WG8.11/WG11.13. Delaware, USA (2015)

22. Deterding, S., Dixon, D., Khaled, R., Nacke, L.: From game design elements to gamefulness: defining "gamification". In: Proceedings of the 15th International Academic MindTrek Conference: Envisioning Future Media Environments, pp. 9–15. ACM, New York (2011). https://doi.org/10.1145/2181037.2181040
23. Jordan, P.W.: Designing Pleasurable Products: An Introduction to the New Human Factors. CRC Press, London (2000)
24. Zhang, P.: Technical opinion: motivational affordances: reasons for ICT design and use. Commun. ACM **51**, 145–147 (2008). https://doi.org/10.1145/1400214.1400244
25. Blohm, I., Leimeister, J.: Gamification - design of IT-based enhancing services for motivational support and behavioral change. Bus. Inf. Syst. Eng. **5**, 275–278 (2013)
26. Thiebes, S., Lins, S., Basten, D.: Gamifying information systems - a synthesis of gamification mechanics and dynamics. In: Proceedings of ECIS 2014 (2014)
27. Shay, R., et al.: A spoonful of sugar?: The impact of guidance and feedback on password-creation behavior. In: Proceedings of the 33rd Annual ACM Conference on Human Factors in Computing Systems, pp. 2903–2912. ACM, New York (2015). https://doi.org/10.1145/2702123.2702586
28. Creswell, J.W.: Research Design: Qualitative, Quantitative and Mixed Methods Approaches. SAGE Publications Inc, Thousand Oaks (2014)
29. Orne, M.T.: Demand characteristics and the concept of quasi-controls 1. In: Artifacts in Behavioral Research. Oxford University Press, New York (2009). https://doi.org/10.1093/acprof:oso/9780195385540.003.0005
30. Wheeler, D.: zxcvbn: realistic password strength estimation (2012). https://blogs.dropbox.com/tech/2012/04/zxcvbn-realistic-password-strength-estimation/
31. O'Brien, H.L., Cairns, P., Hall, M.: A practical approach to measuring user engagement with the refined user engagement scale (UES) and new UES short form. Int. J. Hum.-Comput. Stud. **112**, 28–39 (2018). https://doi.org/10.1016/j.ijhcs.2018.01.004

Author Index

MIX
Papier aus verantwortungsvollen Quellen
Paper from responsible sources
FSC® C105338

If you have any concerns about our products,
you can contact us on
ProductSafety@springernature.com

In case Publisher is established outside the EU,
the EU authorized representative is:
Springer Nature Customer Service Center GmbH
Europaplatz 3, 69115 Heidelberg, Germany

Printed by Libri Plureos GmbH
in Hamburg, Germany